Advance Praise for

For many decades as a rabbi-scholar-educator, Rabbi Mel Gottlieb inspired and educated generations of Jewish leaders. He brings to this task intellectual sophistication and profundity and *neshama*. This volume of his sermonica stimulates the mind and touches the soul.

—**Rabbi Elijah J. Schochet**, Professor of Talmud Academy for Jewish Religion-California, Author, *The Hasidic Movement and the Gaon of Vilna*, Rabbi Emeritus, Hamakom Synagogue.

Rabbi Dr. Mel Gottlieb is a brilliant thinker and dynamic teacher we should all learn efrom. He combines insights from classical Torah commentators with psychology, philosophy, and mysticism. Further, he humanizes our traditional wisdom by making it morally and spiritually relevant to the contemporary reader. His Torah is a treasure for all people to reflect on and to inspire growth in our intellectual journeys, character development, and soul flourishing.

—**Rabbi Dr. Shmuly Yanklowitz**, President & Dean of Valley Beit Midrash, Author, *Forty Arguments for the Sake of Heaven*

Rabbi Mel Gottlieb provides deep and cogent insights on the weekly Torah portions. He makes us think, evaluate, read and re-read the texts. He is a master teacher who invites us to explore the complexities of Torah and its eternally powerful teachings.

—**Rabbi Marc D. Angel**, Director of the Institute for Jewish Ideas and Ideals, Rabbi Emeritus, the historic Spanish and Portuguese Synagogue of New York City.

When an eminent teacher and spiritual guide offers his contemplations on the Torah, we should sit up and take notice. In this book Rabbi Mel Gottlieb shows how the stories, laws, and parables of the Torah point to the character-building insights often known as Mussar, but also how the same material can awaken mystical depths and provide spiritual inspiration. He gives us a combination of worldly realism and stretching toward the heights that can help us face our own challenges and ultimately contribute to a better world.'

—**Tamar Frankiel**, PhD, Author, *The Voice of Sarah: Feminine Spirituality and Traditional Judaism*

Rabbi Gottlieb is a man of profound wisdom and *menschlichkeit*, whose thoughtful teachings are deeply rooted in a love for all Jews and all human beings. His dedication to spreading knowledge and spiritual insight are truly inspiring.

His Torah commentary offers invaluable perspectives that guide readers toward a profound understanding of the Torah's depths and many layers of meaning. By connecting its texts and commentaries to contemporary dilemmas, he makes the Torah's teachings relevant and important for today's readers. I believe his *sefer* will be a valuable resource for anyone seeking to explore the profound wisdom of our tradition.

—**Rabbi Kalman Topp**, Senior Rabbi, Congregation Beth Jacob, Beverly Hills, California

An inspiring and illuminating collection of *divrei Torah*, full of insightful and meaningful revelations. Rabbi Gottlieb's wisdom, sensitivity, and brilliant mind help enlighten and enliven the beautiful teachings contained in each Parsha. I found the content inspiring and very meaningful in contemporary terms.

—**Dr. Jacob Zighelboim**, Author, *From Fear to Awe* and *Paradise Lost, Paradise Regained*

Rabbi Mel Gottlieb is an independent thinker deeply rooted in Jewish tradition, yet he is sensitive to contemporary needs. He possesses a wealth of knowledge accumulated through years of ever-thirsty inquiry. A forward thinker, Rabbi Mel has shaped generations of American religious leaders. He transcends denominational boundaries, inspiring and articulating the dialogue between Torah and reader.

His comments on the weekly Torah reading allow us to learn ancient traditions through a contemporary lens, brilliantly executed and thought-provoking. In his writings, he highlights ethical issues, probes with depth the complexity of the human condition, our place in the world and the subtlety of our behaviors. Throughout his weekly writings, he challenges and inspires us to grow to become the very one we are meant to be! You will be uplifted by this work!

—**Cantor-Rabbi, Dr. Arik Wolheim**, Beth Jacob Congregation, Beverly Hills, California

Mel Gottlieb: rabbi, therapist, and teacher of Torah to generations of appreciative students, draws upon a broad range of classical rabbinic texts, medieval and modern commentaries, and Hasidic teachings, to provide his own, fresh insight to understanding and applying Torah to our daily lives. He writes: "We must bring the melody of soulful Torah to the world." This book is a wonderful contribution to that endeavor by a master educator who embodies the teachings that he so ably unpacks and explains.

—**Dr. Gil Graff**, Author, Executive Director, Builders of Jewish Education (BJE-Los Angeles)

Rabbi Mel Gottlieb has written an insightful, enlightening book for everyone, accessible to scholars and laypersons alike. With its keen focus on personal development, it reflects both his rabbinical understanding of the weekly Torah portion as well as his knowledge as an accomplished psychologist. Connecting ancient wisdom with modern psychology, he breathes new life into the Torah's spiritual heroes, exploring their deep character through their trials and ordeals. "Even if there are obstacles" he exhorts us, "one must keep moving. Investigate what your soul calls you to encounter, and do not get caught up in habits, security and cultural influences that deter you from your path." Rabbi Gottlieb's TORAH TRAVELS is a gem that seamlessly applies the Torah's deep and subtle teachings to our everyday lives.'

—**Michael Gellert**, Jungian Analyst, former Director of Training at the C.G. Jung Institute of Los Angeles, and author of *The Divine Mind*

Rabbi Dr. Mel Gottlieb masterfully weaves psychological and philosophical insights with traditional Torah commentaries. His knowledge of mystical and Chassidic sources is vast and expansive. This book offers novel and pertinent ways to read Torah in light of today's questions and challenges.

—**Rabbi Dr. Tal Sessler**, author and former Dean of the Rabbinical School and Professor of Jewish Thought, Academy for Jewish Religion-California

Rabbi Mel Gottlieb's Parsha commentaries bring light into our perilous times. What a gift to have Rabbi Gottlieb's teachings available for all. He is a unique teacher whose wise heart and brilliant soul open the depths of Torah for all. The abundance of *ahavah* (love) flowing through his words into the heart of the reader is a treasured offering.

—**Rabbi Susan Goldberg**, Founding Rabbi, Nefesh

Rabbi Gottlieb's insights on the Parsha of the week enable the reader to apply the eternal messages of the Torah to the modern life of a Jew in the 21st century in a way which is both innovative and deeply rooted in tradition. The author draws upon his extensive knowledge of Judaic sources, his experience as a community leader and educator, and his academic background to offer the reader a tapestry of ancient, modern, and practical wisdom. Hasidic teachings, Kabbalah, and traditional commentaries are interwoven with lessons about communication and interpersonal interactions, thus making the book more than a commentary on the Parsha; it is a guide for life.

—**Rabbi Haim Ovadia**, Founder and Dean of Torah VeAhava.

Torah Travels

A Psycho-Spiritual Journey Through the Weekly Torah Portion

Rabbi Mel Gottlieb

Ben Yehuda Press
Teaneck, New Jersey

Published by Ben Yehuda Press
122 Ayers Court #1B
Teaneck, NJ 07666

http://www.BenYehudaPress.com

To subscribe to our monthly book club and support independent Jewish
publishing, visit https://www.patreon.com/BenYehudaPress

Ben Yehuda Press books may be purchased at a discount by synagogues, book clubs,
and other institutions buying in bulk. For information, please email
markets@BenYehudaPress.com

ISBN13 978-1-963475-60-9 pb 978-1-963475-61-6 epub

24 25 26 / 10 9 8 7 6 5 4 3 2   20240916

BEREISHIT
Genesis

SHEMOT
Exodus

VAYIKRA
Leviticus

BAMIDBAR
Numbers

DEVARIM
Deuteronomy

Introduction

I wrote this book as a journey to share the deep inspirational insights found in the weekly Torah portions. I have been inspired by great insights into the human condition by our Sages, great thinkers and writers—religious and secular—and how they teach us to grow into our unique destinies. They offer a blueprint on how to create an optimal society of peace and loving kindness, as our Torah Sages and commentators have articulated..

I was raised on the Lower East Side of New York City and had the great blessing in my youth of praying on Shabbat in the Mesivta Tifereth Jerusalem (MTJ) Synagogue of the Gaon Rav Moshe Feinstein, *zt"l*. As a child I was inspired by the humility, warmth, and Torah genius of this great sage, who exemplified the elevated qualities found in true *tzadikkim*. My grandfather, R. Abraham Baker, was the Torah reader for over 40 years at MTJ, and was a great sage and close companion of Reb Moshe. He made sure I attended services every Shabbat, and sat me right in front of Rav Moshe's desk.

Those early years left a deep imprint on my soul and influenced me to pursue Torah knowledge and ethics. I also thirsted to studythe psychology of human behavior and the mysteries of the universe. My spiritual journey was filled with "opposites." Raised in an Orthodox Jewish environment, I received a yeshiva education from an early age and I also had family members who were secular and university educated. As a youth I was exposed to contradictory Jewish lifestyles and philosophies. In addition, my mother died when I was a young child due to a hospital mishap (an overdose of anesthesiology). My fate turned into a destiny which included pondering the meaning of life its mysteries, and the unique role that I must live to contribute to self-actualization and elevation of our world.

When I was 11 years old, I entered the philosophy section of the Lower East Side public library on East Broadway. When the librarian suggested I was not in the correct section for such a young man, I protested. I told her I was old enough to know I wanted to understand the human condition; what the great masters' thoughts about our lives were about, and how our destiny could be most authentically and uniquely actualized. And so I stayed.

As I grew into my college years, I was blessed to study at Yeshiva University which taught us Torah literature, and also gave us a secular education enriched by the study of literature, psychology, philosophy, and other courses. Each area of study enhanced my learning, challenged my perceptions, and motivated me to continue to probe the minds and hearts of the great think-ers. I was drawn to the great rational thinkers, and to the intuitive/mystical expositors sharing their thoughts and experiences. In psychology, I was drawn to masters such as Freud, Jung, Rank, and the humanistic psychologists and absorbed many of their ideas and points of view. I loved the literary masters Shakespeare, Dostoevsky, Joyce, Hesse, Gabriel Garcia Marquez, and others who pondered the human condition. I studied the mythologies of the world religions, the works of Joseph Campbell, and the great Jewish philosophers in my rabbinic training. My life became a quest for truth, and more accurately my own personal truth.

At Yeshiva, I was blessed to study the wisdom of Rav J.B. Soloveitchik, Rav Aharon Lichtenstein, Rav Yitz Greenberg, Rav Shlomo Riskin, and others. I was enthralled by the modern Jewish philosophers such as Eliezer Berkovits, Walter Wurzberger, David Hartman, Martin Buber, Rav Kook, Elie Weisel, and A.J. Heschel.

I also resonated with those who acknowledged the complexity of the hu-man condition, and that it was the journey encountering all the "opposites" within and without that brought one closer to wholeness. I was drawn to the Neo-Chassidic Kabbalistic and Jungian model which seemed to contain a broader taste of wisdom by acknowledging the dark side ("shadow"—the mystery within our existence) and our individual responsibilities to develop a humane, empathic, kind, interconnected existence on our planet.

I studied in yeshiva in Israel for two years after graduating from college. During my first year, I studied at Mevaseret Yerushalayim led by Rav Noach Weinberg, Rav Aaron Feldman, Rav Mendel Weinbach, and Rav Nota Schil-ler. Due to the Six-Day War in 1967, the yeshiva closed down. During my second year, I studied at Yeshiva Mercaz Harav Kook. The first year exposed me to the teachings of the Mussar movement: *Mesilat Yesharim*, *Chovot Halevavot*, Rav Yirael Salanter, Rav Eliyahu Dessler and others. The second year exposed me to the inspiring teaching of Rav Avraham Yitzchak Hakohen Kook and his mystical love of all creation, and introduced to the writings of Chassidic commentators such as the Sfat Emet and Netivot Shalom.

When I returned to the United States, I enrolled in the Semicha program at Yeshiva University and studied Jewish Philosophy at its Bernard Revel Gra-duate School of Jewish Studies and Social Work at its Wurzweiler School. My first job as a rabbi was as Hillel Director at M.I.T. Then I returned to New York and entered a PhD program in Social Work at Columbia University, and my academic career began. I taught Jewish Philosophy at Wurzweiler School of Social Work, Comparative Theories of Psychology at Columbia University School of Social Work, Human Growth and Behavior at USC School of Social Work, and was Hillel Director at Princeton University for a year. After a decade in the rabbinate, I went back to school for a PhD in Depth Psychology/Mythology at Pacifica Graduate Institute. My doctoral dissertation was about "King David's Journey Towards Wholeness." After earning my doctorate, I taught several courses at Pacifica, including one called "Myth, Literature and Religious Studies."

In 2000, a new transdenominational rabbinical school, The Academy for Jewish Religion, CA (AJRCA), opened in Los Angeles, and they asked me to teach. It was a wonderful, creative educational endeavor that shared deep ideas and spiritual wisdom of the Jewish tradition from all Jewish denominations. I taught courses on Chassidic Masters, Mussar Wisdom, Kabbalah, Parshat Hashavuah, and more. This book is based on the Parshat Hashavuah talks I gave at the Academy over a two-year period. I was appointed Dean of the Rabbinical School and President of the Academy and served for two decades. Our 200 outstanding graduates serve the American Jewish community as rabbis, educators, chaplains and cantors.

The inspiration for this book came from the sublime, distinguished faculty of the Academy, its dedicated and talented student body, and all the great teachers who have revealed the beauty, wisdom and depth of the Torah throughout my years there. I am truly indebted to the school's loving staff, administration and alumni for their caring, their sharing, and their talents as educators and spiritual models.

I would like to thank my editor Jeanette Friedman for all her hard work, superb insights and help in bringing this book to fruition. I would also like to thank my wife Annette for all her support, patience, and assistance as I worked on the book; and my children, Adam, Akiva, Floryn, and Micah, their spouses and my six grandchildren—whose wisdom I constantly cherish.

Blessings,
Rabbi Mel Gottlieb, PhD

BEREISHIT
Genesis

Bereishit

With the beginning of the New Year, as we prepare to end and restart the annual cycle of reading our Torah with Parshat Bereishit, we experience new beginnings and insights found in its very first parsha. Bereishit is tightly packed with important philosophical, ethical, and teleological teachings and is so rich in midrashic and rabbinic commentary, it is frustrating to spend only one week studying it.

Bereishit is the extraordinary parsha of our creation myth, the basis for many philosophical principles and psychological foundations upon which our tradition relies, including free will. The Torah posits free will as the pillar that places moral striving within our reach.

But it appears that appealing to a human being's ability to do the right thing by exercising one's free will seems insufficient. Quite often, the more often we exhort a person to "do good," they do the opposite. This insight is important if we wish to educate the character of others effectively. Telling another to "do good" will not work. We must inspire them with spirituality that reaches their souls if we want them to "do good." Because of the *yetzer hara*, the inclination to do evil things, the *yetzer tov*, the inclination to do good things, will fail as often as it will succeed. As the Torah says, "*Yetzer lev adam ra b'niurav*/The inclinations of the human heart are evil from youth" (Gen. 8:21). However, the Torah also says, "*Halo im tativ se'eit*/If you lift yourself up, you will succeed" (Gen. 4:7). You must *be uplifted* in order to succeed.

So when God asked them not to eat from the Tree of Knowledge, they chose to do the opposite, with consequences that came back to haunt them.

We might wonder what was wrong with eating from the Tree of Knowledge in the first place. Our Sages suggest that there was nothing inherently wrong in eating from the Tree of Knowledge and that seeking knowledge is honorable. However, Adam and Eve's mistake was eating from the Tree before the Sabbath, before living through a spiritually inspirational experience that would make the search for knowledge a search enhancing the glory of God—that's why God wanted them to wait before eating from the Tree.

Our Sages suggest that the difference in consciousness after they ate from the Tree is that bodily consciousness, the desire to bring pleasure to the body, transformed the state of absolute truth and spirituality to the subjective pursuit of pleasure. If they would first have eaten from the Tree of Life (*Etz Chaim* in the Midrash), then knowledge from the Tree of Knowledge would have led them to greater awareness of God. But they ate before the first holy Sabbath, the day sanctified for rest and meditation, which led to subjectivity. Therefore, their knowledge was disconnected from the Primordial Light rather than a unified perception of the Presence of God in all of Creation. The disparate truths they gained in the knowledge gleaned constituted a narrow search for truth that leads to many insights through art and science, but not to the unified perception of the Presence of God in everything we experience.

Our Sages also comment on the words of the parsha and elaborate on the choice of each of the letters within it. One erudite insight is captured by asking why the Torah begins with the second letter of the Hebrew alphabet, the letter *bet*, instead of the first letter of the Hebrew alphabet, *aleph*. The answer to this question presents an elaborate philosophy.

Aleph, which is also the number one, connotes unity. Because it is not the first letter in the Torah, we understand that this world is not based on pre-existing unity, but that unity must be created through our actions and by partnering with other human beings and God. If we assume we are already in a state of unification, a "naive consciousness" arises, leading us to a "cursed" existence (a naive consciousness is intimated by the word *arur*—curse, which begins with an *aleph*).

The Torah begins with the second letter in the Hebrew alphabet to teach us that this world is one of *bet*—two-ness, a world filled with disparate energies and opposites that must be integrated into a unity-based consciousness. We are to partner with God and other human beings to create this world. We are to work to make this world one of justice and overcome oppositional forces. Hence the shape of the *bet* is closed on three sides but open on the fourth side, since it is up to us to fill in this fourth side. We are moved to create wholeness by integrating opposites as we journey toward our unique destiny. This challenge, this directive, gives meaning to our existence as we discover new layers of opposites and reconcile them as we move through our life cycles. Through our new insights and unique contributions, we uplift our world. Through this challenge growth emerges and, ultimately, so does joy and satisfaction of purpose.

This process continues throughout our lives as we encounter new opposites along our journey, new discoveries and new ways to contribute to the elevation and unification of our world. It is why the letter *bet* is the first letter in *bracha*—blessing, and is the first letter of the Torah, a Torah of blessing! (Ramchal, Derech Hashem, Ch.1).

Another profound teaching is found in Bereishit/Genesis 5:1, subject of an argument between Rabbi Akiva and Ben Azzai as to which is the most important verse in the whole Torah. Rabbi Akiva chooses the verse in Leviticus 19:18, "You shall love your neighbor as yourself," and Ben Azzai says there is a verse even greater than this found in Genesis 5:1—"This is the book of the generations of Adam, every human being is created in the image of God." The Rabbis agreed with Ben Azzai that this verse found in Bereishit embodies the greatest principle in the Torah, for it instructs us to love our neighbors by teaching us that every human being (even those who may appear different from us) is created in the image of God and thus has absolute value, is unique, and must be treated as an equal (Sifra 4:12). This profound insight is the guiding principle for all humanity. It teaches that we are all God's children, interconnected and bound by a common destiny, one that can lead to the blessed existence which God intends for us. It is love for all our fellow human beings, those who are like us and those who are different, so that we expand our consciousness as we discover the beauty of God's creation, even in the most hidden places.

Another teaching is found in Genesis 2:15—"And the Lord put the man in the garden to cultivate (*l'avda*—to serve) it and to take care of it (*l'shamra*—to watch it, to keep it)." As the Midrash says, "Look, Adam, at my works! See how beautiful they are! For your sake I created them all. See to it that you do not spoil and destroy my world; for if you do, there will be no one else to repair it" (Kohelet Rabbah 7:13).

As I read this verse, I am distraught and moved by what we face today as we witness the abuse of our planet. The Torah teaches us to take care of our world and yet we deforest our beautiful and essential rainforests, we pollute our waters with plastic and mercury, we destroy our plants and diminish the plethora of animal species. Our use of fossil fuels causes terrible climate change, global warming and melting ice caps. We have multiple, destructive fires in California, rising oceans, hurricanes, droughts, enormous floods and storms, extraordinary heat—all influenced by ignoring the mandate we were given to serve and take care of our earth. As the Midrash poignantly states, "If we do destroy it there will be no one else to repair it!"

Indeed, these are vital teachings—to work to build a world that is not yet complete; to work for justice and equality for all human beings, and to realize how interconnected we are. We must learn to love, recognize and see one another as created in the image of God. Finally, we must wake up to deal with the crisis of the hour. We are mandated to serve and guard our earth, the home that God bestowed upon us with Grace and Blessing.

May we all have uplifting Shabbatot and begin again to live out the calling of Bereishit. It is time! Each new year blesses us with a new opportunity. Let the love of Shabbat surround you and may you be blessed with joyous and committed weeks.

Noach

In Parshat Noach we read of his heroic trial enduring the massive flood. He also encounters doves and ravens, experiences a rainbow, attenuates his stress by drinking wine and brings a sacrifice of thanksgiving. Sometimes Noach is compared to Avraham and is deemed lacking in comparison. (Some say that Noach was "Only righteous in his generation," which had a low threshold for morals and behavior). But not one of us is perfect, and to focus on his flaws rather than the unbelievable endurance and commitment that Noach manifested is not helpful. It is not helpful when people compare one person to another. (Ask any teenager whose parents compare them to their older siblings or their friends.) For example, in sports, when you ask, "Who is the greatest hitter in baseball or best basketball player or quarterback?" you're not acknowledging the greatness and uniqueness of other athletes who have extraordinary qualities of their own. They are all great in different ways. To say one is "The Greatest" diminishes the greatness of others. Thinking either/or creates a culture of winners and losers, although the losers are not losers at all.

Of the many unique qualities of Noach, one quality that can inspire all of us and that we can learn from is his independent spirit. The name Noach means quiet, restful, a man who marches to his own tune, who takes a different path than others and listens to a voice the masses do not hear. He may have been considered "maladjusted"—judged by his peers for doing something bizarre, something different than all those around him, the same way hippies from the mid-20th century were considered a threat to normative society. But like the hippies, Noach made history for more than being pious and ethical. He was truly a genuine and authentic individualist.

Just imagine hearing a voice no one else heard, warning you about a massive flood and following that directive, building an odd-shaped, strange-looking boathouse/ark in your backyard. And then you are instructed, by that same silent voice, to lead a parade of animals through the streets of your neighborhood into this ark. Imagine what your friends and neighbors say behind your back. You would have to be strong enough in your belief and in what you feel you are called to do to be able to ignore the majority and the naysayers, to take that different path.

The Midrash tells us Noach's neighbors were judgmental. The confident, successful people of his community sneered at him, laughed at him behind his back, and mocked him. They said, "Imagine! He says we are all wicked and God is going to save him and those animals, and we will all drown for being evil." Noach ignored their ugly gossip and continued to build the ark and gather the animals, hoping the people would wake up and change their ways so the flood would be averted. He hoped they heard his message, for his mission was a passion he had to follow in order to save the earth—as stipulated in Bereishit!

Only a powerful individual with a strong independent conviction could withstand that kind of social trolling. In our day, social media has tried to beat down many good people dedicated to missions to save us from ourselves and from the results of our abuse of planet Earth. They stand up to the ridicule and courageously follow the call of Noach to save our planet!

Another astounding and revealing midrash is the description of the fault they ascribe to Noach. They claimed Noach was lacking in *faith*! He was listening to God and doing what was asked. How could he do that without faith? Here one can see *courage*, a rare quality Noach possessed. He was the man who defied his society, who built this odd-looking boat, who preached that the very Earth would rebel against the immoral conduct of its inhabitants. That man, say the rabbis, "lacked faith, and thus did not enter the Ark until the surging waters tugged at his knees—perhaps he thought there won't really be a flood." And they added, "Later, when he was in the ark, and the waters rocked his boat, he was still afraid he would die and prayed frantically, 'O Lord, help us, for we are not able to bear the evil that encompasses us!'" They faulted Noach, who proceeded with such courage, and endured ridicule because of his belief and faith, because he still had moments of doubt and fear during his journey.

This teaches us that even our greatest heroes, men and women of great faith, are not free from moments of doubt, from the "dark night of the soul." King David, a man of great faith, uttered many verses of anguish and doubt along with his great songs of praise to God. He shouts out "O Lord, why have you abandoned me?" (Psalm 22). We learn that people of faith—even great individualists—are not always certain of their choices. They proceed with fear and trembling. They experience the risk of uncertainty, the risk of being incorrect, of failing if their ideals and hopes are not realized. Though they are not absolutely sure, they still allow their faith to carry them through. According to the Midrash, in Noach, there is a recognition of that trace of doubt found in every great individualist. He was not completely certain God would unleash the flood or that he and those with him would survive it. And if the flood did not happen, he would have to endure the possibility of remaining a social outcast in his larger society. But he possessed the strength to bear the possibility of failure in the eyes of society, family, and public opinion. He had the courage to be himself even when society did not approve of that self; the courage to do something right and good, though unpopular; the courage to follow his conviction even while being poorly regarded.

Noach exemplified the basis of the greatest kind of faith—to proceed despite the doubt that accompanies it. It necessitates courage to proceed even in the face of failure. Paul Tillich, in *Dynamics of Faith*, writes that great faith is always accompanied by doubt and courage. Absolute certainty without risk does not require courage and is sought only when one is ruled by fear.

Today, in our society, we all must conjure up strong faith to be our true selves. We live in a society pressured and shaped by mass opinion and judgments. Our ideas and opinions have to be acceptable to others, our manners must be pleasing, and we must avoid at all costs the anxiety of being unpopular.

When many nations of the Earth are intoxicated with selfish goals and ignore the path of ethical conduct; when hordes of politicians wantonly dismiss the rules designed to preserve our planet, its resources and inhabitants; when inertia, fear and ignorance rule the crowds who oppose progress and safety; we must be courageous and speak out to promote the necessary action for survival. God, in our parsha, proclaims, "I will not continue to curse again the ground because of man, since the inclination of man's heart is evil from his youth; nor will I again continue to smite every living being, as I have done. The days of the Earth—seedtime and harvest, cold and heat, summer and winter, day and night shall not cease." (Genesis 8:21-22).

God promises never to destroy the Earth, but we (human beings) are in danger of doing this by ourselves. We must stand up to the masses and their rulers, as Noach did, to save our Earth from destruction; the floods, the fires, the droughts are upon us through the work of our own hands. It is up to each of us to reverse this destruction of our planet!

When the 40-day and 40-night ordeal was over, Noach got drunk after leaving the Ark! Perhaps he did this to celebrate his survival; perhaps he wanted to obliterate the memory of the destruction that he witnessed; perhaps he suffered survivors' guilt, or perhaps he suffered intense exhaustion and needed to de-stress.

Noach then offered a sacrifice of gratitude to God for saving him and his family.

God rebuilds the Earth, and creates a rainbow as a sign of beauty for a promising future. Let us continue to walk with Noach and the Lord and build and rebuild a world of love and beauty as the Lord expects us to do. May we be blessed to revivify our capacity to be independent individuals and, together, save our beautiful planet!

There are many other important messages to acknowledge in our parsha. Let us look at one very insightful theme worthwhile to illuminate and that is "The challenge created by our usage of Words"! The Rabbis indicate that the Hebrew word *teivah* means not only ark but it also means word; so Noach not only enters the ark, but metaphorically enters the Word! Accordingly, the Tikkunei Zohar says the word *Bereishit*/In the Beginning can be read *Bet Reishit* (two beginnings)—suggesting our current world is God's second creation of it. The previous creation was soundless, yet it was where one's hearing was so acute, one could hear God walking in the Garden (Gen. 3:8). In that first creation, everyone felt heard, all relationships were intimate, and one truly heard the soul of the other.

The second creation, our world, (a world where Noach enters the *teivah*/ word), is a world of words. It contains within it the challenge of potentially reducing the power of relationships because of the mistake of using words superficially. Words are like eggs; sometimes surrounded by a hard shell, but they can be cracked open and nourish our bodies and souls when we enter their living essence and truly *hear* one another. Noach heals our world by truly "entering the Word," by redeeming its usage and recreating intimate relationships.

In a broken society, instead of "entering" the true meanings of the words we utter and making them "real," we sometimes use words in a way that leads to the objectification of others. I may call you a man or woman, but that may not differentiate the uniqueness of a particular man or woman. I may call you a friend, but there are different levels of friendship that the general usage of the word does not capture. This leads to a breakdown in communication and relationships and prevents the possibility of true, honest, authentic knowledge of the other. It destroys our elevated dream of interconnection and unity. It can lead to a world of violence, mendacity, exploitation of others through words, and the breakdown of civilized society.

This describes the dangerous, insensitive misconduct—the evil behavior—of Noach's society at the time of the flood. Noach was asked to help redeem and heal this breach, by "entering the word"—to redeem authenticity and intimacy, and thus create true knowledge and discovery of the other.

Our mystical commentators offer us a deep teaching on the word *teivah*—that as Noach enters the *teivah*/ark, he is being asked to actively enter the "word." Words carry great energy! They can be used superficially, without embracing the import and meaning of the word. This can cause egregious harm. For example, we can glibly say someone is a "friend," but we do not truly engage with them, we do not actually carry the deep meaning of the word "friend." What does it mean to truly relate to a friend? Do you actually know them? Do you feel their pain? Do you actually relate to the word in an authentic way? Do you "enter the word," and genuinely allow it to enter your heart and the relationship?

The Kabbalists suggest our current existence, created through words ("And God spoke and created the world"), is a world that needs healing. Because words can be used glibly, superficially and dishonestly, we are frequently not connected to their deeper meaning.

How did Noach learn to "enter words?" He was tasked to bring animals into the ark, feed them, relate to them, and name them with the depth of intimate knowledge developed through relationship rather than superficial objectivity. With his hard work, his giving of himself, he developed a true knowledge of each animal and was able to give each of them the correct name—based on the knowledge of the uniqueness of each one, gained through his caring relationship to them.

The way to overcome superficiality and the objectification of others is through authentic relationships where one makes an effort to know the other, as Noach did with each of the animals that he nurtured. He entered their world, where a feeling of true intimacy could emerge.

Today, can we learn to "enter the word" and take the time to know another intimately? Can we connect to the words we use, rather than using words superficially without really feeling them, without really connecting to the other? Can we slow down, perhaps move our heads away from our computers and cell phones, and speak to and hear one another? The Hebrew word "to know" (*lada'at*) is equated with the deepest form of knowing; it is the same word used to connote sexual intimacy in the Torah as in the verse "Adam knew Eve" (Gen. 4:1), suggesting that it is through the deepest relationships that true knowledge is born.

Noach's task was to create a tikkun, a repair, a return to the exalted level of the first creation, one of intimacy and openness brought about by "entering the word." If words are used with consciousness, connected to feelings from the heart, they will open the hearts of others and the plague of flood, fire and heat will be mitigated.

May Shabbat slow us down enough so that once we are centered, we can truly use words of praise and love and healing. May we feel harmony as we connect with the knowledge of God's Presence and respond with love and kindness in our world of words and let us say, "Amen!"

Noah was a virtuous soul in many ways. His care for the animals and his naming them through his relationship with them created the awakening of love that emerges when we connect to one another. This promotes the strength, courage and power to actively work together to elevate our world. The model of knowing the other creates intimacy and empathy so essential to the salvation of our planet and is the key to peacemaking. We are all interconnected; knowing that, each of us can fulfill our task of returning to a humane, moral way of being on our Earth.

Noach the *tzaddik* was righteous, independent, and virtuous in his committed and consistent caring for a plethora of hungry animals, getting to know each of them individually through his tireless giving and caring. May we learn from his example!

Lech Lecha

Lech Lecha is about life as a journey. This takes commitment, learning to pay attention to our soul's calling and the effort to keep moving even in the face of life's inexorable obstacles.

Both Avraham and Terach start off on a journey to the Promised Land, but Terach did not get there. He stopped in Charan because Avraham's commitment was greater than his. This commitment came from the depths of Avraham's soul, which was connected to God. God told him he must keep moving in the face of change and not remain still or settle for a path that is not truly his life's path, his heart's desire. Even if there are obstacles, one must keep moving. Investigate what your soul calls you to encounter, and do not get caught up in habits, security and cultural influences that deter you from your path.

Noach taught us the importance of relationship, of empathy (*rachamim*), to truly know one another through giving—whether to animals or to human beings—and Avraham *Avinu* (our father) teaches us abundant kindness (*chesed*) by sacrificing his riches and opening his doors to all he encounters.

Avraham left the prosperous, powerful capital city of Ur to follow a calling: *Lech Lecha*, go forth, go for yourself, walk away from what you know, move from the center of a highly developed civilization to create a new model of civilization in the land of Israel. He moved from a life of affluence to a tent in Beersheba or Hevron. It was a major adjustment—abandoning the unlimited cultural opportunities of life in the big city. But he was called to leave his father's house to follow the one God, his Father in heaven, who could be reached only in the Holy Land.

There are times in our life where we risk the unknown, our place of security and habit, to journey to "a place which will be shown to us" when something in our soul draws us there (Genesis 12:1). Abraham and Sarah became zealous teachers of a new path that appeared in their souls that led to their connection with the Infinite, with the One God. They continually welcomed guests into their home and shared their awakening. Through their lovingkindness, humility, and passion for justice they attract humankind to the highest ethical monotheistic ideals.

The Lord calls to Avraham, "*Lech Lecha*," and our commentators offer several antithetical interpretations of what these two words mean.

The Divrei Elimelech, Rabbi Elimelech Szapira of Grodzhisk (1823–1892), says it means, "Get yourself out"—distance yourself from being centered on yourself. Get the "you" out of your work. Do not focus your whole work on the improvement of your own, solitary self which is "spiritual hedonism," a misguided quest for your own private salvation. This misidentification diminishes the truer interconnected unified perspective that unites us all in the work of uplifting our world. The Ishbitzer, Mordechai Yosef Leiner (1801-1853), on the other hand, says it means "Go into your own self."

You cannot find life in the external things of this world. They are not life-giving. The most basic life-giving qualities can only be found within your own self. Go therein! Follow your bliss, your inner voice that informs what you are drawn to; discover the unique gifts that Hashem has bestowed upon you. Have the courage to let go of allegiance to values and habits from your homes (*bet avicha*) and communities (*artzecha*) and cultures (*moladitecha*) that may not be resonant with your calling (Gen. 12:1).

The Sfat Emet, Yehudah Aryeh Leib Alter (1847-1905), wrote that it means a person should always "be a walker, and keep moving"; be a *mehalech*, always marching from one rung to another. He suggests this journey is also "soul-traveling," referring to the intellectual and spiritual movement of one's soul from level to level as one continually searches for God.

Habit and routine make things seem natural and this nature hides the inner light. This is true even of Torah and commandments, when we do them out of habit. They become our second nature and we forget their inner meaning. Therefore, we always need to seek out some new meaning, risk the new and die to the old (transformation and rebirth). Thus, the verse says, "Get thee out of the land"—a person should always keep walking "to that which I shall show thee." A new discovery will be made if we continue to move forward and "risk the new." That is why a person is called a "walker" rather than a person of habit who follows the same routine every day. Those who stand still are not renewed, for routine holds them fast—therefore a person must keep walking to discover life's wonders.

"Go to a land which I will show you" (Gen. 12:1). It takes faith to risk the unknown, to trust the inner calling, especially when the tangible evidence is not yet visible. "Go to a land which I will show you." Have courage, take a risk even if the goal is not before you now. It will appear if you have faith. As the Sfat Emet teaches, "Habit and routine make things seem natural, and this nature, this habitual proclivity, often hides the Inner Light." Follow the guidance of your soul, and the promised land will appear. "Which I will show you" refers to that which a person cannot see on their own, but if you take the first step, the Lord will reveal the blessing that was meant for you. "Blessed is the one who trusts in the Lord" (Psalm 115).

When you follow your inner soul-calling, your bliss, "you will be a blessing" (Gen. 12:2). The light will shine forth from you and you will be enlightened even without saying or doing anything. The transmission of blessing from you will be instantaneous and anyone who even comes close to you will become blessed. You will have become a blessing! God's Presence will emanate from you. Those who have been blessed to encounter a soul whose "light shines forth" like this recognize that unique moment. It is electrifying and unforgettable.

Every place to which we travel is a place of discovery, a place where we can share our kindness, wisdom and friendship and the unique gifts the Lord has bestowed upon us. Indeed, this is our purpose and responsibility in life: to discover our gifts and to share them with the world. Then our soul is satisfied, our meaning is embraced and we will find great joy.

Avraham was very aware how one's environment can be a major influence on one's psyche, and therefore one must be constantly connected to Soul and to Torah values. The Ba'al Shem Tov insightfully points to a verse in our parsha (Gen. 12:11) that states, "And Avram said to Sarai, 'Behold I know that you are a woman beautiful to see.'" He notes Avram was amazed at the shift in how he perceived Sarai. Previously, he never experienced Sarai's visual appearance as being somehow separate from her spiritual beauty—they were one to him. Suddenly he noticed her visual impact without any reference to her character, her intuition, and her spiritual universe. He realized that the superficial vision of the place he was visiting had infected him. Are we also infected by the materialistic and hedonistic values of our environment? We must keep vigilant and connected to the distinction between Torah values and that which may be distinctly different in our culture. We always need to "keep moving."

Abraham's example teaches us that even though we have a unique path, it is always subsumed under the goal of kindness. At the end of the parsha we read of the law of circumcision (Gen. 17:12). Circumcision marked a certain segregation of Jewry from the rest of humankind. Avram's name was changed to Avraham at that time, connoting his role as "*Av Hamon Goyim/ Father of a Multitude of Nations*" (Gen. 17:4). This separation (particularism) was necessary to strengthen us through the commandments to carry out the universal ideals that include all humankind. This separation dwelling within the ideals of a spiritual community leads to the strength necessary to actualize the universal ideals that benefit all of humankind. It is a journey that gives birth to the best of us, and the manifestation of our unique destiny.

The obligation and purpose of *Brit Milah* (circumcision), therefore, will only be fulfilled if Jews uphold their part of the contract, namely, to couple their suffering of the procedure with a commitment to uplift the whole world through the covenant of Abraham. Jews must be dedicated to the amelioration of both the physical and spiritual elevation of the world. The concept of Jewish "chosenness" was based on a goal, a task, and a responsibility rather than privilege, and it is this idea which distinguishes the Jewish dimension of particularism from other forms of independence and separation from the masses ("a people apart, a chosen people"). We are a people whose particularism leads to a universalism; a mandate that is enhanced by our particular commandments—whose goal is the elevation of all humankind. It is for this reason Abraham underwent the *Brit Milah*.

In this incident the Torah elaborates on his kindness and dedication to all humankind. We read that on the third day after the Brit, when his pain was most acute, God visited him to comfort him in his pain. Avraham sat outside the tent in the scalding heat of the midday sun, even though he knew it would aggravate his pain (Gen. 18:1). The Lord created this scorching hot day to prevent strangers from traveling on that day. For God knew that Abraham's physical pain would not prevent him from his natural proclivity to bestow kindness on other human beings. However, it became clear that Abraham's spiritual pain of isolation clearly outweighed the physical pain of his existent circumcision. His inner core compelled him to bestow generosity and hospitality to total strangers. And thus he was elated to see strangers (angels sent by God) now passing by. The strangers appeared to Abraham as Arabs passing on the road (he didn't know they were angels sent by God). He ran toward the people he thought worshiped differently and pleaded with them to enter his house and partake of a meal that Sarah prepared. He excused himself even from God in order to devote himself to show kindness to strangers—for the segregation which came as a result of *Brit Milah* was accompanied by the most sublime ideals of universalism (A *Brit Av Hamon Goyim*). Our Sages teach two profound ethical and psychological insights from this story: first, that doing kindness to human beings is even greater than dwelling with God! And second, that spiritual suffering (Abraham's isolation) can at times be even greater than physical suffering!

Is it not amazing that right after undergoing his circumcision in the parsha, still filled with pain, when he sees three strangers approaching, he runs to invite them into his tent and to feed them? He even excuses himself from God, who comforted him in his circumcision, so that he might devote himself to show kindness to strangers! I believe this is the goal of the Jewish people—to spread kindness, generosity, and hospitality in the world. Our separateness is important only to strengthen our convictions to carry out our goal and to not be overinfluenced by the negative impact of our environment. We must imbibe the strength a strong community imparts and bring the powerful love it teaches to the rest of the world. Our path must be a particularism leading to a universalism of kindness and living under the Light of God. May we all be blessed to follow this holy path and heal our world in this time of distress and bifurcation. Let us all be "walkers" like our ancestor Abraham. And feed the hungry like our mother Sarah, and may it be so!

Vayera

We live in contentious and stressful times, and certainly in an election season, with media and politicians engaging in mendacity, falsification, stereotyping, and belittling of "the other;" when extremism on both sides prevents the listening and empathy necessary to carve out and create a path of peace and respect for the dignity of others created in the image of God. Thank God the gift of Shabbat invites us to enter a space of harmony, to connect to the Light which always waits to be revealed by the soul within, as we find time for deep breathing, learning, song and fellowship.

There are many deep ideas from our parsha to share, including soul-filling commentaries from the sublime, mystical Rav Kook. The parsha is so resonant with what we face today, and his analysis of our modern challenging reality rings so true. We absorb the words of Light radiating from his soul that are meant to be shared with our world. The words of our Torah are uplifting and revealing of the Healing Light that we are to spread through our universe from generation to generation. Our study of Torah strengthens us with wisdom and strengthens our faith to bring forth the world we deserve: a world of peace, justice for all, beauty, enjoying the gifts of nature and loving our fellow human beings filled with God's Light and splendor. Let us learn from the stories in this packed parsha and see what Rav Kook has to say in conclusion.

There are rich stories and moral lessons and quandaries in this parsha. This includes Hashem "lying" to Avraham about Sarah's reaction when she is told that she would be giving birth. Sarah laughed and said, "How can it be that I will give birth? I am so old!" She actually said, "How can that be? My *husband* is so old!" Rather than hurt Avraham's feelings, the Lord tells a white lie, as it were! (This suggests that there may be times when it is not necessary to hurt another person if there is an alternative to spare them hurtful feelings). We also read about Lot's wife wistfully looking back at the destruction of Sodom because she was so attached to the material life there and was therefore turned into a pillar of salt. Lot's daughters try to save humanity through incest, which results in the birth of Amon and Moab, parents of Ruth and David. Hagar and Yishmael (the "others") are sent away, causing a psychological wound in Yishmael for the rest of his life—and one that has consequences to this very day. And, of course, the parsha contains the numinous, perplexing, enigmatic, profound trial of the *Akedah* (the sacrifice of Isaac), perhaps the most terrifying and mystifying tale in all of Scripture. There are also three other important and relevant stories in this parsha that affect our lives today.

We begin with the continuation of the story of Avraham and his three visitors (Gen. 18:1) that began at the end of last week's parsha. Our Sages say, "Hospitality to visitors is even greater than residing in Hashem's Presence" (Shabbat 17a). The verse (Gen. 18:1) says that God visited Avraham on the third day after his *brit* (circumcision) to comfort him on the most painful day in his recuperation. Avraham was waiting in the scorching sun, ready to receive any guests who might pass his way. His tent had entrances on all four sides to make it easy for his guests to enter.

God made sure the day was extremely hot in order to discourage travelers and protect Avraham from his natural inclination to invite them into his home. But as Avraham's spiritual pain of not being able to follow his inclination to feed visitors became greater than his physical pain (since he was a man of *chesed*), Hashem's initial act of protecting him from strangers (by making it a hot day) was rescinded.

From afar Avraham saw a group of wayfarers (some say angels) headed in his direction. He ran to greet them and entreated them repeatedly to stay, relax, and enjoy a sumptuous meal. When they agreed he ran back home and hurried to prepare the meal with Sarah. The Torah stresses that at every step, Avraham hurried and ran to perform this mitzvah. He was not deterred by the heat, the pain, or the fact he was inviting a group of strangers into his home. When one has a sense of purpose, severe physical pain can be overcome. When one doesn't have a clear inner purpose, everything is "painful."

As we are all the children of Avraham and Sarah, it behooves us to carry on their legacy of *chesed*—to invite those who need a meal to our homes, and to share with others our blessings and friendship. It is a mitzvah and is a potential opportunity to uplift our world with *chesed*. Let us put on our "running" shoes like Avraham and manifest kindness and humility. This will give us a sense of purpose and a sense of meaning as we follow the mandates of our tradition.

Next in the parsha is the story of the destruction of Sodom and Gomorrah (Gen. 18:20-19:38). Why did God divulge the plan to destroy Sodom and Gomorrah to Avraham, where Avraham's nephew Lot and his family lived? Why destroy Sodom and Gomorrah in the first place? The Rabbis say it was because the inhabitants of these cities were wicked and showed no indication of improvement. This was proven by the fact that one could not find even 10 righteous people in those cities, so it seemed the only solution for the ultimate good of humanity was their destruction.

The people of Sodom were not depraved because of poverty or want—the possession of material goods is what corrupted them. It made them greedy and the attitude was, "Why should we share what we have with strangers? We will only have less and everyone will come for a handout! The fewer guests we have here, the more there will be for us." In ancient times there were no inns, hotels, or restaurants. Only the inhabitants of the city could invite strangers into their homes, so refusing to offer shelter to travelers was the height of cruelty and corrupted the morality of the whole region. As a result, they treated visitors badly to distance them and pressured others in their community to follow these norms. Furthermore, as far as the cities' residents were concerned, if a person was not successful, it was a sign that the Creator did not like them, ("blaming the victim") or that they did not try hard enough. The way of the cities led to eventual degradation of the masses, because people do not help those who have not helped them. This is contrary to the Jewish way, which is designed to strengthen trust in others and society through deeds of kindness.

The Jewish way is why Avraham helped those in need. He gave spontaneously with an open heart, and gave what the other person needed—not just what he thought they should need—and thereby helped build the other's trust and self-esteem. By being a "giver," Avraham became richer—in character as well as materially.

The Midrash says the Sodomites issued a proclamation saying, "Anyone who strengthens the hand of the poor with a loaf of bread shall be burnt by fire!" They had raised this awful social norm to a legality and carried it out. Pelotit, Lot's daughter, was one of their victims. She saw a very poor man in the street and her heart was grieved, so every day, when she went out to draw water, she hid provisions in her pitcher and sustained the poor man. When she was caught, the Sodomites brought her out to be immolated. She cried out to God, and her cries ascended to the Throne of Glory. When Hashem went down and observed the truth of what the Sodomites were doing, their destruction was inevitable.

We often think of the sins of Sodomites as being those of sexual debauchery, but they were punished for their social iniquity. As the Ramban says, "The Sodomites intended to prevent the entry of all strangers, because of the fertility of their land. They didn't want to share their bounty with others. They accepted Lot on account of his wealth or out of respect for Avraham. According to our Sages they were notorious for every kind of evil. But their fate was sealed for their persistence in not supporting the poor and needy. No other nation could be compared to Sodom for their cruelty."

In Mishnah 5:13 in Pirkei Avot/Ethics of the Fathers we read, "One who says what's mine is yours, and what is yours is mine, is an unlearned person. One who says what is mine is yours, and what is yours is yours is a pious person. One who says what is yours is mine, and what is mine is mine is a wicked person. And one who says, what is mine is mine and what's yours is yours is characteristic of Sodom."

This is relevant to our societal behavior today. The Torah teaches us that we are responsible for all members of our society. We cannot close our eyes to inequities and care only about our own welfare. We are charged to follow the *chesed* of Avraham and support such policies as a society. On a practical level, if we ignore the poor, and choose to only protect our own wealth, we create strife, anger, and a damaged society. If we have wealth, we should be joyous and show our gratitude to God by sharing with others so they can also benefit from the blessings of our plenty. Following the behavior of the Sodomites, who chose greed and were filled with fear of losing their wealth through sharing, only leads to destruction and wrath.

When it came to finding righteous people in Sodom and Gomorrah, a third idea is found in Genesis 18:24 which says, "Would you not spare the city if there are fifty righteous people (*tzaddikim*) in the midst of the city (*b'toch ha'ir*)?" Our Sages make the profound point that a righteous person must dwell in the midst of the city in order to be called a *tzaddik*. A righteous person must always care for the welfare of his surroundings, and not be privately righteous just for themselves. One must act on one's convictions even in a hostile environment. This is true righteousness.

The fundamental charge to our leaders is to be aware and care for the place in which we live. We cannot turn a blind eye and obey the *mitzvot* solely for our own salvation. We are interdependent and hence responsible for that which calls us to repair our social fabric. We are individuals, but we are also members of society—a society that always can use improvement.

Rav Avraham Isaac Kook writes in *Orot Hakodesh/Lights of Holiness* of matters that strongly relate to this parsha and the story of Sodom.

"All the defects of our world, both the material and the spiritual, derive from the fact that every individual sees only the one aspect of his existence that pleases him, and all other aspects that are not comprehended by him seem to deserve purging from the world. And this tendency leaves its imprint on individuals, groups, and on disparate cultures, holding that whatever is outside of one's own is destructive and disturbing. The result of this is a multiplication of conflict" (*Lights of Holiness*, Vol. 1, p. 121).

This is an apt description of our current world. Rav Kook's solution is to move away from the perception that we are each isolated individuals to the more elevated faithful reality that we are all interconnected under the Light of God. Thus, all our actions have an impact on others, and this consciousness leads us to think differently and to act differently. We are all here in a joint venture to bestow loving interactions with others and with the Earth as a whole.

What a gift it is to open our eyes to the wonder of Creation, to the assortment of animals, plants, tastes, smells, and sounds of the universe. How blessed are we if each of us can truly gaze into the eyes of another and see each other as beautiful beings of God? The love of God and God's creation leads to the love of our fellow human beings, a gratitude for the gift of being alive in this world, and thus there should be a natural desire to help our brothers and sisters as we inhabit this Earth together.

Rav Kook suggests, "It is in the grand and true perception of the idea of the Unity of all existence, all contributing to the whole under the Canopy of God, which promotes the expansive abundant energy of loving kindness, with joy out of the abundance of all. This can occur when we do the Mitzvot connecting to and reminding ourselves of God's love, which we want to bestow upon all. The distorted love that loves only the dimmer spark seen in our myopic vision (born out of a radical individualism, leading to a narrow-isolated experience) and misses the Greater Love, creates a false philosophy and a deprivation of connection to the Source of All, that is found in all the detailed specifics of our blessed creation." (*Lights of Holiness*, Vol. 2, p. 586).

Our world today, suggests Rav Kook, with its exaggerated individualism, has created a chaotic, dangerous world that can and must be healed through a new enlightened spirit of faith that will create reconciliation and unity. This goal of unity is realized not by suppressing differences, but by disciplining generalizations and exaggerations, and honoring and understanding the outlooks of others, not only in their outer expression, but in the depths of our complicated fears and the reactivity of others.

Rav Kook felt that all our endeavors must be directed toward disclosing the Light of general harmony that can only come from an ideology of interconnection (seeing unity in the disparate whole) rather than a philosophy of radical individualism and separation. By bringing each of the valuable feelings and opinions under the canopy of Great Faith, we realize that we are all children of God, here to elevate the world and see and feel our fellow human beings with a spirit of warmth, support and benevolence. As Rav Kook poetically puts it, "Whoever contemplates the Divine in nature and the Divine ideas in their purity (Torah), cannot hate or be disdainful of any creature or any talent in the world, for through each does the Creator Reveal Him/Herself" (*Lights of Holiness*, Vol. 1, p. 327).

Friends, let us heal the world with the spiritual vision of Rav Kook, and *chesed*, the kindness of Avraham, so that we pass this chaotic time of narrowness to emerge in a time of broad vision, a time when we realize we are all children of God, blessed to be on this earth, charged to heal it, and discover the Unity that is always there as we "Journey toward Wholeness."

Chayei Sarah

The Torah portion begins by informing us of the death of beloved Sarah. Avraham chooses an appropriate burial ground and goes to the children of Chet and asks them to approach Efron, the landowner, to purchase the land in Chevron (Gen. 23). Efron offers him the land for free, an indication of Efron's respect for him, but Avraham insists on paying rather than accepting the favor. Why does Avraham reject Efron's offer and why did he assign the children of Chet to approach Efron rather than going to him directly?

Our Sages look at the text in this parsha and extract an important ethical lesson from this incident. As a model for the future that would establish certain attitudes concerning our relation to the Holy Land of *Eretz Yisrael*, Avraham, instead of demanding the land, went out of his way to legitimately purchase the land, and make it known publicly. Instead of making a private real estate deal with Efron, he asked the people of Chet to approach Efron. In this way, the entire community was aware of his intention.

This is a very important principle to be applied in all our acquisitions today! Avraham wanted to show the people of his generation and future generations that you do not use the word of God or personal power and prestige to gain advantage over others. God's promise to Avraham that his children would inherit this land did not give him carte blanche to take advantage of others (to hide behind the Divine word). God will fulfill this promise at the appropriate time, not when humans decide it should be fulfilled. The human responsibility, having been blessed with a Godly promise, is to behave in a Godly manner, so people will see a people with elevated human character, admire it, and want to emulate this holy behavior, and thus come closer to such a conception of God. This aboveboard transaction is a blueprint for all future purchases; every purchase must be done by mutual agreement and public acknowledgment.

Avraham insisted on paying for the land to avoid any future accusations that implied he used some sort of trickery or imposed his position of power in order to obtain it. He paid full value and behaved as an honorable righteous leader should. He exhibited generosity of spirit, courage, honesty, and integrity. By making the acquisition ethically, with both parties publicly agreeing to the deal, he manifested the highest values of the Jewish people.

Avraham acted as a leader should when he acquired the Cave of Machpelah in Chevron. The transaction became a vital lesson in how to be an outstanding, respected, worthy and honorable leader. It is the responsibility of those who wear the mantle of leadership to behave in a Godly manner. A leader must be bound by ethics and thereby bring holiness to the world and make this world a blessing and a home of beauty and harmony. The deal was also a leadership lesson in a different way—one in how to interpret a Godly promise. God's promise does not give us license to behave unethically. God's promise was a mere glimpse into the ultimate reality. Until that reality unfolds, it is the responsibility of those who were bestowed with God's promise to behave in a Godly manner. The way to behave in a Godly, humane/ethical manner is to leave the matter of exercising power to the Omnipotent and exercising *menschlikhkeit* (basic human decency). This may complicate deals to secure land in Eretz Israel that may benefit us in important ways, but Avraham's behavior makes it clear that ethical behavior is the optimal path in our decision-making, even if it means sacrificing our maximal desires. This takes great faith, but it is a prime value in our tradition. "'Not by faith and not by Power, but by my Spirit alone,' saith the Lord'" (Zechariah 4:6).

Why did Avraham take such pains to acquire the Cave of Machpela in Chevron, and what is its significance? Why does the Torah give such a lengthy description of this acquisition? In addition to modeling the proper ethical way to make a purchase, the Midrash states that the Holy Land is the place chosen because it is where the consciousness of the source of worldly blessings is the highest. The Holy Presence permeates the land, and Chevron is the place of "joining/*chaver*," where heaven meets earth. Therefore, our holy ancestors are buried there, and it is identified in the Midrash as "the entrance to the Garden of Eden," signifying the joining of heaven and earth.

We find the theme of the "uniting of the opposites" here as we observe that our ancestors were buried in pairs—husband and wife together. The concept of pairing partners suggests that through "joining," each of the partners can achieve together what neither could achieve alone. They support one another with great spiritual sensitivity and appreciate each other's goals. Their spiritual well-being leads to an actualization of their unique gifts in this world. In these marriages of the ancestors the presence of God made itself palpable and they were buried at the place of union of heaven and earth.

On a national level, says the Sfat Emet, this is the task of Israel: to bring everything in this world back to its source, to recognize God in everything, to bridge the gulf between the material and the spiritual. Thus, everyone buried in the Cave of Machpelah in Chevron had a twofold purpose: They made their physical activities spiritual and engaged in spiritual activities as well, such as prayer, study, and good deeds.

The Midrash says, "Avraham discovered this cave during the sojourn of the three visitors at Mamre. They write that when Avraham went to slaughter a calf for the three visitors, the calf ran off into the darkness of the cave. When Avraham followed the calf, he found Adam and Eve lying in their graves with lamps over their heads, and a sweet odor filled the air. Adam was created from the red clay of fields near the cave. It is said that there are seven gates to the Garden of Eden and this cave is the outermost gate. Adam, burying Eve's body, was overwhelmed by a sweet, divine fragrance and tried to recover his lost home by digging deeper. He was digging his way to the entrance of the Garden of Eden when he was commanded to stop."

Avraham wanted this cave to be Sarah's burial ground. Its purchase was counted among the 10 trials of Avraham, as he made the sale public and legal, doing it correctly (ethically), even as he faced the wiles of Efron. The site retains its holiness for the Jewish people to this very day as the burial plot of our ancestors.

Another important lesson from our Sages about this parsha is taught to us through the behavior of Avraham's servant, Eliezer, who was asked to choose a bride for Isaac. We learn from this story that the most important trait suitable to becoming a family member of Avraham and Sarah was kindness. Eliezer, watching Rivka feeding her sheep, observes that she had a well of kindness within her and the subsequent unfolding of events confirmed his choice. Through his strong faith Eliezer knew Divine Providence would lend a guiding hand to allow him to single out the virtuous bride-to-be. He then used perceptive communication with Rivka's family to effectively achieve his goal.

Eliezer also teaches us to know with whom you are speaking and how to speak to them. Any relationship requires perceptive communication to succeed. One must consider the perspectives and preferences of our partners, not just our own. By relating in this way, Eliezer, instead of being considered a fraud, was respected in the house of Betuel and successfully completed his mission.

Avraham's example of leadership, honor, and elevated character is required in our challenged world today. He teaches us that financial advantage, pragmatic political alliances, and even God's promises cannot replace our responsibility to act morally and ethically. No leader can ignore the exalted values of our tradition and use power or individual needs as the focal point of their privilege. Moreover, when a religious community becomes loyal to an immoral leader for practical benefits, it demeans the holiness of character that our first great leader Avraham epitomized and our responsibility to make God's name holy in the world as a people bound by the Torah and its ethical demands.

As Rabban Gamliel in Pirkei Avot cautioned us, "Beware of rulers, for they befriend someone only for their own benefit; they act friendly when it benefits them, but do not stand by someone in their time of need" (Pirkei Avot 2:3).

May our community and our world be blessed by the holy and the ethical values of our tradition. May we meet each other with love and respect, even when we may differ with each other's opinions and perceptions. Each of us is blessed with the ability to give a unique contribution to the world, and we are challenged to grow along the way in humility and in greater love. It is a long, arduous journey for all of us, and we are presented with many serendipitous blessings. Our journey is our challenge; we must meet it in gratitude, and know that if we are open to learning, greater truth will emerge.

Toldot

We have already read about the greatness of Avraham, the father of our nation, the originator of our tradition, and the man of *chesed*/kindness. Soon we will read about Yaakov/Israel, another giant who boldly stands out in our history. In our parsha we read about Yitzchak, the bridge between Avraham and Yaakov, who seems to fall short of the grandeur of the two praiseworthy ancestors who fit the heroic mold in our tradition. We do not find the numerous traditions and legends in our literature about Yitzchak as we do with Avraham and Yaakov.

But when we take a deeper look, we can find the innate greatness in our ancestor Yitzchak, as well. The one outstanding incident in his life was his readiness to be the sacrifice his father was to offer up at the bidding of God. His faith in Avraham and in God was valiant, steadfast, and unwavering. Moreover, as a result of this traumatic event, his personality developed an innate sense of awe, discipline, diligence, deliberateness, vigilance, and strict attentiveness. After all, if his father was able to lift up a knife to murder him, life must be a pretty frightening place and an unfathomable ordeal. Life becomes an experience of constantly surviving random, inexplicable suffering and one which demands bravery while living through many trials and tribulations. Thus, our tradition describes Yitzchak's essence as *pachad* (dreading) *Yitzchak*. Avraham was defined as the essence of *chesed*, and Yitzchak is defined as the essence of *yirah*/fear and trembling, or awe. After all, in this world, even a father can murder his son. Thus, one must proceed with caution, discipline, and boundary setting in order to interact successfully in this world.

What is so significant about *yirah*, and why is it so underrated, disrespected and neglected in our society? I personally gravitated toward rabbis in rabbinical school who emanated love, and felt uncomfortable around those who seemed overly cautious, careful, and too attentive to every detail of the law. Our Sages, however, proclaim that each energy—kindness (*chesed*) and careful attentiveness and deliberateness (*yirah*)—is a necessary trait applicable to different situations. They suggest that only when one is capable of both can an integrated "self" be actualized.

As I continued my tenure in rabbinical school, I began to realize that the trait of *yirah* had a holy root within it. It contained an awestricken quality that recognized that there was something larger in the universe than our egos. Those who embodied it acknowledged that God demanded *yirah* so as not to harm others, and not to cause destruction of others' property, and to value and respect all whom we encounter in this spiritual, mysterious world filled with splendor and tenuousness. If we are careful about not destroying our world, we will also be open to its magnificent beauty, the "*Mysterium Tremendum*," that dwells within it. I learned more about the value of the trait of *yirah* from observing the inwardness and piety of learned rabbis whose way to holiness embraced *chesed* and *yirah*. I still recall the intentional prayer of those who embodied *yirah*, as they experienced and connected to God in their inwardness. They had this capacity to connect to a level of holiness that went beyond our world of the senses. When they prayed the Amidah, some swayed gently and intensely as if they were in God's presence; some stood erect as a stick, almost in a trance, as they concentrated on every word, asking God for support, and thanking God for God's Grace and many blessings.

So, humble, gentle Yitzchak was happy to serve as a link between Avraham and Yaakov, to carry on the tradition, values and mandate to be passed on from generation to generation. He did not need to live in the limelight, but within his discipline. He accepted the charge placed upon him to serve the Lord as his father had, and to pass his knowledge and experience on to his offspring, Yaakov. This is an important message. Yitzchak teaches us that without those willing to carry out the introverted daily chores of the community, the extroverted leaders cannot succeed, and the community will dwindle and lose its spark.

An indication of Yitzchak's nature is found near the end of the parsha (Gen. 26:12-14). "Yitzchak had acquired wealth, flocks, and herds" because of the success of his father Avraham and his own continuous, assiduous, disciplined work in these fields. This abundance aroused jealousy in his neighbors, the Philistines. So, the Philistines aggressively stopped up all the wells Avraham's servants had dug in the days of yore and filled them with earth.

After this hostile act, Yitzchak departed from there and dug new wells in the valley of Gerar. But the herdsmen of Gerar quarreled with Yitzchak's herdsmen and said the water belonged to them. Yitzchak instructed his servants again to move and dig new wells; the herdsmen of Gerar quarreled over those as well. So, Yitzchak and his people once more relocated from there and dug other wells. Finally, at this point, his neighbors ended their quarreling and Yitzchak said, "Now God has created ample space and we can be fruitful in the land" (Gen. 26:22).

One might surmise that Yitzchak's passivity, his unwillingness to fight for his land and instead move on from a confrontation, comes from fear. This behavior was very different from Yitzchak's father, Avraham, who waged war with others and argued with God. Yitzchak had grown up around violence and confrontation. He watched his brother Yishmael be cast out in the desert with Hagar. He had experienced his father's knife at his own throat! This is why Yitzchak actively chooses another path, turning away from confrontation and violence when possible, preferring to dig new wells than to fight over the old ones. Are we to presume and infer that he did this from fear and weakness, or was it an active choice, to deliberately choose a different energy from his father's?

It is the latter—an active, alternative way of being, using *yirah*, discipline, deliberateness, and caution to search out ways that do not lead to violence. He had already experienced too much violence and aggression in his life. This affected his temperament, and his way became the way of *yirah*, conscious necessary restriction, deliberateness, and patience. This became the guiding light in his life. His patience and discipline led him to a successful end, a path to survival and peace. The result at the wells shows us that this alternative was the wiser course of action. Yitzchak finds new water, his neighbors seek a treaty with him, and he is blessed by God after the incidents of the wells.

May we all have the capacity to apply both *chesed* and *yirah* to create peace and harmony with one another and raise the level of our interactions through thoughtfulness, caring, patience, and discipline for the sake of the welfare of others. May both the energies of Avraham and Yitzchak bless us to create a more loving world.

On a personal note, I would like to acknowledge that during this week of Thanksgiving and Toldot, our family learned of the loss of a dear, beloved friend who had suffered from a major illness for months. Death alters our plans and our perceptions and awakens us to the fragility of life. We learn to appreciate the preciousness of what we have and not to take our blessings for granted. We learn that there are factors in life that we cannot control, to which we must yield and accept. The awareness of life's limitations awakens us to the importance of living every day with greater appreciation.

When Death arrives at our doorstep, it also humanizes our soul. It moves us to become more sensitive to the suffering of others. We may be moved to retreat from our self-centeredness, our pride, and our worry about trivial matters. Our quality of empathy is strengthened when we suffer loss, a quality so sorely needed in healing our fractured world. It reminds us that we must truly get to know the "other" who also suffers as we do.

Longfellow once wrote, "If we could read the secret history of our enemies, we should find in each man's life sorrow and suffering enough to disarm all hostility." Thus, suffering may lead us to a heightened sensitivity and compassion, to a capacity for healing and the powerful blessing of creating peace between brothers and sisters.

Let us also remember, in the spirit of this week's celebration of Thanksgiving, that our tradition sensitizes us to all that has been given to us through the commandment to recite 100 blessings every day, from the moment we wake up with gratitude, until we lay down to rest in the evening. When we live with gratitude, aware of all the gifts with which we have been blessed, we inevitably find our connection to the bestower of all these gifts, the Holy One, whose Light shines throughout creation. We are awakened to the infinite complexity and beauty that is always present. Gratitude is our most cherished companion in a life of faith. Moreover, living our life with gratitude leads us to give to others out of a sense of our inner joy and our innate responsibility to share abundance with others.

We are called to share with those who are hungry; with those who need our help to provide affordable housing; with those who are dependent on our resources and blessings to find the joy they deserve along their journeys. We are all interconnected, all God's children, all linked in our limited journeys on our blessed Earth.

On Thanksgiving Day this year, let us be awakened by the inevitable losses, the transience and fragility of life, to deeply appreciate all the gifts we do have: dear friends, nourishing food, the singing of the birds, the dancing of the waves, the blessings of smiles and welcoming eyes, the barking of friendly dogs, the sweet scent of Thanksgiving flowers on our tables, the gift of the wise ideals of our Torah, and the breath (the soul) that has been given to each of us.

Our family's thoughts are filled with memories of our beloved friend who now takes her journey to God's Palace. May she rest in the luminous, loving Light of the Lord and all those who have gone before her, as she now dwells in our fond memories and in the depths of our hearts. We carry both tears and sublime gratitude for all the years in which our friendship flourished, and we say, "Thank You."

Vayetze

In Parshat Vayetze, the Torah teaches us about the dynamics that fill Yaakov's psyche and are familiar to our own experiences.

In Genesis 29:11, we read, "Yaakov kissed Rachel and wept with emotion," for he saw that his soulmate would not come with him to the grave (Rashi). What is kissing? Answers the Zohar, "The cleaving of Soul to Soul." Indeed, Yaakov's life seems one long quest for the repose that was snatched away from him whenever he thought he had attained it. Lavan cheated him; Rachel eluded him on his wedding night; Yosef is taken from him; he has to leave the promised land in order to reunite with Yosef after years of separation and loss.

In Genesis 47:9, he tells Pharaoh that his troubles had made him old, not his natural physical process of aging. His kiss is filled with longing and the anguish of loss. Though Rachel is not buried with him (she dies and is buried in Bethlehem), our Sages teach that the depth of Rachel's tears served to influence the Heavenly Court to bring the Jewish people home from exile, comforting the people along their way home. Her tears, the result of separation from Yaakov, were so powerful that they influenced the Heavenly court to promote the redemption. We feel the longing of Yaakov, as all of us have had moments when our deepest desires are not fulfilled and our hearts are broken, but we find acceptance and continue to benefit from that which remains with us.

A second poignant message is found in Genesis 29:2-3. "He looked and there was a well in the field. . . . and the stone was large on the mouth of the well, and the shepherds would roll the stone from the mouth of the well and water the sheep." The Sfat Emet teaches that the field symbolizes the environment that surrounds us and what is within this well is a life-giving source we must discover. Every human being is capable of discovering the life force (the Light within), the truth within ourselves, the truth of the infinite.

But there are many inhibitions to self-knowledge and our destiny (the stone was large). We must gather all our faculties under the higher self and know what we have always known; that our inner spark of God is within us, and then we can roll the stone, remove our material proclivities and con-fusion. Rolling away—*vayigal*—the stone, removing that which prevents us from growth (resistance), creates revelation of truth, *gilui*, and redemption, *geulah*.

This is a superb insight into the human condition; it reveals the insight that is necessary to remove that which inhibits growth. The Jewish belief is that the Light, the soul, is always within our reach, waiting to be revealed.

In the same parsha, Yaakov experiences an unusual and transcendent dream as he travels from Be'er Sheva to Charan. "Behold a ladder is set up on the earth, and the top of it reaches to heaven, and behold angels of God are ascending and descending on it" (Gen. 28:12). The dream continues with God assuring Yaakov of God's support and watchfulness, and that his future offspring will be blessed. Yaakov awakens in awe and erects a holy monument to mark the place—Bet El, God's house—and pledges to give a tenth of all his bounties to God's world.

At times in our life, we are blessed, like Yaakov, with the "Great Dream." Or intuitive insights that alert us to our destiny and responsibility. We can attempt to live out our dream or we may dream away our lives! We can honor our encounter as a gift from the Holy One, and honor God by committing ourselves to actualizing our insights and carrying out our soul's calling in this world. Or we can allow the gift of the dream to fade away.

Yaakov, because of this numinous experience, immediately commits him-self to carrying out God's ways and immediately builds a symbol to mark the event. He knows how easy it is to allow even an inspirational event to flee one's consciousness and become lost unless inspiration moves to the realm of action.

What does this important dream symbolize for us? The ladder is a join-ing instrument with many rungs that teaches the importance of connecting Heaven and Earth. It teaches us that we are either ascending or descending, always in a state of change, and that we never really remain the same. It teaches us that each of us has a specific rung on the ladder and if we try to grab an inappropriate level or jump too quickly, we may fall.

We read in the dream that the angels first ascended (implying that they are on earth) and then descended, returning as in a circle. Should not the angels have logically come down first, and then returned to the heavenly realm? Instead, we are exposed to the angelic love of the lower levels of being, of the Earth and God's creations, reaching a higher level of development in the attempt to connect to the higher realm—and then bringing the heavenly energy back to Earth and embracing the lower world with love and care. After ascending again, they come down once more, as in a full circle, to continue their presence on earth rather than remaining in Heaven.

The angels' journey suggests that correct spiritual behavior includes the attempt to transcend this world while remaining responsible to care for all creatures on Earth. It is tempting to study Torah and feel inspired as a result, not wanting to be encumbered by our daily material duties. Our allegiance to Heaven, to the optimal imaginations of our psyche, may lead us to also feel judgmental toward others who have not ascended the heavenly ladder.

This is a trial for those who ascend and want to remain ensconced in this comfortable "high" space. If we don't integrate the higher light and share it with the world, we will alienate all those with whom we come into conflict. We will assume we are the elite, or sometimes we may fear we will be "compromised" by following the lures of the world, and so be inclined to flee from, rather than embrace, our fellow human beings, alienating them with our "judgments." Yaakov's dream teaches us that at each step of ascent, the lower rung must also be embraced. Judgment must be tempered with compassion, or a split within the self and the world will be created.

We encounter this very problem in our contemporary society. The zealots' extremism inhales shards from the upper world and "totalizes" this flavor, unable to compromise and engage with the "lower rung," making them unable to "partialize" their so-called idealism, polarizing our world rather than uplifting it. When there is no incorporation of the lower rung, this zeal, this desire, to impose this "upper Light" which can create a "utopian, messianic reality" can be harmful. The ascending striving, otherwise so appropriate, can become energy that is filled with hate—intolerant of the "imperfections" prevalent in our earthly human world. The extremists have no room for compromise and view compromise as weakness, rather than a necessary virtue to promote harmony. When the value of the "lower rung" is honored, this expansion of thinking can magnify the idealistic view and add new insights to previously held ideologies. Openness to change is a requisite for growth. Thus, the angels first ascend, but equally important, they always come back down to complete the cycle, to create the true messianic realm on Earth.

Unless we strive to become integrated in this way, acknowledging Earth as well as Heaven, we will painfully discover that hatred, and ultimately violence, lurk beneath "the love of the higher" professed to all. One who ascends but does not descend is dangerously disappointed by reality, willing to destroy this world to reach the utopia they have experienced in their messianic dream. If the ladder is not connected to this Earth, the process of construction will be destructive because it ignores our reality. The promised land cannot exist in Heaven, but must exist here on Earth, honoring the natural laws of this Earth.

Moreover, those who only descend in a frantic attempt to embrace the lower world are equally dangerous. In an attempt to make this secular, material world into a world of full value while ignoring the spiritual dimension, they inevitably create a world of such emptiness that it self-destructs, robbing us of all of that which elevates us.

Our current society exists in an era of polarization where political, religious and cultural differences seem to be stuck on opposite ends of the ladder. We must find a way to meet in the middle, absorbing those elements that can expand our limited views. There is no perfection on either end of the ladder, but progress and growth can occur if we take the full journey, make the full circle. Then we can wake up and realize that every rung of the ladder has some wisdom we need to learn.

Let us learn from Yaakov's dream how to keep moving up and down; to keep learning, to find the rung that inspires us and share that unique message to help heal the rifts in our world. Slowly but surely, by not falling off the ladder, we will progress toward a livable, nurturing society, one that can be a messianic realm here on our Earth.

May the wisdom in the depths of our Torah continue to promote growth and the actualization of the vast, unique gifts each of us possess since we are created in God's image. The faith that emerges from Torah study is a prerequisite for the hard work we must do to rid ourselves of the fears and insecurities that prevent us from moving forward to our life's destiny. May we all be successful and help each other with love to support the life journey of our brothers and sisters and delight in their success.

May that day come soon and may every Shabbat bring us the dream blessedly meant for us. Shabbat is but a taste of what a world of peace can be—a world of fraternity, respect, and the curiosity to learn from one another and from the song of the Torah.

Vayishlach

Among the many salient themes in our parsha this week we find insights into the impact dreams have on our psyche. Yaakov's dreams teach us the way to approach those who frighten us and show us how fear-based prejudice prevents reconciliation and harmony. A dream is a gift, but only if we use its message in the concrete world. We each can live out our dream, or dream away our lives.

At the beginning of our parsha, we read about Yaakov's return to his home-land for Isaac's funeral and his confrontation with Esav. After being away from home for 34 years (20 years dwelling with Laban and 14 years studying in the Yeshiva of Shem and Eber), Yaakov begins his journey back to the Land of Israel. As Yaakov advanced toward Israel with his family and entourage, Esav advanced toward him and there were 400 men with him. Yaakov prays, sends messengers with gifts for Esav, and, just in case, prepares for war.

He was hoping that Esav may have forgiven him after all this time. But when his messengers inform him that Esav is approaching with 400 men, the verse then says, "Yaakov was both frightened and distressed" (Gen. 32:8). Why the repetition? Rashi says that he was afraid he might be killed, but was also distressed because he might have to kill Esav.

Our Sages teach that the proper way to approach a potential war (enemy) is first to pray for peace and the wisdom to negotiate a successful outcome, then to send gifts to the aggressor to hopefully avoid war, and then to arm for battle.

Peace is always our fondest hope. Yaakov acknowledges that entering war creates the fear of defeat and death and, poignantly, the distress of having to kill another. This is very painful to a spiritual soul.

Yaakov divided his people and possessions into two camps, so if one is attacked the other may survive. During the night he took his wives and 11 children and crossed the Yabbok River (Gen. 32:23). They crossed with their possessions, perhaps to protect them from Esav, and Yaakov remained alone on the other side of the Yabbok. Some commentators suggest the word

Yabbok is very similar to Yaakov and thus intimates he was "crossing over into himself."

He had reached a stage where his soul was ready for transformation (a night journey of the soul). The time was ripe for him to overthrow his fear and adaptive trickster personality and evolve into the higher destiny of "Israel." At that point, the Torah tells us that he meets a man/angel, and they wrestle until the break of dawn. This wrestling is generally viewed as a symbolic struggle or a prophetic vision. Is Yaakov still filled with fear and the impulse to run away or is he now finally ready to face his fears? After all, Yaakov's fear was the catalyst for the "trickster" coping mechanism that was a pattern in much of his early life—lying to his father, tricking Esav about the birthright, and being surrounded by lies for 14 years while living with Laban, a consummate conman.

On the eve of his dramatic confrontation with brother Esav, will he leave his "trickster" defense, and grow into a higher being with nobler ideals? It is reasonable to assume that because of his fear, he was trying to escape the danger he intuited was awaiting him by once more escaping through a lie and abandoning his family. As he falls asleep alone on his side of the river, he dreams he wrestles with an angel (his higher self), and his thigh is wounded in the fight. In that dream, Yaakov reached a state of consciousness that transformed him to a higher level of being: he could no longer run away from truth with trickery. We learn from his dream that the essence of lying stems from fear and avoidance of perceived consequences we assume will be painful. Yaakov was ready for this dream and future reality to emerge; we can only enter and decipher a dream when our consciousness is ready to receive it.

The angel wounds his thigh so he cannot run away again. He must now face his new destiny as the one who struggles with God, or the one who sings to God, or one whose soul is now oriented toward becoming one who engages in righteous and just behavior. It is a mystical moment, a progression to becoming "the very one he was meant to be—recognizing and choosing his destiny—with a new name to symbolize his new path.

His name is changed; no longer will he be called "Yaakov" (the trickster) but he is transformed into a man of truth, and will be called "Israel." This word can either mean "He who struggles with God," or "He who sings to God" (as Rav Kook suggests *Shir Eil*), or "The one who does Righteousness (*Yashar*) for God."

This is the second elevated dream Yaakov experienced as he grew into his destiny. The first dream occurred in Genesis 28:11-22, the dream of the ladder with angels ascending and descending, with God promising to be with him and his children. When he woke up from that dream, Yaakov experienced awe, the Light of the unique essence of the Divine, the root of his own soul and his unique destiny.

But the whispers of a dream's revelation sometimes get lost in our daily encounters with life. They can remain suspended, random, delayed in a circular dance of unconsciousness for generations, until we become capable of hearing the whispering voices waiting to bless us. We must sometimes wait for the next dream to awaken us again. Yaakov's dream of wrestling with the angel is such an event.

Yaakov had yet another dream. The third dream appeared after he spent many years with his immoral father-in-law, Laban. It was a dream (Gen. 31:10) about material opulence, about goats and flocks. Yaakov realized his dreams had changed, and this one let him know that he had become immersed in the material world of Laban and had to leave to reclaim his destiny. Laban had worn away his dream of a higher destiny, the destiny of Israel. He became Yaakov again, so God told him to go back "to the land of your fathers," to recapture the meanings of the dreams of the angels so that he could once again be Israel.

A final message reveals itself in the reconciliation of Yaakov and Esav. After wrestling with the angel, Yaakov returns and the brothers meet. When they finally meet, Esav runs up to Yaakov, falls on his neck and kisses him, and they both weep (Gen. 33:4).

It seems Esav forgave him after all ("time is a healer"), and their poignant meeting is one of love and longing. A further indication of this is when they appear together at their father Isaac's funeral. Reading the text in this way reveals the capacity for change and forgiveness that each of us has, even when we have been wounded. *Teshuvah* (return to the soul within) is one of God's greatest gifts to us.

And here we have two divergent views in the rabbinic tradition regarding the attitude toward Esav (Rashi 33:4; Sifrei Bamidbar 69.2). One attitude leads to peace and reconciliation between enemies, and one remains eternally distrustful of Esav and does not imagine that he has the capacity to change ("Esav will always hate Yaakov").

The latter rabbinical view says that Esav was trying to bite/nashko Yaakov's neck and that Yaakov's neck turned to marble, so Esav cried because he hurt his teeth while Yaakov cried out in fear. These Rabbis see the old Esav. But other Rabbis took the view that after all these years there had been a true change in Esav's character, that the kiss was sincere, and the weeping was a show of true reconciliation on the part of both brothers.

The Rabbis who feel that Esav cannot change hang on to their animosity and see Esav's character as unchangeable, as they are convinced that Esav's initial betrayal by Jacob (stealing his birthright) is a wound that cannot be healed. They view him as a man filled with a desire for vengeance. Esav is stereotyped as the symbol of evil who will always try to destroy Israel. As one midrashic rabbi states, "Esav only cried because he tried to bite Yaakov's neck, but it was turned to stone, so he cried tears of pain, not forgiveness."

This negative view continues throughout history with the dictum that Esav will always hate Yaakov ("*Eisav soneh et Yisrael*"). It becomes a self-fulfilling prophecy, expecting the worst and never being open to the possibility of change, creating negative energy on both sides. This rabbinic opinion transformed the complex character of Esav into the archetype villain who appears throughout history and whose intent is to destroy the Jews.

Another rabbinic voice also claims Esav only came to the funeral to claim his inheritance and not to reconcile with Yaakov. The view that antisemitism is built into the psyche of all opponents of Israel is a dangerous notion that prevents the reconciliation of enemies.

This view is considered by many to be contrary to the heart of the Torah, which teaches love, compassion, and forgiveness through acting in the ways of *Yisrael/Yashar Eil*. Every individual has the innate ability to do the right thing and is capable of *teshuvah*/returning, and reaching harmony with others.

There is definitely an alternate understanding of this rabbinic Esav which is crucial for us to create a more peaceful world. True, the young Esav was no saint, impetuously selling his birthright for fast food (Gen. 25:33). And the seed of revenge does enter his mind when Yaakov deceives his father in order to receive the firstborn blessings from Isaac (Gen. 27:41).

But 20 years later, when Esav could exact revenge on his brother, what did he do? He ran to embrace his brother; he kissed him, and he cried (Gen. 33:4). It is simply inconceivable to a second group of Rabbis that Esav is the same old manipulator. They imagine and proclaim that after 20 years of soul-searching, Esav has matured into a respectable human being. They acknowledge the capacity for change, and that even Esav is capable of *teshuvah* and new understanding. They proclaim that brothers can reconcile and that forgiveness can be achieved. Clearly, anger and hatred poison one's soul.

One consequence of following the Rabbis who claim that Esav is unchanging is that we have internalized Yaakov's fears and continue uncharitable judgments toward "the other." When Yaakov's messengers tell Yaakov that Esav is coming toward him with 400 men, he panics and assumes that Esav is coming to destroy him (Gen. 32:7-8). Thus, the cautious rabbinic commentators align with Yaakov's mentality before his numinous night journey/encounter with the angel of God. They see him as one still filled with a fear/trickster mentality and conclude that the prudent response to all adversaries who contain even fragments of hostility is to be on guard and not trust them.

An alternate reading of our Torah text by other rabbinic commentators recognizes that the text does not say that Esav's men were armed; it just says that he was accompanied by 400 men. Surely, the messengers would have conveyed that vital piece of information if they were indeed armed. This group of commentators includes Rashbam, Rashi's grandson, who looked at the exact wording of the passages in the Torah, rather than interpreting them in their historical context.

They say that Yaakov sent messengers to seek Esav's favor (Gen. 32:6) and Esav responded favorably by coming with a large greeting party to show Yaakov his happiness, respect, and love. Moreover, a further indication of their reconciliation is that Yaakov and Esav attended their father Isaac's funeral together and buried him together. (Gen. 35:29).

May we all find the courage and discernment to allow for growth and forgiveness so that we can forge peace with previous enemies and make a world worthy of the Messiah. May Yaakov and Esav find the capacity for peace and love in our time, so that our energies are free to reach the highest potential of which we are each capable, to discover the God within and the abundance of God's Grace in all the beauty of our creation.

We ask to be blessed to achieve reconciliation with those who have harmed us. May we follow our great dreams, and always seek peace before hostility. May Yaakov's angel meet us and guide us to the beauty we are meant to share in this world! Amen!

Vayeishev / Hanukkah

There are three themes raised in this parsha, and each teaches us something about the way we treat one another.

The first is favoritism. The Talmud in Shabbat 10B attributes the initial cause of the animosity between Yosef and his brothers to Yaakov. Yaakov favored Yosef by giving him a coat of many colors (*ketonet passim*). Yaakov appointed Yosef to be the leader among the brothers and gifted him with this special garment as a symbol of his leadership. The brothers were jealous of Yosef because of this. Most often, when someone has a son in his old age, older siblings accept their father's extra show of love to the youngest and do not resent this added affection. In this case, however, there was an unexpected factor that upset the normal dynamics. Yosef was a tattletale and carried stories about their evil doings to Yaakov. When the brothers observed him trying to turn their father against them, their hatred for him was aroused. Once that happened, they hated him for the favoritism Yaakov had shown him as well. For this reason, the Talmud teaches us to avoid showing favoritism to any child (Shabbat 10b). One never knows what additional factors will come into play. It was gossip, *lashon hara*, that brought Yosef down into Egypt and subsequently led to the slavery of the Hebrew people.

The second theme is fear: Our reading begins with the words, "And Yaakov dwelled in the land of the sojourns of his father." The Hebrew word for sojourn (*megure*) can be derived from another root to mean *fear*. This leads the Ramban and the *Kedushaht* Levi to understand the verse to say, "And Yaakov dwelled in the fears of his father Isaac." This is a very profound insight. To modern ears, it sounds as if it were taken directly from Freud. In large measure, we do live "in the fears of our parents." We take on such apprehensions as the fear of failure and success, the fear of ridicule, the fear of the unknown, and thus the need for control. In a deeper sense, we draw into ourselves the unexpressed fears of our parents, about their parenting, about their experience with their own parents, about the meaning or meaninglessness of their lives, and about their insecurities. We as children take these into ourselves by a living osmosis, and we pass on our own fears and anxieties to our children. So, we do, indeed, dwell in the land of the fears of our parents!

What was Yaakov's fear? His father Isaac had been bound to the altar and nearly sacrificed to God. Isaac experienced the truly awesome power of God. Even if Isaac had never spoken about it to Yaakov, Yaakov would have known of the total devotion of that moment, of its utter holiness. And so, despite God's promise of protection, Yaakov feared that he would not be able to worship God with the awesome commitment that Isaac manifested, and he would thereby bring disaster upon himself and his family.

The Berdichever Rebbe teaches that this anxiety, this fear, is not bad or to be avoided. Fear is a natural part of life that can motivate us to grow. But these anxieties must have a framework, a dimension of transcendent meaning that is gleaned from a communal culture, or a personal soul journey. Only when fear is rooted in significance is it worthy of our human energy. Meaning comes from this larger destiny, not from our personal pain.

In our modern world, we tend to spend a lot of time dealing with our personal fears, those drawn from experience, and those drawn from the experience of our parents insofar as they have been absorbed into our own psyches. But what is one to do with these fears? There is no life without fear. Owning the knowledge that our bodies will perish creates unavoidable anxiety. But if we have a religious (transpersonal) context that gives some meaning to our lives, fear can find its place. There is a spiritual (and social) reality that guides anxieties, giving them a larger context beyond the self.

There is holiness which gives meaning to a life which is otherwise only personal. One needs meaning, and one also needs the ability to be creative and actualize one's unique vocation, gifts, and destiny. We must always find a larger context if our anxieties are to be attenuated. One of the main problems of our modern age is that many people are unable to find a larger meaningful context that allows them to overcome their anxieties, the main one being the fear of death. Many in the modern world have lost faith in traditional religions, myths, and communities. Our challenge is to share the depth and wisdom of our Jewish tradition and make it engaging, comprehensive, and dynamic for modern people. We must also allow each person in his or her uniqueness to search honestly within and without, and allow God's grace to enter.

Destiny is the third and main theme woven through the parsha and the thread of Yosef's life. His faith and commitment to an inner conviction of his exalted destiny is palpable. It was his guide through every challenging experience he encountered. Yosef trusted his dreams, he believed in himself, and that his destiny was to become a leader. Though he was incarcerated with slaves in Egypt, he submitted to God's will with faith. His deprivations led to him building the necessary spiritual strength to become a leader in Egypt and allowed him to look back without vengeance at the hardhearted mistreatment by his brothers. He felt everything that happened to him was necessary and divinely ordained. It is why he was called Yosef the Righteous One (*Yosef Hatzaddik*). Whether residing in a lowly prison or living in the opulent palace of Pharaoh, his faith never wavered. He felt every experience was ordained, and that he needed to respond appropriately without malice, disappointment, or anger—for "God's will" was present on this journey. He embraced his fate and chose to make it the destiny that God bestowed upon him.

This recognition of the Divine is what distinguishes the deeply religious person from the cursory religious person; each of them behaves differently under adversity. When their good fortune has turned away from them, one can readily determine whether their religion was deeply felt or not and whether they retain faith in God's benevolence under adverse circumstances. We usually associate happiness with something pleasant, never with suffering. Yet religion connects the two because it looks beyond the pains of the moment to consequences in the future. We may be better off because of the afflictions that come upon us if borne in the right spirit.

This was true of Yosef. His misfortunes were also experienced as blessings yet to be revealed. Had his life run smoothly, he would not have achieved as much as he did under the stress of hardship. His early dreams made him aware of his destiny. He felt he was destined by God to play a great part in the history of his family by occupying an exalted position. Imagine this young, vulnerable man having to become a servant in Potiphar's home. He was a slave. One would have imagined his ambitions would have been completely shattered by his hard fate, but he clung to them all the while. He never lost faith in his destiny because he knew it was God's will.

Yosef believed his life was controlled from on high. If troubles befell him, he felt they were sent by God and must be beneficial and not harmful, and were all part of the plan. And so it was. The very misfortunes that appeared so inexplicable were the stepping stones to his ability to save his people. His faith gave him unwavering trust in the purposes of God. He never thought of taking revenge on his brothers for their treatment of him, and felt that what happened to him at their hands was part of God's plan. He waited until they showed regret for their deeds before revealing himself to them, since he felt their regret and *teshuvah* were necessary for their healing and reconciliation.

Yosef teaches us all to believe in our dreams and our unique destinies and to be guided by our soul's intuitions and the outer signs and provisions that life presents to us under the guidance and benevolence of Hashem. But this necessitates our looking inward, trusting our inner voice, and looking outward with faith to discover the blessings set out for us. We then take the necessary actions that we are meant to bring into the world.

Let us now turn to Hanukkah.

Hanukkah is one of those times we should seek out the Light that binds us together and helps us define our lives, just as Yosef did. In these most challenging times, when Earth itself confronts one tragedy after another—constant wars, pandemics, the climate crisis, painful hunger, unemployment, and cultural divisions that keep us apart—Hanukkah reminds us of the Light that always dwells within the darkness. In this darkness, there may be no better time to join in Hanukkah singing, in soaking up the Light of Hanukkah, and affirming our belief that Light will enter and transform the darkness, and faith will transcend skepticism.

In facing the darkness together, we will rekindle the divine spark in our souls as we connect to each other, to Torah, prayer, and song. As challenging as it might be, each of us can rekindle our faith. We must always remember the deep truth: All our thoughts and actions, our daily decisions, and how we see and relate to the world have a profound impact on bringing light or creating darkness; everything we do (or do not do) can have a profound impact on those with whom we share our planet.

As we observe the wonders of nature, peering at powerful, white shiny waves in the ocean, surrounded by majestic life-sustaining trees, we can feel the impact of the extraordinary connection between people, animals, plants, the air, the water, and the soil. Staying conscious of the interconnection between all things can help us intuit and appreciate the miracle of life and how we, as part of this interconnection, impact the whole world. We are each God's candle—given the power to always impart Light into darkness.

In addition to the blessing of Light and faith/miracle that Hanukkah brings, Hanukkah also brings us the message of religious freedom with the story of the uprising of the religious community against oppression, and the importance of the religious tolerance the Jews brought to the world. Hanukkah also reminds us of the threat of our assimilation into the larger cultures we live in and the loss of our Jewish roots. Just as the culture of Hellenism overpowered the majority of the Jewish people in ancient times and their specifically Jewish identity was threatened, we, too, Jews in America, face a similar challenge. We all too often celebrate the holiday of Hanukkah only in relation to the universal ideal that we venerate as American Jews when we associate our holiday with the celebration of Christmas, stressing the nature of its universal celebration of Light and miracle for all people.

However, unlike Purim, which is celebrated as a holiday of triumph over the impending physical destruction of the Jewish people, Hanukkah is instructive of the equally powerful threat of the spiritual destruction of the Jewish people as we forget who we are when we take in the overwhelming culture of the society around us. Jewish survival was threatened by the overwhelming lure of the outer Hellenistic culture at that time (second century BCE) and many opted to give up their unique Jewish customs to assimilate and be accepted by the outer culture. This ever-increasing threat lives with us today. Hanukkah reminds us that if we are to survive as a Jewish people, our particularistic uniqueness must be honored along with our assertion of universal values. Many of us today live first as Americans and only pay lip service to Jewish traditions that at times are at odds with the values of the larger culture. We prefer to blend in rather than suffer the stigma of being a people apart, and abandon practices and values that are distinct from Western values of exaggerated materialism and hedonism.

Jews and members of each unique culture must own and contribute their uniqueness to the larger whole for true unity to occur. We may aim to "blend" but opt not to "melt into a pot" where our uniqueness is obliterated or negated by the majority culture. This is a major challenge; some in our community, like some Hasidic sects, opt for extreme separation because of the power of the outer culture. They, as our Maccabees, may become the surviving remnant of our community, unless we learn to honor the beauty and obligations of our unique tradition and live in this world as Jews in a blended society. In this way, Hanukkah teaches us the importance of particularism which must be respected if we are to survive in a culture of universalism. A Jewish universalism without particularism is doomed to obliteration, but a particularism that denies our ideal of universal love and respect for all people will lead to tribalism and isolation that denies our mandate of bringing our Light to the entire world through interaction and faith.

May the Light of Hanukkah strengthen our universal calling, strengthened both by the universal Light that surrounds us and the particularistic traditions that sustain our identities and promote our universal mandate of spreading God's Light in the world.

Miketz / Hanukkah

Miketz continues the Yosef story and reiterates what a life of faith looks like. Out of all our ancestors, Yosef is the one who is called *Yoseph Hatzaddik*— Yosef the Righteous. He was the embodiment of a very strong faith in God and the destiny designated for him. As a result, he accepted everything that happened to him as the path God determined for him. He saw his journey contained meaning and purpose, whereas another human being might see it as a path with no rhyme or reason, one that was torturous at times. He believed so firmly in his dreams of his special destiny, that he acted righteously in every circumstance that befell him. That is the definition of a *tzaddik*—one who believes in God not only during the good times, but more importantly, when darkness befalls them.

This is visible in Yosef's interaction with his brothers. They sold him into slavery and let Yaakov think he was dead. Yet Yosef did not contact his suffering father once he rose to prominence. Our commentators suggest that Yosef so strongly believed his journey had a meaning that would lead to a positive resolution for all, that it would ultimately result in reunion and the healing of his father. He believed he was sent to Egypt to save his people and the Egyptians from hunger, and his brothers were part of the plan to bring about the fulfillment of his dreams. He delayed revealing himself to them because part of the fulfillment of his journey had to contain their complete repentance—their taking responsibility for their actions; their acknowledgment and contrition for what they had done to him and their asking for forgiveness. He saw them taking responsibility and being sorrowful for what they had done. He saw that although they faced the possibility of abandoning their youngest brother Benjamin, who was at his mercy, they stood up to protect him and sacrificed themselves in the process. He knew they had evolved into better people from their earlier misdeeds and jealousy and were now virtuous and upright. He created the opportunity for them to show their righteous behavior, and so he forgave them and poured out his love for them.

At the time of their reconciliation, he poignantly asked, "Is my father at peace, is my father still alive?" The repetition suggests that he is asking if his father is vital and living his life despite his loss, and is not living a superficial and depressed existence. He wondered if his father might be at peace, but was he truly alive? He was elated to learn Yaakov was alive.

The difficult questions raised by Yosef's sometimes puzzling behavior can be answered by understanding that he behaved as one who believes in his dreams and destiny. After all, Yosef's behavior from the moment he first arrived in Egypt, and then when his brothers came in search of food, was bewildering. Why didn't he send a message to his father after being released from prison and being appointed to an influential position in Potiphar's household? Yaakov thought his beloved son may have been killed, so why did Yosef let him live with such uncertainty? Yosef also must have known there was hunger in the countries surrounding Egypt, including Canaan. How could he not help his own family? He may have been angry with his brothers for having sold him, but his father and his brother Benjamin were also in Canaan. And the moment he discovered his brothers' identity, he failed to help them and put all kinds of obstacles in their way. He even accused them of being spies and thieves. Could Yosef not overcome his resentment? Did he want to take revenge?

Yosef's story challenges each of us to learn to live our lives believing in our destinies and to act in sync with them. Let us view each day of our lives as a miracle and march heroically to live out our destinies and contribute to our world. Let us do this with faith and with joy, as it is for this we are created. Even when we perceive things as simple little deeds that do not hold much import, we must know that each deed is part of the destiny that contributes to our larger world. Each of these deeds, indeed, carries a miracle within. So let us each learn to listen to our destiny, live it out, and love ourselves in the process, feeling God's Presence with us.

Miketz is also the parsha that falls during Hanukkah. At the heart of the festival is the joy of the Temple rededication in Jerusalem after the incredible victory of the vastly outnumbered Maccabees over the Syrians who had defiled it.

Our Sages ask, "Why is the miracle of Hanukkah an eight-day miracle?" After all, when the Jews entered the Holy Temple, they found enough natural oil to burn for one day, so the miracle should have lasted seven days. The Sages responded by saying that this is the difference between the way the Hellenists look at the world and the way Jews look at the world. Whereas the Hellenists make a distinction between the laws of nature and those "beyond nature/miracles," the Jews see even natural laws as miraculous. That's because the energy and causality of God are manifest in the workings of the natural world. The natural world is not to be taken for granted, but looked at in amazement as the work of the Creator.

This explanation is fascinating as it awakens us to the glory of everyday creation—in nature, in architecture, in the amazing accomplishments of human beings created in God's image to build a world of technological complexity—to pave highways, to build subways, to build telescopes in outer space, etc. All these achievements should not be taken for granted, as they truly reveal the miraculous and awesome glory of God's creation. God is the creator of creators, and the ingenuity of human beings made in God's image elevates the faith in our souls, showing us how the Lord dwells among us.

The historian Josephus describes the intense struggle that took place between the Maccabees and Assimilationists in the Jewish community of the second century BCE, one which led to civil war. Different factions in the community fought to shape the future direction of the Jewish people. The Maccabees clashed with the Hellenistic Jews, and the Assimilationists opposed the senior, committed Jews.

But the rededication of the Temple would have been impossible if the Maccabees had not had a powerful commitment to their heritage and their faith. And our Sages remind us that we should remember to rededicate our personal temples, the temples in our hearts, at this time. We must continually bring more light into the world amidst the transient darkness. Just as the community of Israel is instructed to build a sanctuary for Hashem, so too are we each instructed to build a sanctuary for Hashem in our hearts. Just as we were given the mitzvah of purifying the oil in the Holy Temple, so too must we ensure that there is pure oil in our personal temples.

We know not all Jews in the second century BCE had this sense of dedication, and in every generation, we are tempted to assimilate into the cultural values of the larger community surrounding us. In those days, there were Jewish Hellenists content to assimilate into the larger Greek culture. They adopted Greek gods, the Greek language, Greek sports, Greek modes of dress, and Greek names. Hebrew was neglected. The Sabbath and Jewish festivals were gradually replaced by pagan observances. Some Hellenists even underwent a painful surgical procedure to undo their circumcision so that they might appear in the public arena in the nude.

But there were enough Jews who cared about preserving Judaism, our distinctive way of life, and our spiritual identity who decided to oppose this vast assimilation. Without their fierce determination, there would have been no temple rededication.

This is true today, too. We live with very tempting opportunities that can lead us away from our tradition, yet Hanukkah reminds us that there is always a strong contingent of Jewish people who will fight to continue the beauty of our tradition. These souls recognize the importance of ensuring that our tradition thrives and flourishes in the culture in which we live and that we use it to be a light unto the nations.

However, Yosefus points out that although the traditionalists were victorious, they did not banish Greek culture in its entirety. Hundreds of Greek words and concepts entered the Talmud and Midrash. Greek science, philosophy, and aesthetics found a place in the writings of Maimonides and other commentators. The Septuagint, a translation of the Torah into Greek, also suggests a mutual influence that was prevalent. The Talmud (Megillah 9b) says that the Sages permitted the Torah scrolls to be written in Greek.

Though this allowed the reading of the Torah in the vernacular to increase the spread of the Torah amongst the masses, the commentators also suggest that this translation to the vernacular was a curse. It had detrimental consequences, since it allowed people to read the Torah text without mastering the holy Hebrew language; and though the superficial knowledge of Torah was available to a wider number of people within the community, the deeper level of Jewish knowledge was diminished.

The Midrash Shachar affirms the positive influence Greek culture added to Jewish tradition. As it states in Genesis 9:27, in Noah's blessing to his sons Yiftach and Shem, "May the beauty of Yiftach dwell in the tents of Shem." The Midrash identifies Shem as the forerunner of Israel and Yiftach as Greece in the future. This suggests the validation of extracting the positive aspects of Greek culture, (music, art, philosophy, and poetry) and adding beauty to the sublime concepts of our eternal Torah and its communication with the Divine. As Heinrich Heine, the 19th-century German romantic poet, born to assimilated Jewish parents, famously said, "For the Greeks, beauty is truth, and for the Hebrews, truth is beauty."

Can the positive aspects of modernity (science and art) integrate and complement our Jewish tradition today with our eternal values of ethics, humility, and awe before God? Can this dance increase the harmony in our world? Can Jewish culture make a positive impact on the outer culture and inject ethical values, values of justice, of loving behavior within our community as images of what an enlightened ethos can achieve?

There are those traditionalists who believe that our modern culture is too crowded with temptations, with excess materialism and hedonism that can lead us away from a life of holiness. They believe it is prudent to live separately from the outer culture—as do the Satmar Hasidim who live in Kiryas Yoel and Williamsburg in New York State, or the Tosher Hasidim who live in Kiryas Tosh, a suburb of Montreal, Canada.

And then there are those who believe that our encounter with the larger culture enables us to introduce our enlightened values to others while engaging with the positive dimensions of modernism. The latter view claims that Judaism throughout our history has integrated positive dimensions from various cultures throughout the ages and introduced new customs as we grew and changed through history. Yosefus confirmed this about our second-century BCE encounter with Hellenism. Yet we must be cautious because the lure of the outer culture can be so intense, that it may sometimes require the balancing voice and practice of extremists—such as the Maccabees—to ward off a disastrous, extreme assimilation.

The different energies prevalent at the time of the second century BCE and the story of Hanukkah awaken us to the complexity and tensions of living in modern culture. At the same time, we are preserving our unique destiny as a people of Light who bring a unique message to our world, one that emphasizes holiness, justice, love, awe, and gratitude to our Creator. Yet we are vulnerable to assimilation. The tensions that different groups within our community create to maintain their cherished view as the correct response to modernity make our challenge all the greater. Only with increased tolerance for the views of disparate groups can we create an example of harmony that will be the example, the guiding Light of Hanukkah necessary to create the messianic world that we are charged to create.

May we be blessed by the beauty of the shimmering candles, always giving off light, light that is never diminished. May we be inspired by this Light and the shining candle within each of us and rededicate the pure oil that burns within each one of us. May the light of the Shabbat candles combine with the light of the Hanukkah candles to make this Shabbat the brightest revelation of God's Light, the light waiting for us to spread its beauty throughout our world!

Vayigash

In Parshat Vayigash, we learn Yosef is unable to control his emotions follow-ing Judah's moving appeal to save Benjamin. The verse says, "Yosef could not restrain himself in the presence of his brothers who now stood before him, so he called out, 'Remove everyone else [the Egyptians] from the room.'"

Only his brothers remained when Yosef made himself known to them (Gen. 45:1). Rashi says Yosef asked the Egyptians to leave because he did not want to shame his brothers and reveal what they had done to him in front of his courtiers. The Midrash explains that he took a great risk in doing that, for his brothers feared he intended to avenge himself on them for selling him into slavery. Yosef's previous behavior seemed to point to this conclusion—he accused them of being spies; he imprisoned Simon; he planted the cup in Benjamin's sack and forced them to return to Egypt.

They were baffled. Why did this viceroy (Yosef) bear them ill will? Once he revealed himself, they were so worried about revenge they might have killed him in self-defense. Yosef realized this and that taking revenge might jeopardize his yearning for a reunion with Jacob.

Neither of these rationales mattered to Yosef as much as his desire not to embarrass and shame them in front of strangers. These were the same brothers who had caused his terrible suffering for the past 22 years. He thought it would be better to die than shame them in front of the Egyptians. This exemplified his exceptional character and his powerful inner faith. Only someone with extraordinary faith could act this way.

His words of reconciliation are based on his unwavering faith in God and his destiny. He told them, "Don't be distressed, Hashem sent me here as a source of sustenance to provide for you, to ensure your survival in the land and to sustain you for a momentous deliverance" (Gen. 45:5-7). He continued, "It was not you who sent me here, but God, and I am fully aware that the interpretations of my dreams were divinely inspired. I harbor no hatred toward you, you were only acting as God's instruments. Tell my father Hashem made me master of all of Egypt, to please come and not delay so that I can provide for you when you will join me here" (Gen. 45:8-9).

Because of Yosef's faith in God, he was able to avoid focusing on the wrongs inflicted upon him or see life through a glass darkly. Instead, he saw life through the lens of faith. Yosef could have remembered how his brothers mistreated him; how they cast him into a pit where he might have perished had an Ishmaelite caravan not appeared; how they coldly traded him away without any remorse. Instead, he remembered how he provoked them, how he brought tales of malice about them to their father Jacob. He may have remembered how he taunted them with dreams of his destined domination over them. Yet instead of remembering the wrongs he suffered at their hands, he chose to remember the wrongs he inflicted on them. Rather than exacting revenge, he chose to make amends.

What took Yosef such a long time to reveal himself? He was waiting for and anticipating a sign of his brothers' regret about their past behavior. He did not blame them or take the opportunity for revenge. When Judah protected Benjamin, telling Yosef that if Benjamin did not return with them their father would die of grief (Gen. 44:29), at that moment Yosef realized his brothers were regretful of their past actions. They were united and ready to fight for their younger brother. They had come full circle as he had hoped and expected they would. And so, he proceeded with the reveal.

One of the main messages of the parsha is that we can only survive and thrive as Jews if we have the ability for reconciliation and are united—if we approach and become close to each other (*Vayigash*/And Judah came close) (Gen. 44:1). "Every Jew, every human being, must say to his brother and sister *Geshu Eilai*/Come near to me" (Gen. 45:4).

We are all interconnected. Because of Judah's genuine concern for Benjamin, Yosef said, "I am your brother" (Gen. 45:3). I want to be part of our family, I want to live with loyalty, love, and devotion. This strength to reconcile is our salvation and our blessing. Without this capacity, we will live in a world of acrimony, hatred, and danger. With faith, and appreciation of the Divine in our life, who Loves our love, we will create a better world. So let us identify and become conscious of our memories and our wounds and learn to focus on our capacities and resilience to live as Yaakov and Yosef have done in their lives despite all their challenges.

In addition to the pain, heartbreak, and the outpouring of Yosef's love for his brothers, this story explains the importance of memories—of what we remember, and how our memories define us. We can remember darkness and negative feelings toward others or we can remember the positive events that affected our lives. It is imperative to work to search out and strengthen those memories that are uplifting while revealing suppressed memories that may influence our outlook, unbeknownst to us. Perhaps Yosef's years in prison enabled him to confront negative memories and move on from them as he released his feelings and found forgiveness. He moved from the realm of unconscious influence to conscious clarity of the deeper Light within and recaptured his destiny.

Often, we repress uncomfortable memories, and unbeknownst to us we are controlled by their intense imprint. Thus, we must work to unveil deep memories and release their intense influence upon us by remembering them and unveiling the strong emotions attached to them. After this important work, our memories can become redeemed and our darkness lifted.

It is not unusual for us to see the dark side of life. We all carry inner wounds. It may be easy to notice people who are mendacious, insensitive, greedy, and self-centered. But Yosef teaches us that we can also see the nobility and generosity of the human spirit, the sacrifice and kindness many people manifest daily. If we only remember another person's faults, we are doomed to remain cynical, critical, and probably depressed. Though Yosef's wounds were deep, the strength of his faith was an antidote to depression and anger.

A more positive memory balance sheet is a holy requirement to create a better world. When we model faith, humility, and virtuous action, we create holiness in the world and fulfill our mandate as a "holy nation." When we focus on the positive, we create positive energy and uplift others. Thus, it is important to recognize what we are "remembering" and how it affects us and those around us. We may not have the innate strength of Yosef, but we do have the capacity to become more aware of our thoughts and the impact they have on our behavior. Our Jewish tradition teaches us that we are required to focus our minds in prayer every day. We are to take a moment to examine where our minds and memories are and through this consciousness, create the new habit of remembering with positivity the gift God bestowed upon us in this glorious creation. It is our duty to uplift our world and make it a blessing through our memories.

And so when Yosef asks his brothers (Gen. 45:3), "Is my father still alive (*chai*)?" Reb Shneur Zalman of Liadi says Yosef was asking more than "Was Jacob not dead," he was asking if he was still *alive*. The word *chai*/alive takes on special meaning. Was Yaakov living with vitality despite his loss and suffering? To be alive on the level of chai is to be infused with the energy of the inner Light connected with one's soul and God's grace. It is the quality that allows us to live with joy and gratitude, even accepting suffering as God's benign providence containing meaning and eventual blessing. It is our connection to the latent Light in the universe that fills us with faith and trust. In this way, we are truly *alive* to God. Shabbat is a wonderful, special day to rest, to remove the repetitious, unconscious chatter of worry and toil, and get reconnected to *chai*, to Life and Light!

May we each find strength and *commit* ourselves to *practice* positive remembering, to count our blessings, to love and appreciate the gifts of our Creator, and to become, through the practice and holy training of our life of mitzvot, a candle of Light in our world.

Vayechi

The word *Vayechi*/And he lived, contrasts sharply with the parsha's opening theme which begins with a deathbed scene. Yaakov is taking his final leave from his family. He blesses his children and grandchildren. "And when Yaakov finished blessing his sons, he gathered up his feet into the bed and died, and was gathered unto his people" (Gen. 49:33). The Torah then describes Yaakov's burial and the mourning that preceded and followed it.

Perhaps with this parsha title dealing with death, our tradition wanted to reduce the pain of loss by focusing on life—*Vayechi*/And he lived. When a loved one dies, we are overwhelmed by the awareness of what death takes from us. At such a time our tradition would have us remember the gift that we had sharing our years with those we lost.

Death can take from us what might have been. It cannot take from us what has already been. It cannot rob us of our past. The days and years we shared, the adventures and joys, the acts of kindness and love; all these are part of our everlasting memories. Even death cannot erase them. Our loved ones will always remain a living presence. Thus, we say Kaddish on the date of our loved one's passing every year, light a yahrzeit candle, and say the Yizkor memorial prayer during the High Holiday and other holiday services. Life transcends even death, and we are taught to honor our beloved family members and friends through acts of memory and rituals that support that. We are taught of the soul's invincibility, its permanence, and are sustained by the faith that even though the body dies, the soul lives on in our memories.

Another reason for beginning our parsha with "And Yaakov lived," is that for 22 years Yaakov lived in mourning for the loss of his precious son, Yosef, believing him dead. During those years, *Ruach Hakodesh*/The Holy Spirit, which is manifest only upon one who is in a state of joy, did not rest on Yaakov. When the brothers returned from Egypt and reported that *Od Yoseph chai*/Yosef is alive, the Torah says the spirit of their father Yaakov was revived. Yaakov was once again in a state of joy, and *Ruach Hakodesh* returned.

Human nature is such that when a person comes upon something precious after having been deprived of it for a period, there is a heightened joy and affection, a reduction of anxiety, and a replenishing of equanimity. When Yaakov felt his soul once more becoming bound up with the Divine spirit after a separation of so many years, his soul was once more ignited with a great spiritual ebullience and he soared to new heights of inner faith and gratitude. He lived again; for living in harmony with the soul brings revivified energy and joy. Yaakov was even able to reach new levels of spirituality while surrounded by the moral decadence of Egypt. In being truly alive again, his feelings were reawakened to a true realm of living.

To feel is to live and to reject feeling through fear is to reject the life process itself. As he learned Yosef was still alive, Yaakov may have reviewed his life experiences, his questionable choices, his mystical dreams, all that he had suffered, the losses of Rachel and Yosef, the deceptions of Laban—and was ready to manifest his future in harmony and soul satisfaction. Beneath Yaakov's fears was his inner knowing and he could now live out his life with serenity and heightened faith. Personal growth always results when you let yourself expand beyond the farthest borders of what your life has been so far.

On his deathbed, Yaakov wants to bless his children by revealing to them that all will be well with them at the end of days. But Rashi points out that an angel prevented him from doing so. The Sfat Emet points out that this was because if this truth were to be revealed to his children they would become complacent and not work to seek to create and advance truth. Thus, this withholding necessitated the development of faith and the "Journey toward Truth." Indeed, the goal of this world is the development of faith to lead us toward greater, ever-evolving truth. It is only in the next world where Absolute Truth can be revealed. If it were revealed here there would be no development in this world. Thus, the Kotzker says, "The assertion that one knows the full truth is the demise of religion, the journey toward truth is the flowering of religion."

Yaakov is taught that we must struggle to find truth, and that is where creativity and insights are developed. Thus, the healthy dynamic, the energetic movement toward greater truth and eventual wholeness, is supported by faith and not by easy truths. The whole development of the deep insights in the Talmud is due to the search for truth that is not easily accessible. Through dialogue among the rabbis, new perceptions and insights are revealed. Indeed, these truths, sometimes ever-evolving, would remain dormant if the need to discover them was not necessary.

When Yaakov called his sons to give him their blessings, he used the words "*Heosfu*/gather together, so that I may tell you what shall befall you at the end of days" (Gen. 49:1). Yaakov in his prophetic vision entreated his sons to gather together to live together in harmony and not be torn by conflict and dissension. He urged them to see the harm done by discord, lack of respect for one another, placing one's needs and views above others; and that the antidote to discord must be abundant love (*ahavat chinam*), togetherness that recognizes we are each unique but interconnected as God's children.

Yaakov knew the exile in Egypt evolved from the quarreling and discord between Yosef and his brothers. It is through dialogue between brothers and sisters that the holy bread of truth is revealed, with each person contributing their unique insights and gifts to reveal even deeper truths. When there is strife, anger, and hatred between brothers, an exile and enslavement like that in Egypt occurs, or the destruction of the Holy Temple follows. All dialogue is lost and bright gems that can only be discovered through struggle remain darkened. The Light remains lonely while waiting to be rekindled. Shabbat Shalom to all!

SHEMOT
Exodus

Shemot

We now begin the second book of the Torah, one that concentrates on Moshe's leadership and the reactions of the people he led—emphasizing his ability to lead them and teach them the importance of the rule of law (the Torah), justice, empathy, compassion, and freedom. It is not only the foundational story of our people under the Divine Providence of God, but also the tale of liberation from slavery, and the mandate that leads to the charge that all people must be free from enslavement and lead lives of dignity and equality ruled by justice and compassion.

Why was Moshe chosen to be the leader of his people? What were his special virtues? Our Sages point out his caring for his people. He stood for justice, he embodied humility, and he empathized with the enslaved Israelites, even though his "status" was higher than theirs. He was compassionate and thoughtful, meditating on his own in the desert, trying to discover what his soul needed; he found God and was told he had been chosen to liberate his people from slavery.

Once he convinced Pharoah to let his people go, he shepherded his people through the rigors of desert living for 40 years, as he led them into new lives and freedom, while possessing modesty and humility. He was righteous and attentively led his flock with caring and alacrity. It is told that when a sheep went astray he carried it on his shoulder back to the flock.

Moshe was open-minded and compassionate toward others because he experienced many traumas and also the privileges of living among the elite. He knew the narrow line between acting out on impulses such as anger and reactivity and restraining himself. Thus, he had compassion and empathy for others. He experienced a vast arena of human living and the many challenges that it brought forth. He went from being abandoned as a child to living in the house of Pharaoh with all its power and opulence. He went from living in an urban environment in Egypt to one in the vast deserts of Sinai. He even knew what it meant to take a life (as he murdered an Egyptian)! He experienced many character traits and their opposites. He was a stutterer and did not feel capable of speaking to Pharoah, yet he found the courage to do so with the aid of his brother Aaron. He struck the rock out of anger, yet he pleaded for forgiveness for his people; he was at times impatient with them, yet showed deep patience in discovering the burning bush. Our Sages state that Moshe was capable of every character trait and its opposite. And the Torah states, "Now the man Moshe was very humble, more so than all the men that were on the face of the earth" (Num. 12:3).

Due to his inner character traits and his exposure to a wide array of life experiences, Moshe became the guiding light and leader of his people by actualizing the ideals of caring, empathy, justice, courage, and humility. Verse 2:11 of our parsha states: *Vayigdal ha ish Moshe, vayetze el echav, vay'ar bi-sivlotam* ("And Moshe grew up and went out to his brethren and observed their burdens"). To "grow up" means to go out, to notice, and to care. Maturity equals caring. We are born selfish. Growing up is the slow, painful process of learning to also sacrifice our needs for the sake of others.

It would have been understandable if Moshe chose not to notice his brothers and sisters, and instead continued to enjoy the protection, privileges, and security of the palace. But he "grew up." Most of us are afraid to venture out and give others a claim over us, to risk vulnerability and the unknown. Perhaps being an outsider while being raised in the regal space of the house of Pharaoh gave him the strength and courage to rebel against the plight of the slavery of his people. He learned about the narrow line between anger, murder, and restraint which, upon reflection, allowed him to become empathetic and compassionate toward others. His failures taught him that imperfections are part of the human condition, and the best we can do is to learn from those experiences and not be judgmental of ourselves and others. Indeed, the search for perfection can lead to self-flagellation; the more prudent path is the journey, the movement toward greater integration, toward growth and wholeness, and using our growth and insights along the path for the betterment of our world.

Let us observe a few of the incidents in Moshe's life that affected his character. In our parsha, young Moshe stands up for justice in three distinct instances. In the first, he sees an Egyptian oppressing a Hebrew slave and notices no one else stood up for the Hebrew man—"*Vayaar ke ein ish/*There was no man to rescue the Hebrew" (Ex. 2:12). Realizing no Egyptian court would bring the Egyptian to justice because they hated the Hebrew slaves, Moshe took the law into his own hands. He couldn't bear the suffering and injustice he witnessed, so he intervened. In the second instance, two Hebrews were fighting with each other. Unable to ignore the internal strife within his people, Moshe tried to stop the altercation. He asked the wicked one, "Why would you strike your fellow?" (Ex. 2:14) and tried to help them settle their argument peaceably. In the third instance, he notices two non-Hebrew shepherds oppressing the daughters of Yitro at the well in Midian, chases them away and waters the women's sheep (Ex. 2:17). In each instance, ignoring tribe or ethnicity, it is justice that motivated him.

After marrying Yitro's daughter Zipporah, Moshe becomes a shepherd. As he guided his sheep in the wilderness, he noticed a burning bush in the distance (Ex. 3:2). Many people would have ignored the bush and kept on walking. But Moshe noticed the bush was not being consumed by the flames and so he "turned aside" to observe (Ex. 4:3). It often takes great patience to discover and feel God's presence. It took Moshe some time to realize the bush was not being consumed. He had the patience he needed to notice this remarkable incident that prepared him for God's revelation.

Patience is crucial to discovering our souls. The ego is always in a rush, but the soul needs quiet and time to emerge and break through all the chatter and worry and anxiety that inhibits its emergence. As God witnessed Moshe following his inner instinct/soul, God's voice became manifest in the burning bush and was able to be heard by Moshe in the wilderness (Ex. 4:4).

At first, overwhelmed by God's presence, Moshe's humility instinctively caused him to resist God's call. He assumed he did not have the ability to carry out this overwhelming task, but Hashem reassured him, and he slowly felt himself strengthened by the Presence of God. God also assured Moshe that his brother Aaron would aid him in his holy work.

And so Moshe went out, gave up his own security and fulfillment in order to serve, and felt the pain of his people. To serve is to become connected through giving, and we grow in new ways. Our soul is nurtured; our being is transformed from incessantly chasing our ego's needs to one of greater equanimity. We become faithful and calmer as we live in the present, connected to our souls within, and can recognize the manifestation of God throughout our lives. This recognition allows us to care for others and to stand up for justice as Moshe, Shifra, and Puah did—they each felt God's presence, enabling them to transcend their fears.

Moshe had four qualities that made him an ideal leader. First, he *cared* for others as well as his brothers and sisters. He even ran after a lamb that strayed and carried it home on his back.

Leaving the privilege of the palace was a sign of Moshe's maturity and caring. Freud says we are born selfish—"polymorphously perverse"—and Genesis 8:21 claims the heart of man is evil from youth. It would have been understandable if Moshe chose to ignore everyone and everything to remain secure, but he grew up and did what was right. It is often imperative to do the right thing, even if doing it risks danger for yourself. So, he went out to his brothers, felt their pain, and gave up his own security and fulfillment to serve. To serve is to become connected through giving. It is in our connection and relating to others, to get to know "the other," where caring and empathy are developed.

The second quality was his sense of justice and the courage to stand against injustice. We have already pointed out the three key incidents that illustrate his commitment to those values. In the first incident with the slave master, one might say he intervened out of solidarity with his people and not because of justice. In the second incident, the fight between two Hebrews, he may have tried to prevent internal strife within his people and not because of justice. But when he intervened between two gentiles who treated the women badly, we see it is because of his sense of justice, and not reward. We may surmise that pursuing justice was a part of his motivation in all these cases (See Pinchas Peli's commentary, citing Nehama Leibowitz and Ahad Ha'am).

A third quality was Moshe's patience and sense of focus. While it is true that he showed impatience and impulsiveness at times toward his people and their failures, his awareness of these proclivities allowed him to focus on overcoming these faults, and increased his openness and humility. This quality of great patience and focus is glaringly obvious in the incident of the burning bush. "And an angel of the Lord appeared to him in a blaze of fire from amid the bush. He saw and behold the bush was burning in the fire but the bush was not consumed!" (Ex. 3:2). We all have burning bushes surrounding us and within us. But we must be patient, and look to them to discover them. Many of us may never have noticed the bush. Moshe had the patience to see that it wasn't consumed. He had the ability to spontaneously "turn aside," and thus this incredible discovery. Patience is a crucial requisite to discover the spiritual dimension within our lives. The soul is eternal; the ego is always in a rush.

Moshe's fourth quality is his courage, which gave him clarity of purpose. The verse says, "And Moshe saw into their suffering" (Ex. 2:11). He saw their place of freedom and their potential. Every human being has some inner place where they are a free person; a part of us that has never submitted to the bondage surrounding us, but knows the place of freedom. Finding that place within us and allowing it to help us become free from our inner Egypt is how we will find our way out of Egypt. That is the time when we are not willing to put up with our suffering anymore (Sfat Emet).

"*Shalach et ami v'ya'avduni*/God tells Moshe to say to Pharaoh, send out My people that they may serve Me" (Ex. 7:26). Moshe had the courage and clarity to confront Pharaoh. The path to freedom is not to serve the Pharaohs of the world with their selfish interests, blinded by power and cruelty. It is the following of God's commandments that leads to freedom from ego-consciousness to soul-consciousness. It is the connection to a higher calling that leads us from slavery to freedom. Though subservience to a tyrant may create the illusion of security, it is a false hope that leads from fear to servitude. Our Sages teach us freedom must come through a path that leads us to a higher plane of life-soul consciousness (*Ein charut ela cheirut*/the Tablets lead to freedom).

One may ask, Is there such a thing as absolute freedom? There are times when we are closer to the Light and times when our choices lead us down darker paths. Judaism's solution is a recognition of this creative tension. The bearing of this tension creates an inner reliability and authenticity to help us follow an inner higher calling.

Absolute rejection of the Law can bring confusion and lack of identity, as too many choices lead to a potential lack of discipline; the alternative may be submission to an absolute authority. But Judaism's solution is neither the path of dogmatism nor the road of unrestrained freedom. It is a path that leads us to soul growth while encountering a myriad of choices, each of which must be discerned as either soul-enhancing or a distraction from holistic meaning.

Let us learn from the qualities of our hero Moshe so we can each be caring and courageous in our own ways, and lead our world to true freedom as we embrace the spiritual path set out for us by our holy tradition.

To discover our unique souls, each of us must be capable of moving from our secure places (the palace in Egypt) to risk the unknown. When we are blessed to take this risk, we can then be led to discover what is meant for our souls. It is up to us to take that first challenging step, to leave the flimsy security of the outer world to the stronger inner security required to discover the Presence of God within. Then we are required to return to our people and share this blessed knowledge, this God-given gift, with others for their benefit and blessing. Though we are tempted to dwell with this shining, scintillating gift without returning to our challenging realities, Exodus teaches us that we must go back to strengthen and uplift our world together! No one is free until we are all free!

Shabbat is a most wonderful time to reflect upon this; to quiet down the chatter, to be patient, and wait to discover the ever-present burning bush. We must turn away from our habitual distractions and our impatience as we run through our daily routines. We can then move from the realm of habitual wanting to the realm of habitual having. This is our peaceful Shabbat gift. May Shabbat be our restorative and may we all work together to heal the world as we confront the crises that impact our world today Shabbat Shalom!

Va'eira

Parshat Va'eira gives us many deep insights about the nature of freedom, leaving our servitude, and our move from our *Mitzrayim* (the place of restriction) to the land of Israel (our place of freedom). Our verse states, "And I will bring you out from under the burdens of Egypt, and I will save you from their bondage" (Ex. 6:6).

This verse seems repetitive because if the Jewish people are taken out from under the burdens of Egypt, undoubtedly, they are saved from their bondage. The Kotzker Rebbe suggests that there are two necessary steps to complete liberation. First, the slave must be set free physically and then his slave mentality must be cast off. One who is freed physically but still mentally subservient is not actually free. (You can leave *Mitzrayim*, but has *Mitzrayim* left you?) The word *sivlot*/burdens may be derived from the word *savalanut* which means acceptance, tolerance, or patience.

Pharaoh's strategy was cunning and successful. Our people could not hear the Call of the Soul "because of the pressure of their hard labor" (Ex. 6:9). Sforno says, "They could not settle their minds to contemplate."

To know the truth, we must have time to ponder and absorb our experiences. Pharaoh did not give the Israelites time for this deep contemplation. This was the pressure laid upon them. Pharaoh wanted to kill the very faculty of thought, meditation, and spiritual activity, says Ramchal. But the suffering that we experienced eventually became a powerful motivator to seek liberation.

To live is to experience sometimes deep suffering as well as sublime joy. Yes, we all suffer in our lifetimes! Whether caused by our attitudes and actions; our inner turmoil seething in a world filled with darkness and light; perhaps because of outer circumstances that bring destruction, frustration of goals, and pain. But suffering is also a necessary crucial ingredient in the creation of substantial growth. Change takes strength and we often face challenges that cause us to suffer. The attempt to avoid suffering and the resistance to change further deepen pain and slow the process of growth. Yet, within each of us there is the powerful counter-force, the life force called the Image of God that informs us that we each have a unique destiny. Thus, our suffering allows us to grow as we begin to understand the roots of our fears and inhibitions. When we own our strength, we find the rhythm of our path to growth; we accept who we are, and take pride in what we are meant to contribute during our time on our planet.

Suffering is the first step in the growth process; it can motivate us to understand ourselves better, to assist us in becoming conscious of behaviors and beliefs that inhibit progress and fulfillment. The insights developed as we try to understand the roots of our suffering are the start of the journey to a more conscious life that reduces the suffering heretofore experienced. Insight will also run into resistance, as we have to confront the challenges, fears, and hard work it will take to change. The temptation to repeat past behaviors grows stronger as we grow. Thus, one requires passion, emotional intensity, and the will to accompany insight if one is to keep moving. The final step is to translate our insights and emotions into concrete action, to act on our gathered insights and intensified emotion to reinforce our insights as we truly grow into our destinies, into the people we were meant to be. We are, after all, God's creations, blessed with the gift of life and unique talents that are meant to be expressed in our world.

In this week's parsha we see how this process of necessary suffering leads to change and growth. Pharaoh must undergo a series of painful plagues before he is willing to allow the enslaved Jews to go free. He resists and resists until finally, the intensified suffering awakens him to alter his behavior.

There is a Hebrew word, kaved, related to the heart of Pharaoh in our par-sha—meaning hardened, heavy, or stubborn. The term is repeated a number of times in this parsha and next week's parsha as well. The word's numero-logical equivalent (gematria) is 26, the same number as the word for God: Yud-Heh-Vav-Heh. The suggestion here is that God's Presence is revealed in the suffering. As noted, the dynamic of suffering is often necessary to make us aware of realities and perceptions that open the way to change. The word kaved—chaf, vav, dalet (26) is mentioned five times in this parsha, in Genesis 8:11, 8:28, 9:7, 9:3, and 10:1. "Hashem said to Moshe, 'Come to Pharaoh, for I have made his heart and the heart of his servants stubborn (kaved) so that I can put these signs of mine in his midst'" (Ex. 10:1).

It is sometimes only the experience of deep suffering that can break through our stubbornness, our refusal to change habitual patterns created and reinforced in our lives. The secondary gains we benefit from secure patterns can only be shattered by individual or communal suffering. What the world suffered with COVID-19 ("Covid" is also 26 in Hebrew!) taught many of us to readjust our attitudes toward our lives and make commitments to a life of greater meaning and spiritual connection.

Of course, the suffering in Egypt was so great that only God and his chosen leader Moshe could help the people to move forward. During their stay in Egypt, the Jews gradually accepted the rulership and values of Egypt. They lost their special identity. That which had been considered as oppressive had become their accepted burden. God therefore tells Moshe that God's supreme power would redeem the people from their physical affliction and from their mental and spiritual bondage as well. For true freedom does not mean merely physical liberation from a master, but also the ability to choose and make proper decisions free from the fear and inhibitions inherited from an alien culture.

Freedom brings with it anxiety, choices, and the unknown rather than the sure habitual lifestyle, directed by strict authority. The pressure to conform to the authority of the leader increases when a whole group follows the strict norms of the group (groupthink). That is why it takes great courage to deviate from the group norm. The ostracization becomes too great a burden to bear, and the choice of conformity and abandoning one's freedom often emerges.

The road to freedom (inner and outer) is long and full of obstacles, and there are no shortcuts. It does not come because of an overnight revolt of the oppressed masses or a one-time act. Often, the suffering masses do not even want to recognize the fact that they are being oppressed—perhaps as a coping mechanism to allow for survival. But it also may be a result of the challenge of growing up and facing responsibilities and new choices. Sometimes the unknown brings greater fears than the oppression people experience, and they rationalize and accept the status quo as tolerable. Redemption comes about through many stages—the final one being a deep commitment and a conviction that somewhere far away, a land is waiting for them, expecting them to come to freedom.

As a therapist for years, I had many patients who left the East Coast to get away from their families but still called them every day! Or they forever hear their family's voices in their heads telling them what to do. Thus, the verse in our parsha "V'hotzeiti etchem metachat sivlot Mitzrayim, v'hitzalti etchem may'avodatam, v'goalti etchem" (Ex. 6:6) states that God liberates the Jews physically and also redeems them from bondage of the spiritual and mental burdens of their slavery.

How could it be that despite their bondage and hardships, the Hebrews did not really want to leave Egypt as our Sages suggest? It would seem that in our psyches we unfortunately have this proclivity toward obedience to authority (a phenomenon Stanley Milgram discovered in his experiments at Yale University in 1961 and described in his book *Obedience to Authority* in 1973), where we easily yield our power to an outer authority—even a despotic, autocratic one—as a result of our lack of clear core values. Due to our insecurities, it would seem that at times we would rather follow a tyrannical leader, rather than make responsible choices on our own. Moreover, psychologists have pointed out the insidious dynamic of identification with the aggressor (aka Stockholm syndrome) where, when we have lived in abusive circumstances, we take on the characteristics of the abuser to feel protected and able to survive. It takes courage and determination to break away.

The Torah points out the four stages of the liberation, expressed in four different terms found in Exodus 6:6-9. "*v'hotzalti, v'hitzalti, v'goalti, v'lokachti...*/I will bring out, deliver, redeem, and take you..." First, I will *bring you out* from under your burden. I will have your consciousness raised to realize that being in exile is an unbearable burden. As pointed out in the previous parsha, the Hebrew word for burden is *sivlot* which is close to *savlanut*/patience. Only when people run out of patience with the status quo and feel that their helplessness is intolerable are they ready for the second stage—the delivery from actual bondage. Mental freedom is thus a prerequisite for physical freedom.

Moreover, a freedom-loving people does not exert itself to build magnificent palaces for others, but dedicates its efforts to its own needs. Hence God's promise, "I will *deliver* you from their bondage." That is followed by the third stage in the process of redemption: "I will *redeem* you with an outstretched arm." A proud, self-sufficient people will stand up resolutely for its rights as an independent nation. And only then, when they are free, self-reliant, and independent, are they ready for the fourth, and final stage, "I will *take* you as my own people."

One of the requisites in the movement toward freedom is the ability to listen to your inner place of freedom, to the Soul Within. The verse says: Moshe claims, "The children of Israel have not listened to me" (Ex. 6:12). The Sfat Emet says that listening requires emptying the mind of distracting thoughts. Our inability to empty ourselves of our fears and illusions and clear our minds and hearts to hear the Call of the Soul without any distracting thoughts delays our journey to freedom, to the "Promised Land."

The Torah has been given to Israel to provide a voice that can lead us to a higher calling when that is commensurate with what we know in the deepest part of our hearts and minds. We recognize this calling when we are not distracted. It is a powerful voice that temporary chatter will not silence. But we have to hear it. That is the precise reason that as Jews, every day we say "Sh'ma Yisrael/Listen O Israel the Lord is calling you, open your heart."

The Voice has never stopped, but we must listen, we must clear out a space in our hearts and souls to hear this powerful voice and not be sidetracked by other "pressing" concerns. Idolatry—whether an obsession with money or other addictive aspects of our society—is anything that keeps us from hearing the Divine voice, and we become enslaved to those secondary interests. Our involvement with those interests occupies most of our attention and inhibits our ability to receive the deeper voice of the soul. Studying Torah, praying with concentration, doing acts of compassion—these things, being in the Light, open us to hearing the voice. Since the Torah has been given to us early in our history, we must rediscover the voice from within ourselves via a lifestyle in which we engage in doing mitzvot.

Torah study, prayer, and good deeds lead us to a freedom of connection to the soul and to a higher calling rather than to the slavery of outer materialistic proclivities. The power to hear the Voice of God's "I am" as Moshe did requires powerful concentration. It is to recite the Sh'ma with powerful energy and concentration. It is to go out into the green field and feel the miracle of creation. It is to allow the waves of the ocean to meet us with all the power that derives from the Creator. Both the sound of the waves and the silence of the trees whisper to us that there is something majestic in the blessing of our existence. The power of silence, the power of intense prayer and openness, can liberate us from the slavery of our everyday distractions to the higher Call of the Soul.

In the sheer flurry and chaos of daily hard labor and set routines, we do not make the time nor find the peace for this inner exploration so necessary for the experience of freedom. When we become submerged in myriad details and responsibilities so that our life goals and plans are obscured, that part occupies us at the expense of the whole. We become our work and lose sight of the fact that we are more than that. Yes, our work can be holy and a blessing, but we must also remember that we have unique identities that encompass something larger than our work. Pharaoh trapped us in that "work" and did not give us the time needed to imagine who we truly are as children of God. He did not give us the time we needed to understand what we are meant to express in our world that is soul-edifying and gift-giving. This ability to do that is our movement from slavery to freedom. Our intense suffering and God's liberation from our work burdens moved us toward our eventual liberation.

May we all be blessed to own our suffering as an occasional gift, perceive it as a growth trial, and discover the depths of our soul, enabling us to grasp more deeply who we truly are. We are souls created in the image of God with unique gifts and purposes designed to uplift and heal our world. May we absorb its beauty and bring joy and love to others.

Shabbat gives us time to contemplate where we are on the continuum of slavery and freedom. Are we achieving the balance necessary to integrate both work and leisure to a defined goal that uses our talents and bestows these gifts to our world? Are we fulfilling our destinies? Have we truly left *Mitzrayim*? Our parsha teaches us that this is the time to enter or continue our journey toward freedom so that we can identify the unique gifts that God has placed within us, embrace them, and share them with the world that awaits our blessing. Shabbat Shalom!

Bo

We've learned that quiet isn't always peace
And the norms and notions
of what just is
Isn't always justice
And yet the dawn is ours.
—Amanda Gorman

When Joseph Biden was elected, many of us were exhilarated. His inauguration manifested the energy of Martin Luther King, Jr. with the sublime, eloquent words recited by the elegant, ethereal poet Amanda Gorman which were like Manna from Heaven to those of us who understand the fragility of Democracy, the fragility of our lives. The poem sounded like the sweet trumpet of freedom, soothing our souls. Finally! Exalted noble words, spoken by a woman with the powerful blessed gift bestowed upon her by the heavenly angels, were expressed as a symphony elevating the human spirit. We were inspired to soar to the heights, to hope to be true to the image of God for which we have been impatiently yearning. The words were so familiar to our souls, words that have been absent and missing from the American scene for decades.

L' Havdil, every week, the Torah, with its words of sublime poetry, brings us closer to this deep wisdom and calls us to action on its behalf. Let us join hands and hearts and bring forth the light that awaits us as we challenge darkness with faith and strength, dancing to the rhythm of God's words. We have the capacity and responsibility to march forward even when despair has shackled us. When we bring our own Light, and see hidden Light emerge from its cocoon, we dance with joy as the new morning arrives.

We are inspired to grab the present moment, the *now*, and begin the daily work to give birth to action. We look into the Torah and roll up our sleeves. We reach out to those who have different insights from ours, and expand our vision, respect, humility, and serendipitous surprise. We venture out from our places of safety and sameness to take risks to build a new world. This does not mean we ignore the darkness that must be addressed and transformed. It does mean we have the faith and strength to march forth with our own truths and the willingness and strength to be open and transformed by the truths of others. At the very least, we must be open to increasing our consciousness through dialogue and encounters with other people. We are obligated not to recreate the plague of Darkness.

In this week's parsha, two verses are very instructive. The first is Exodus 10:33 where we learn the Darkness is so thick that people could not see each other. Our Sages ask the question, "What kind of plague was that? They could have lit lamps and been able to see despite the darkness. Isn't that what they did every night when it got dark?"

Our Sages explain the darkness from which the Egyptians suffered was a special kind of darkness. It was not a darkness that affected the eyes; it was a darkness that affected the heart. Physically they were able to see, but they did not feel for each other, they did not care for one another. This is what the Torah means when it says, "They did not see one another." They were blind to each other's needs. Each person saw only him or herself. And this is a terrible plague. Judaism expects of us that we shall "see" and hear each person as a human being who has needs, feelings, fears, hungers, and hopes, just as we do; they are children of God just as we are—fully entitled to be treated with the dignity, justice, and compassion we claim for ourselves. This is the essence and the prime teaching of our tradition, and the hope for our world!

The Torah tells us that during the plague of darkness in Egypt, "All the people of Israel had light in their dwellings." This is the basic challenge that confronts each of us—to keep the light of understanding and caring aglow to enable us to truly see each other—for it is only when we see the humanity in another that we can preserve it in ourselves.

Rabbi Aaron Shmuel Tamares, in his 1906 "Sermon on Liberty," talks about a different aspect of the darkness—the thickness of the darkness, and the command for the Israelites to stay indoors that was to prevent them from witnessing violence. Hashem told Moshe Hashem alone will deal with the plague of *Makot Bechorot*, the death of the first-born Egyptians, carried out during that profoundly dark plague. Hashem—not an angel, not a seraph, but God alone—would be responsible for this devastating plague. Hashem did not want the Israelites to become a violent people like the Egyptians, so they were confined to their homes for their own safety and did not bear witness to the violence of the Tenth Plague, which was one of the ways they were prepared for the later receipt of the Torah in Sinai.

The second verse is Exodus 10:26, where Moshe tells Pharaoh that when the Israelites leave Egypt all their flocks and cattle must leave with them, "For we shall not know how we are to worship Hashem until we get there." (The animals might be needed for the worship process).

Our Hasidic masters claim this teaches us an important lesson for our spiritual growth. When it comes to the worship of God, one should not expect to find ready-made formulas. True worship of God requires renewing wonder and discovery through sometimes painful trial and error, from making new decisions and taking leaps of faith. Rav Chaim of Tzanz recounts how he asked one of his students, "Tell me, if you happen to come across a wallet full of money on Shabbat, what would you do, would you pick it up?"

"Of course not," said the student. The Rebbe responded, "Fool!"

The next student said, "Of course I would pick it up." The Rebbe called him a sinner.

The third student, after hearing the master rebuke the first two students, replied hesitantly, "Well I do not know. At finding the wallet full of money, I would struggle with myself in deciding whether or not to take it. I hope I will be able to make the right decision."

"At last, we have the right answer!" said Reb Chaim. "Truly we shall not know how we are to worship the Lord until we get there."

The Torah orients us through the mitzvot, to help us develop moral and ethical character, and to bring us closer to the love and ethical behavior required by God. However, new circumstances, new insights, and new responses specifically appropriate for the "now" moment are often called forth from the depths of our souls. At the "now" moment we may humbly call upon God and ask for guidance. We hope that our studies and our teachers and loving partners have prepared us for the call of the moment, but ultimately, we alone choose to increase holiness in the world, or we can tragically miss the moment.

Thus, Judaism teaches us how to behave ethically and uplift our world, but it also teaches us about the nature of the world, its inevitable changes, its contradictions, and how we are to proceed with all its complexity, using our faith as the Life force that guides us to maturity.

Maturity in the human psyche means an increased capacity to hold opposite ideas at the same time and to be open to uncertainty (to keep moving forward "until we get there"). Faith emerges from patient reflection, and in the process, we must be able to endure some uncertainty. If we only hold a single idea (*sheker*/lies) we only see the world through a narrow lens. Great tension may arise when we see the world moving in a direction that is contrary to our previous beliefs. At that point, we may have to see the world differently and hold some contradictory ideas or competing perceptions in our heads at the same time (*emet*/truth). We have to learn, as Moshe did, to be open, to be present in the midst of potential conflicting ideas and challenges.

There is a danger of being unable to bear this creative tension and to opt out to obviate the opportunity to experience "the new" that emerges. There is the temptation, because of the tension, to close "the new" and hold rigidly to the familiar and secure. This attempt to reduce the tension instead of recognizing that change is inevitable, and renewal is essential to the life force, to the ability to grow. We must be able to keep going "until we get there."

We must be open to focusing on discovering the burning bush. We must be courageous enough to leave the secure place in the Palace to trek through the desert and discover the "new;" to miraculously experience God in every place if we are centered enough to open our eyes and hearts and embrace the Light that is always there waiting for us. This calls for risk-taking and the knowledge that creativity comes through new ways of seeing that are very different from the habitual pattern that closes off the "new" waiting to be born.

Amidst all these inevitable uncertainties our true calling can emerge. Our fearful ego/self may feel that we cannot continue with this apparent chaos. The deeper Soul, however, is not defeated by the confusion that raises its head. Our faith carries us forward. We know why we have been created, and for what our lives are intended. The life of *emunah*/faith, even with uncertainty, aligns us with the path of true meaning. We understand we can endure the tensions of life and we have the capacity, the gift, and the responsibility to contribute to the healing and renewal of our world.

We must be able to trust and know that we will get to the place where we are meant to be and must always be open to the Light within the darkness. The Light within our hearts will clearly see the Light within each of us created in the image of God.

May each of us continue to bring forth new gifts from within as we continue to encounter our trials, and bring forth Light from darkness. Shabbat Shalom to all!

Beshalach

There are many parallel themes and moral instructions found in our Torah portion Beshalach. We are taught about the virtues of courage, the spontaneous urge to sing, the importance of compassion, the need for faith, and the necessity to combat radical evil.

After the Israelites leave Egypt, Pharaoh realizes that the people of Israel are walking in circles and assumes that they are entangled in the land and that the wilderness has shut them in. So, he sends out his army to destroy them. The Israelites, at the edge of the sea, see the Egyptian army coming toward them and are terrified. Before them is the sea and behind them the ominous Egyptian army. There seems to be no plausible escape route. They are paralyzed as they reach the Sea of Reeds (Red Sea) with no way to cross it. They face imminent danger and are at risk of an impending massacre.

Suddenly, one man, Nachshon ben Aminadav, stood up and began walking toward the Red Sea. Our Sages tell us that the minute his feet touched the water, the sea started splitting and an unexpected new escape route emerged. He chose to take initiative with his great faith, and believed that a new reality would present itself if he risked taking this first step. The Midrash reports that Nachshon ben Aminadav's intrepid response—the response of one man who has the courage to jump into the sea and save his people, literally turns the tide. His valiant act calls forth a responsive miracle from God, who parts the waters so the Israelites can move through to dry land. As the Egyptians enter the sea, the waters come crashing back and destroy them. Without the courage of Nachshon, the people might have been trapped.

When we have faith, we create hope even against all odds; with faith, a crisis becomes an opportunity and potential transformation. Sometimes taking that first step may lead to a "miracle," a concretization of a dream or vision of a new future. Then others may follow this dream and create a new reality, a new society of hope, justice, and beauty. With faith, we may find creative solutions that may at first appear unrealistic. Suddenly, new opportunities open up to us and lead us to the future we are meant to create.

When Nachshon experienced this miracle, after his first courageous step, it was time to show gratitude to our Creator, to sing the song of Praise for our salvation, and new freedom. And thus, "When the people witnessed this miraculous event they believed in the Lord and in his servant Moshe. For when the horses of Pharaoh with his chariots and his horsemen went into the sea… The people of Israel walked on dry ground in the midst of the sea. Then Miriam, the Prophetess, the sister of Aaron, took a timbrel in her hand; and all the women went out after her with timbrels and dancing." (The Sages in the Talmud (Sotah 11b) point out that it was "Due to the merit of the righteous women of the generation that the children of Israel were redeemed from Egypt"). And Miriam sang to them, "Sing to the Lord, for God has triumphed gloriously; the Egyptian horses and rider have been thrown into the sea by God…" Then Moshe and all the people of Israel sang this song to the Lord, saying, "I will sing to the Lord, for God has triumphed gloriously" (Ex. 15:1-22).

The Rabbis point out that the language expressed in the text of *Az yashir Moshe*/Thusly Moshe will sing, is a causative tense, connoting a future event that foretells that Israel's leaders, like Moshe and the Israelites, will cause and create a reason for everyone to sing in the future. Human beings and all creation will burst forth in song, to sing in harmony with all the galaxies, animals, plants, and creation. This will be the song we are all preparing for, says Reb Naftali Tzvi of Ropshitz. It is important to sing with joy in recognition of everyday miracles!

All the people sang from their souls as they experienced a whisper from the infinite, and their souls floated upward on the wings of this beautiful melody descending from the heavenly abode awakening them to something beyond their ego confinement. "*Az Yashir*!/I will sing!" They yielded to sounds that brought them to another dimension, a dimension always present but ethereal and hard to grasp with our busy-ness, distractions, and lack of focus. By connecting to the voices of harmony the grace of connection to the Infinite emerges. Song becomes a means of expressing and reaching beyond words, beyond the veil. Sometimes the curtain (veil) is opened, and grace is achieved and then we return to our world blessed, touched, yearning for more, but filled with faith and gratitude.

The secret has been revealed to us in the symphony and we are assuaged and fulfilled, imbued with soul meaning; we have been touched. We know these moments are rare, but they sustain us. It is a moment when we can express the inexpressible *shira*/rhapsody. It is a moment of *shema*—deep quiet, open listening; of truly listening and hearing the deeper sounds of the universe, and the glory of our Creator. *Shema* brings us to a place of the unfinished symphony, the Presence of the Lord. But this moment is ephemeral and transient, as we are limited by our grasp of the Great Mystery.

We must bring the melody of soulful Torah to the world. It awakens us to the cosmic in our soul and to the splendor of nature that surrounds us. We are opened to God's Presence, the still small voice in all of life. Our Sages teach that in the future there will be a reason for all people to sing; all creation will burst into song in harmony with all the galaxies, animals, plants, and creation. This will be the song for which we are preparing (Reb Naftali Tzvi of Ropshitz, Zera Kodesh).

Song is a requirement in ushering in the messianic reality. We are taught that King Hezekiah was punished for not singing after his victory over Sancheriv. And therefore, he could not be the Messiah. He forced people to study Torah without joy and song. His son Menashe became the most wicked king and though there were a majority of Torah scholars studying under his rulership, this soon dissipated, due to the lack of joy and song (2 Chronicles 32:25-32, 2 Kings 18-20, Sanhedrin 94a).

Thus, we must sing and arouse our souls as we touch a deeper level of reality that stems from meaning and expansion of consciousness, but we must also commit ourselves to a practice that sustains our blessed encounters with the numinous. Every week on Shabbat we taste this mystical song but we must then bring it into the everyday tasks of life—studying Torah, caring for others, and praying with the fervor of song and full presence.

The Midrash teaches us another incisive ethical imperative related to this miraculous event. Interestingly, while our Sages praised the song of gratitude by the Israelites for this great miraculous event at the Red Sea, they taught that the angels in heaven were chastised for fully celebrating this occasion. That is because many of God's children (the Egyptians) died. The lesson is that we are never fully happy when death and suffering are present even when we are victorious over our enemies.

Our tradition always teaches compassion, honoring life, and not neglecting our sadness when we are in the midst of the death of our enemies. They taught that God admonished the angels not to sing when God's children (the Egyptians) were dying. Thus, we have the custom of spilling a little wine at the Passover Seder when we read about the Ten Plagues. We mark the fact that we can never be happy with the suffering of others. What an astounding insight that captures and asserts the prime value of Judaism—that above all, we are to develop deep compassion in our souls as a way of being in the world, and therefore we are to weep when our enemies are suffering.

We must also recognize that even a miraculous moment may not be sustained until one integrates the experience, through a practice that strengthens the memory, and through behavior that evokes a relationship with our Creator. For the people, even after the profoundly spiritual experience at the Sea of Reeds, soon lost their faith because of the hardships in the desert and regressively fell prey to the slave mentality they lived within Egypt.

The Lord tested them with the manna from heaven, and it took them 40 years in the desert to truly become free. Perhaps the new generation that grew up, free from the shackles of Egypt, was more prepared and capable of becoming "free" human beings.

As the people continued their sojourn in the desert, God showered them with food, the manna from heaven. They were instructed not to hoard the food, but to rely on God's promise that they would receive the proper amount of food every day. This calls for faith and accepting what they have, instead of gathering more manna than necessary out of anxiety or greed. When we have faith, we live in a state of equanimity and trust that following the way of the Lord will always lead to satisfaction and growth.

Finally, at the end of the parsha, we have an important teaching of how to engage with evil. Amalek attacks the Jewish people to destroy them, and God tells Moshe that Amalek (arch-evil) must be fought in every generation. While we are taught that the prime value is to be compassionate and interact with enemies in a way that can transform them through our inner light and humanity, there is also a category of evil that has lost all capacity for repentance and must be destroyed. This is the category of Amalek. Throughout history, this archetypal seed is identifiable by its sub-human behavior, as exemplified by those such as Haman, Hitler, Hamas, Hezbollah, etc.—those who want to destroy our people without any sense of conscience. If we ignore or deny this kind of radical, evil behavior, we are culpable of enabling even greater evil and destruction. Thus, our response must be "to fight against Amalek in every generation" (Ex. 17:16).

During this parsha week, we also celebrate Tu B'Shvat, the New Year for Trees, awakening us to the beauty and miracle of nature, another dimension of the glory of God and God's blessings become manifest. Not only our

Jewish tradition, but the lore of all world traditions extols the "World Tree," with all its mystery and power and blessing. Among the many comparisons of the Tree to human beings by our Sages is a commentary by the Lubavitcher Rebbe, brought by Mordechai Lightstone, who points out eight ways in which human beings can emulate a tree (Igros Kodesh Vol. 1, pp. 247-250).

First, a tree always grows toward the Light. We too must always grow toward the Light that resides in holiness (Berachot 48a).

Second, even the smallest scratch can have lasting effects on a tree. A small scratch on a young sapling can leave a scar on the fully-grown tree. So can scars remain on young children when we educate them in a harsh, insensitive manner.

Third, trees grow deep roots. Just as a tree is strengthened by the depth of its roots, we human beings can deepen our roots by increasing our connection to the depths of our tradition. By studying the wisdom of our ancestors and their commitment to spreading holiness in the world, and acting in God's image, we grow firmly and confidently into the destiny meant for us. As it says in Pirkei Avot, "One whose deeds are greater than their wisdom, to what are they compared? To a tree with many roots—which all the winds in the world cannot budge from its place (Pirkei Avot 3:17).

Fourth, trees provide refuge for others. Just as a tree selflessly provides shade and shelter, we must be a source of comfort for others and provide resources for those in need.

Fifth, just as a tree grows sweet fruits for others to enjoy in the present and the future, so too we can provide fruits for others to enjoy, sustaining others with our gifts in the present and for their future. Indeed, by planting a tree that will outlive us, we will be providing shelter and fruit for future generations.

Sixth, trees are supple and bend in the wind. Only a tree that can bend in the wind will survive a storm. We too, must be flexible and adaptive, facing whatever confronts us, and use our strength to respond both faithfully and sensitively.

Seventh, trees grow stronger through life experiences. Just as the rings of a tree record its growth through years of trial and the vicissitudes of life, so, too, must we always add deeper levels of insight and nurture others from our culled experiences.

And eighth, trees enrich the ecosystem with their gifts. By using our gifts to make a positive impact on our world we can emulate the trees. Just as trees provide immediate benefits like shade, wood, and food, they also filter the air and give off oxygen; they have a lasting impact on the world. So too, by our honest efforts, we can impact our fellow humans with our grace, humility, and wisdom.

May we each use the energy of Tu B'Shvat to heal many of the ecological crises the world faces today. May we transform the perception that Earth itself is merely a resource to be used for our personal human benefit, rather than a blessing to be shared to benefit all of us. Our air, our water, and our food chain deserve our care and guardianship. We must protect their health just as our trees protect our well-being, and the time to do so is now! And let us say Amen as we march together to create a healthier, sustainable world!

Yitro

Our parsha starts with "*Vayishma Yitro*/And Yitro heard" (Ex. 18:1)—but it does not specify what he heard! Perhaps Yitro, Moshe's father-in-law, was a good listener, so he listened first before giving advice. And Moshe in his humility welcomed the advice of an outsider and observer of his community who offered constructive advice.

But the verse does not specify what Yitro heard. We know from experience that it is beneficial for an outsider, such as the royal Priest of Midian (Yitro), to intensely observe the community and offer astute, constructive thoughts about their established habitual patterns. Their advice is an opportunity for us to examine and improve what we do. Being blind to what outsiders can see and ignoring them because we fear change almost always leads to entropy and irrelevance. We can be deprived of new energy and potential propitious innovation.

We observe that Yitro listens first before he gives constructive advice to Moshe. Listening is difficult for humans, but listening to what others say—and hearing it—provides the basis of decision-making for every aspect of our lives. Listening/hearing is the WD-40 of civilization.

What was it Yitro may have heard about the ordeals of the Jewish people to make him want to join this people? The Talmud in Zevachim 116a offers three opinions.

Why did the Sages feel it was important to know what he heard, and why did they come up with different opinions? Reb Moshe Feinstein *zt'l* suggests that different people are inspired by different things, and this reveals their true nature.

First, Yitro may have heard of the attack and defeat of Amalek at the Red Sea.

Some are inspired by the search for justice and the defeat of evil in an unjust world. Their hearts are immersed in the pain of injustice, and they are elated when they hear of victory over Amalek and the defeat of evil. They have tears in their eyes when justice triumphs and virtuous effort results in victory for a cause. Since sincere effort does not always result in victory or success, it is so moving and inspiring when the results match the effort. They are concerned with righteous justice and therefore would be impressed by the defeat of Amalek.

But why should the actions of Amalek be so important to Yitro to make him want to join the Jewish people? The defeat of Amalek simply may have been the defeat of one army over another. What startled Yitro was the brazenness of Amalek, to attack the people even after all the miracles they experienced. He deplored their cruelty in attacking the weak, the lame, and the elderly from the rear, from their most vulnerable place. Yitro realized the capacity for evil in human beings runs deep, and therefore the love of God is the only antidote. He wanted to join these people and felt all would be lost if he did not.

Who was this Amalek, filled with such bitterness and cruelty? And what were the effects of his outrageous aggression? The Rabbis point out that Amalek was an offspring of the family of Eisav (Sanhedrin 99b). A woman named Timna, the daughter of the local leader (Gen. 36:20-22) wanted to convert and enter into the family of Israel and came to Jacob and his family, but she was turned away. She then went to the family of Eisav, who welcomed her into their family.

Timna became the concubine of Eliphaz, Eisav's son, and their offspring was Amalek (Gen. 36:12). They say Timna's wound of rejection was so deep that she passed it on to her offspring—who carried out their vengeance throughout future generations. This episode also teaches us the importance of welcoming strangers with love, as they contribute greatly to the Jewish community.

One Kabbalist noted that Amalek injected doubt—a severe injury—into the psyche of faith in the Jewish people. Even after all the miracles they experienced, the Jews were still vulnerable to enemies such as Amalek, and this created uncertainty in their previously strong faith. The *gematria*/numerological sum of the Hebrew word for *safek*/doubt is 240, the same as the Hebrew word Amalek. The wound of doubt is an egregious blemish, a spiritual weakening that must be fought by us in every generation.

The second thing he heard, the Rabbis speculate, is of the splitting of the Red Sea.

Some are inspired by the salvation of those in danger by gracious, humane deeds, acts of kindness and courage that save the day—as when the Jews miraculously crossed the Red Sea—so he wanted to join these people. Some are inspired by the salvation of the oppressed, the relief of suffering, as in the salvation of the Jews from Egypt as they crossed the Red Sea. They may also be impressed that a slave mentality can reach freedom.

The rabbis' third speculation about what Yitro heard is that he Divinely prophesied the Israelites' future receiving of the Torah. Yitro could see the greatness of Hashem in the lofty, sublime teachings of the Torah, so he wanted to learn more. Hence, he wanted to join the upcoming revelation at Mount Sinai and be a participating witness to this magnificent milestone. From this we learn it is incumbent upon us to consciously identify what inspires us, what our deepest soul passion is, and to follow this impulse to contribute and actualize this most important gift in our world.

Yitro also advised Moshe about his leadership skills. What did he notice about Moshe's behavior? He noticed Moshe loved to teach his people, answer their questions, and care for their well-being (Ex. 18:22-26). But sometimes, when we love something very much—like Moshe loved his people and loved to teach them Torah—we forget to set limits. Before Moshe heard Yitro's advice, he was overwhelmed by the burden of his responsibilities and lacked boundaries. We learn from this that while we need to love others and love Hashem, it is equally important to love ourselves and protect our mental health.

One needs the balance of loving ourselves as well as loving others. So, as an outside observer, he advised Moshe to change his administrative style. Sometimes the need to change one's leadership style challenges a competent leader, and he needs an outsider to make him aware of more efficient ways of leading. It takes humility as well as confidence not to feel threatened and instead welcome outside help that a competent consultant—such as Yitro—offers.

The parsha shows us that Moshe did not feel defensive or insulted. He was humble and listened to Yitro. He took his advice and decided to delegate some of his authority. He asked other qualified people—"people of great courage, and of integrity, people of truth who reject bribes" (Ex. 18:21) — to help him with his many tasks.

But then, why did Moshe send Yitro back to his land after receiving such prudent and beneficial advice? Moshe wanted to see if Yitro would still have the same heightened desire to join the Jewish people after he returned to his homeland. Quite often, after a natural "high," we revert to habitual norms and decide not to make the sacrifice of uprooting ourselves and moving to a new environment. The comfort of the known supersedes the excitement of the new. So, he sent Yitro back to measure the depth of his commitment.

After examining what Yitro heard, we may ask ourselves what the Jewish people heard at the revelation at Mount Sinai. And why were they worthy to receive the commandments at this time?

The Midrash tells us the Israelites were worthy to receive the sublime revelation of the Ten Commandments because they reached a pinnacle of communal unity and love while camping at the foot of the mountain. At that point, they were worthy of directly experiencing the immanent Presence of God. Love is the lifeblood of all relationships and their feeling of unity affirmed that we are all interdependent, and that separateness is a temporary illusion. Theirs was a lived experience of their own divinity. They embodied faith and centeredness. (And since the Midrash says all of us were there at Sinai, we directly experienced the Presence of God as well.)

The Israelites' spiritual sense was so heightened, that they "Saw the voices of the Shofar" (Ex. 20:15) and heard the Voice of God. Each of them heard the utterance in a unique way, drawn to the specific words that touched their hearts. The Midrash says that each person heard the letter *Aleph*/Ahh, the first letter of the Ten Commandments, and thereby heard God's Presence.

Their hearing, the highest of senses in the spiritual world, was like seeing, the highest of the senses in the physical world. Like is attracted to like, soul is attracted to soul; the Israelites' spiritual sense was so heightened, their bodies were actually dying and their souls were rising to the heavens—so God limited them to hearing only the first letter of the first word of the commandments.

This suggests that connecting to God's Presence is our essential task. Each of us may experience the Presence of God in different ways. This experience should not be limited by words or assumptions from our limited perspective. It is why mystics attempt to quiet the mind chatter which disturbs their ability to sit quietly and take in the Light of the *Shechinah*. After encountering the sound Ahh (Aleph), the Presence of God, and feeling their souls ascending, God revealed the rest of the content of the Ten Commandments through the consciousness and filtered words of Moshe so that the people may continue to live.

The parsha contains the first version of the Ten Commandments. An entire book can be written to interpret them, but here we will comment on just two of the commandments—the first and one and the last one.

The first commandment, "I am the Lord your God who has taken you out of the land of Egypt, from the house of slavery" (Ex. 20:2) is a commandment of faith, and establishes God's Presence. This challenging commandment of faith was understood to be transmitted to the future community of the Jewish people through memory transmission from the witnesses who passed the story of this Revelatory experience from generation to generation, from prophet to prophet (Halevi, Kuzari). This memory was kept alive by Sages and students of Torah throughout the centuries.

As time marched on and the memory became more distant, other avenues toward faith emerged—such as perceiving the grandeur of the Creator in nature or by using reason and logic (the categorical imperative). Intuition, the inner soul's recognition of a moral energy that we each contain and intuit as God's Presence within us, was another path toward faith. The study of Torah and prayer heighten the intimate connection with God. Sometimes sudden manifestations of meaning emerge through reasoning or from a personal epiphany. The Sages explain it is only faith that makes one free from the slavery, worry, doubt, and fragmentation that can impact our psyches in this world. This is the power and importance of the first commandment.

The tenth commandment, "You shall not covet your fellow's house. You shall not covet your neighbor's wife, his servant, his ox, nor anything that belongs to your fellow" (Ex. 20:14), relates to the first commandment. When we have faith, it leads us to be peaceful within, to truly trust in God. It instructs us to move from the realm of habitual wanting to the realm of habitual having. Dissatisfaction and yearning for that which is not ours is based on a lack of faith, and so the antidote for excessive *chemda*/coveting (the 10th commandment) is the first commandment—faith in God who provides us with exactly what we need. If the heart is filled with the love of God, coveting worldly goals and possessions is attenuated.

Each of the ten commandments is powerful. We are taught that fully embodied deeds done with a holy intention also connect us to God's presence. And it is our task to fulfill the commandments with great passion and concentration to uplift the world to holiness and reveal the hidden Light. So, let us ask ourselves which commandment moves us, and what are the ten commandments of our current lives. Each of us must reveal the personal Ten Commandments in our lives to ourselves and discover the Light. This will manifest God's Presence in our lives, which is always extant and longing to be revealed. It is the power of love/light that attracts love/light, and the projection of love influences all it touches.

It is this spirit of great love that impacted the Jewish people after experiencing the many miracles bestowed upon them as they were released from slavery by the power of God. It is this radiant indwelling of love that made them worthy of connecting to the Great Love, the Presence of God.

May we all have the strength to live the Ten Commandments with courage and love and thereby uplift our world. May the teachings of Yitro, to listen, be incorporated into our beings. May we continue to listen to the sublime rhythms of the universe, to the soulful messages of our hearts, and to others' wisdom and pain to help heal our world. Just as our ancestors at Sinai experienced their own essential divine nature in the Presence of God, let us also be inspired to be a force for good in our world of perpetual evolving revelation. May we live always as we did at the foot of Mount Sinai!

Let us pray that our faith allows our lives to become freer, more centered, and filled with inspiration to carry God's mandate to the world in a calm and centered way. May we be blessed to experience the Presence of God's compassion as we enjoy the blessings of our creation. Shabbat Shalom!

Mishpatim

Happy Rosh Chodesh Adar! According to our tradition, every month has a specific energy. Adar is the month in which we are to experience *simcha*—joy and happiness. At Mount Sinai we said "Na'aseh V'Nishma" (Ex. 24:7), that by fulfilling the commandments we will come to understand them. So, how do we "do" joy? Some experience joy by going out into nature—seeing the waves, the trees, and the flowers uplifts us. Some attend concerts and sporting events, some hang out with friends, some of us walk our dogs, and some find immense joy in studying Torah.

When I was a young boy in the yeshiva, I found immense joy in studying the tractates of the Oral Law related to civil law and ethical behavior which are the underlying principles of justice and compassion. Many of these laws are found in this week's Torah portion, Mishpatim.

Mishpatim starts with "V'eilah hamishpatim," the extra *vav*/and emphasizes that these laws were given at Sinai with the Ten Commandments. We learn that our faith is not restricted to the spiritual realm and must deal with the material and financial concerns people face every day. Everyday relationships with others are considered religious issues. The Jewish legal system is juxtaposed with the religious laws of the Ten Commandments because one without the other leads to a limited blueprint for an elevated society. Religion without legal ethics, and legalism without religion, are disastrous. Therefore, the parsha begins with issues regarding criminals and the impoverished, since the test of a just society is how it treats its powerless members.

We know all too well how equal justice is often justice denied and/or unfair. There are many examples of those who attempt to obsessively uphold oppressive laws regarding others who have less power; there are those who want to control everyone at all costs, or who do not respect the rights of those whom they perceive to be in opposition to their way of life. The Torah asserts integration between law and religion with no bifurcation. Religion applies to every part of life, and where it shines most is in the everyday dealings with our fellow human beings. The essence of the Torah is to create a mensch. The more human you are, the more Jewish you are.

This Torah portion begins with the laws of slavery. Why are the laws of the Hebrew slave mentioned first rather than stealing, killing, etc.? It is because the first of the Ten Commandments mentions slavery, and so slavery is mentioned first. The Torah mentions we were slaves in Egypt no less than 42 times and therefore we should not enslave others. One would think slavery would have been outlawed in our Torah since the Hebrews suffered years of bondage and toil. However, Maimonides states that the time was not ripe to prohibit slavery entirely. It was the practice of all cultures at the time, and human consciousness was not ready to obviate it. Thus, the Torah transformed the concept of slavery (*eved*) to one of a hired worker. According to Maimonides, the process of gradually changing the law in accordance with the times relates to other laws in the Torah as well. For example, sacrificial laws which were in common practice at a certain time are no longer carried out. Laws related to bastardy or the rebellious son were made impossible to carry out.

Even as a child, I knew enslavement was unethical, and the beauty of Torah study allowed me to discover how protective and advanced the laws of so-called slavery were in our oral tradition and how they were implemented to progress from an institution of punishment and restitution (simple reimbursement) to one of rehabilitation.

The parsha begins with lists of a slave's rights and the responsibilities of his owner. In the Torah, there are only two categories of people who can become a Hebrew slave: the first, those who don't pay their debts; the second, thieves who also may work to pay back what they stole. The debtor becomes a form of indentured servant and works to repay his debt to the owner (Lev. 25:39-40). The thief becomes a slave as a way of restoring stolen property or goods. Slavery in the Torah is actually a rehabilitation process that makes it more likely that through developing a relationship with the person who was harmed, the offender will develop a sense of remorse and compassion. It makes more sense than putting a criminal or debtor in prison, keeping them isolated or surrounded by those who may be angry and bitter—conditions less likely to reform behavior. This method is more effective than incarceration since it can alter the consciousness of the debtor or thief. They are assigned to live with and get to know the people they harmed.

The Torah transforms the slave into a hired worker since the Torah excludes the Hebrews from slavery. In our times, the current percentage of recidivism is high for released prisoners, because many are released with no funds on hand, no earning power, no vocational training, and no education. The Hebrew servant, when he is released, is given earnings and the capacity to succeed in society. The protections given to the Hebrew slave were such that the Talmud says that he who hires a Hebrew slave hires a master.

The Torah explicitly states (42 times) that we were slaves in Egypt and therefore should not enslave others. Clearly, the first law of human relationships is that no one should be enslaved for life. The Hebrew slave could only serve up to six years—and if the Jubilee year comes before that time or his master dies, he is free in less than six years. If the master refused to provide proper food (the Talmud in Kiddushin 20a states that the servant must be given the best bread, best wine, best mattress, etc.), or if he imposed tasks upon his servant that hurt his dignity, even by saying something like "Put on my shoes," or if he insulted him or beat him, the court (Bet Din) would immediately free the slave.

The Hebrew servant was not allowed to be a personal servant. He must be free to do his usual occupation and when he is freed, he owes no reparations to the master. That pertains even if he created expenses for the owner because his wife and children were given food and lodging, and even if he marries while a slave. He can only work six years, but he can leave at any time if he repays his debt, unless he chooses to stay longer. If he chooses to stay, his ear is pierced because "he did not hear at Sinai that he should be a servant only of the Lord," and not to another human being. He must remember that the Hebrews were freed from the slavery which they experienced in Egypt.

The Rabbis also explain that a thief may not realize the attachment an owner has to his possessions, and may feel that his punishment for stealing is too severe. There is no better way to demonstrate the pain the thief has caused to the owner than having him witness firsthand the attachment that the owner has to their possession and the pain the owner experiences by losing the possession. The thief or debtor might have justified the theft on the grounds that the owner was richer than he is and would not feel the loss greatly. Only by living with his victim can the thief witness the attachment to—and the pain of loss of—his possessions. There may be a deeper connection to our possessions than one realizes—Pirkei Avot 2:12 says, "Let the property of your fellow be as precious to you as your own."

The basic goals of the Jewish Judicial system are the social equilibrium of the community and the moral perfection of its members. The laws exist to teach human decency and moral responsibility, hence the details of the legal system. So, if one steals, one is obliged to pay back double the cost of the stolen object (Ex. 22:3). If the law were interested in restitution, simple reimbursement would have sufficed. However, the Torah is also interested in the thief's rehabilitation. So, he must suffer the same impact. By paying double he is out of pocket the same amount as his victim. The punishment makes amends to the victim and educates the victimizer.

This type of religious ethic, this type of sensitivity, is what led to a respect for law and property. The Talmud proclaims that a few thousand years ago, when people would go up to Jerusalem on their annual holiday pilgrimages, they left their homes unguarded, and on their return, they found everything intact, without any police to guard against thieves. The explanation is that their belief in God, their relationship to the Ten Commandments, and to the ethical laws, prevented crimes—not legislation, punishments, or even capital punishment works as well.

Many of the laws in Mishpatim are commandments to exercise self-control when the temptation to be abusive is the greatest in one's relationship to the weak and defenseless. At times, the natural order of life must be interrupted to protect the weak, unlike Darwin and Nietzsche's propositions of "survival of the fittest." Many ecologists believe that death is part of the natural order, and it contributes to the larger ecosystem. But Judaism teaches that morality transcends nature. We believe that at times we must interrupt the natural order/survival of the fittest rubric to protect the weak, the vulnerable, and the defenseless from the more powerful. The commandment to love and protect the stranger is mentioned 36 times, more than any other commandment in the Torah. "For you know the heart of the stranger," and must protect those who abuse their power to satisfy their personal needs and gains, often rationalizing greed under the guise of their "natural right."

An example of how the Jewish judicial system is created to reform and elevate our nature (l'tzaref et habriyot) and to create peace and justice in our world is the law found in Ex. 23:4-5. As it states, "One must return one's enemy's ox if he wanders off, or if you see your enemy's donkey lying under his burden, help your enemy lift it." The law states that one must help his enemy and overcome hatred by practicing kindness and interaction. Do not intensify feelings that already exist by not returning his ox, for if your enemy hears about it, it will only make him more bitter. On the other hand, by doing him a kindly action, you may restore harmony. The Rabbis attached such importance to this law that they declared, "Should your father tell you to ignore it, this is an instance where he must be disobeyed!"

The order of presentation of the laws in our parsha progresses from the most obvious to the least obvious. After slavery is covered, there is a list of punishments for various crimes. First comes the punishment for murder and other capital offenses, such as kidnapping and striking a parent. In the earlier cases, we are told of the punishment of the one who intentionally murders, but as the text continues, we discover that one is responsible for a lesser blow that strikes a victim at whom the blow was not directed (Ex. 21:12-23). There is responsibility to be taken for destroying a life via manslaughter, and injury to a limb also demands compensation (Ex. 21:24-27).

We read further and discover one is responsible for that which he does himself and also for injury caused by his property. For if someone's ox gores a man, the owner of the ox is responsible (Ex. 21:28-32). One is responsible for injuries toward other human beings, for damaging or stealing animals (Ex. 21:33-37, 22:1-3), or damaging the field of another (Ex. 22:4-5). If one accepts the obligation to watch another's goods, he is responsible if the goods come to harm (Ex. 22:6-15). One's responsibility extends so far that one must see to it that the widow and orphan are not mistreated (Ex. 22:20-23).

Other laws follow and the parsha closes with the mystical vision of God seen by Moshe and the Elders (Ex. 24:10). The vision of God is contingent upon the mundane observance and understanding of God's law.

There are two sets of laws I find deeply inspirational. The first are the laws preventing the oppression of others with words or money. "Do not vex nor oppress the stranger for you were strangers in the land of Egypt" (Ex. 22:20-3, 23:9). We are commanded to exercise self-control just when temptation is the greatest—in one's relations with the weak and defenseless.

The second set of laws relates to how we treat our animals and enemies. We are taught to unpack the loads resting on the backs of the animals that belong to both our friends and our enemies. The latter charge, (including the animals of our enemies) is to help us overcome the hostility that we carry in our hearts through the opportunity to extend an act of kindness in an interaction with an enemy (Ex. 23:4-5).

It is written that if your friend's ox needs unloading, and at the same time another friend needs help loading his ox, you should help the former first because it alleviates the burden of the animal. However, the Talmud teaches that if a friend's ox requires unloading, and an enemy's ox requires loading, the enemy must be helped first, even though unloading helps the animal (Bava Metzia 31a). The reasoning here is that the potential of creating peace and harmony with an enemy through an act of kindness is of utmost importance superseding even the temporary pain of the animal.

The Torah emphasizes the pursuit of peacemaking through interaction and kindness as an important mandate in healing our world from strife. Bringing peace between enemies and healing the world takes precedence even if it mandates sacrifices, and overcoming natural impulses to take vengeance. Forgiveness, healing, and justice are the overlying foundation of our legal system.

As our Scripture teaches, "Its ways are ways of pleasantness, and all its paths are peace" (Proverbs 3:17).

Yes, the study of Torah brings us joy/happiness. Thus, in Adar we are enjoined to increase our Torah study and be joyous. May we all be blessed to bathe in the Light of the Torah as our souls dance to its tunes and hear its uplifting messages. Let us each do our parts to help us create an ideal society and attend Purim festivities drunk with joy and faith. Shabbat Shalom!

Terumah

This week's Torah portion focuses on the construction of the Tabernacle, the *Mishkan*, a sanctuary filled with unusual miracles. Our parsha begins (Ex. 25:1-9) with the contributions for the *Mishkan* from the children of Israel. "…Let them take for me a portion of their resources and set it aside for a higher purpose. In 25:8 the verse reads "…And they shall make a Sanctuary for me so that I may dwell among them."

Our commentators note the text does not say, "So that I shall dwell in it/*B'tocho*." It says, "So that I shall dwell among them/*B'tochem*). For *Am Yisrael* to take a portion of their resources to build the *Mishkan*, means that every individual has an active role to play in the cosmos. The verse does not say, "And I will dwell in the Tabernacle." God wants to dwell within *us*! Our Rabbis teach that each person is a living, breathing Tabernacle where God resides when we make an internal space for God's Presence. We do this by acting ethically, by connecting to God through prayer, by studying the Holy Scriptures, and by observing the magnificence of the natural world created for us. When God resides in us, we live with the Presence of the Creator and are uplifted in gratitude by the splendor of all that surrounds us. And we weep and mourn within, as well, when we witness destructive and insensitive behavior toward others and toward God's creations.

Let each person make themselves into a sanctuary where God dwells. Let the *Shechinah* (God's Holy Presence) reside in their hearts and souls so that each person is a carrier of God's beneficence—a vessel bringing the beauty of God's Presence to our world.

The question is asked: why did God require a specially designated, enclosed space for worship? Rashi and Sforno suggest it is because the Israelites had not yet manifested a consistent ability to connect to God in nature, in the vast complex of awesome, mysterious Creation. That fact was proven by the sin of the golden calf. The golden calf was a "security blanket" that could not move, could not speak, could not hear or see, was made of fixed material, and was a tool to make religion routine. It is hard to believe in an ephemeral being, and thus a special place had to be created to focus the Israelites' energy and recapture intense, rapturous worship. The golden calf was conceived as a mitzvah that became the sin of idolatry. The *Mishkan* was, therefore, a concession to the Israelites' need to focus on something concrete when they worshiped Hashem.

The Ramban suggests that it was not a concession at all, but a necessary construct to promote consciousness that radiates outward. A fixed place, set aside for this very purpose of meeting God within, is a necessary aid to elevating our connection and communication with the *Shechinah*. It is a sacred gift and necessary blessing to create a special space to come together to meet God in addition to the other ways in which we connect to God and the Light.

The Talmud in Yoma 21a says that the Ark had no measurements, that it did not occupy physical space. The Talmud in B. Batra 14a says that the Tablets of the Law filled the Ark to capacity. Other sages view the *Mishkan* as a model of the world—it was indeed a place of meditative intensity and ecstatic desire to connect with God.

The *Mishkan* is discussed at length in Exodus, for the redemption from Egypt was not sufficient to remove the residue of slave mentality. The Revelation at Sinai was a great elevated moment for the Jewish people. But spectacular events do not always have staying power unless they are reinforced by everyday rituals that secure memory. Thus, the *Mishkan* was intended to be the central rallying point, the place where every member would go with their offerings and elevate their spiritual fervor.

The *Mishkan* was built of wood, for a house of God should be alive and growing. The inclusion of the *Mishkan* and the poles to carry it (so that it can be moved from place to place) suggest a universal spirit embodied it. The Midrash tells us that the people were shown a heavenly model of the *Mishkan* that was made of fire. Fire is an ultra-living element and the gold covering the wooden Ark of the *Mishkan* was the static representation of fire.

Our text tells us that God did not dwell in the fixed Ark where the tablets were placed. Hashem lived above the Ark between the gold cherubim (with large wings and the faces of children). The space was surrounded by a fog of incense. It was a mysterious elusive space wherein God was centered. Chasidim say that space is the space of the human heart. Our open hearts make a space for love and desire. God lives wherever we let God in, always there waiting, always loving us. God meets us in the passion of the heart of people seeking Torah, truth, and compassion.

Where specifically is God to be met in the *Mishkan?* "It is there on the top of the Ark that I will set my meeting with you, and I shall speak with you from between the two Cherubim that are on the Ark of the Testimonial

Tablets" (Ex. 25:21-22). This space between the cherubim is the space of desire, where two beings face each other in love and longing, and God resides in that loving space; that is where God meets us—not in the fixed space inside the Ark, for fixity creates complacency. The Lord meets us in a space filled with longing, desire, and passion. The cherubim never consummate their love; they remain two separate entities. The space between the wings, the space of their desire for each other, in the shy oblique gaze from a distance, at opposite ends of the *kaporet* (cover)—that is where God is (compare Keats, "Ode on a Grecian Urn").

There, in the space where the two beings face each other, is where the *Shechinah* reveals herself. It is our deep, loving longing for God that allows God's Presence to emerge. It is the same energy that manifests when we love another human being with deep desire; God basks in that love, in the strong, honest desire that yearns for connection with our beloved human being or directly with God. When we have a passionate desire to connect to Hashem, God's Presence becomes manifest. We must have that desire for Hashem to dwell with us. The vulnerable space in the human heart must be opened for God to enter. This is the space of desire, of longing for our beloved!

It requires energy to traverse the divide in the quest for wholeness between the transcendent and immanent realms in this liminal space. In the space we create within, messages are transmitted between the worlds; messages of prayer, yearning, and gratitude.

When two people say to each other "You are the one," then God dwells in between. For love arouses love. Because the cherubim never consummate their desire, the desire continues to grow and remain strong; God's Presence (*Hester Panim*/Hiding Face) is elusive and conjures up our desire to reach out more and experience the love of the *Shechinah*. Then God's Presence, which is always there waiting for us, is felt deeply in our souls. For love creates reciprocal love, like the two lovers in *Shir Hashirim*/Song of Songs, our holiest book in the canon. Two souls yearning to come close to each other create the Holy of Holies. God says, "There I will meet you and there I will speak with you, from atop the cover, from between the two Cherubim" from the place of desire, the place of eternity (Ex. 25:22).

If we long for God, the indwelling will come again. God waits for our love, "And you shall love the Lord your God with all your heart" (Deut. 6:5). God says, "Let them bring me gifts and show me that they long for me and remember me, and want me in their lives" (Ex. 25:2). Love brings forth love.

King David expresses his longing with the words, "I will not give sleep to my eyes, or slumber to my eyelids until I find a place for the Lord" (Psalm 132:4-5).

The cherubim teach us that God is with us if we love each other, if we recognize that we are all different aspects of the One. Our parsha affirms this unity with the placement of the showbread in the *Mishkan*. They are two faces of bread looking at each other while facing upward. "On the table you shall place showbread before Me always" (Ex. 25:30). This pairing suggests the need for us to face one another, to communicate with each other, and to face God. At the foot of Mount Sinai the people dwelt in unity (*vayichan ha'am*) and communicated with one another, making the Revelation possible. Unity and dialogue make Sinai possible—that love makes God's Presence palpable.

The cherubim also represent unity. In BT Shabbat 89a, our Rabbis teach that during the Pilgrimage Festivals, when the Jewish people marched to the Holy Temple in Jerusalem, they observed the cherubim facing each other. But when the Holy Temple was destroyed due to disharmony in the community, when the Romans entered and destroyed the Temple, the cherubim looked away from each other! God appears when we face each other in love, not when we are in a state of disunity.

The function of the *Mishkan* in the desert was continued later in *Eretz Yisrael* by the worship in the Holy Temple in Jerusalem. After the destruction of the Temples, the continuity of connection to God and God's commandments is found in the miniature temples—the synagogues and study halls of today (Megillah 29a)—where Jews hear the sounds of Sinai through the study of Torah.

Why do we need a sanctuary, a specific holy site today? Isn't God omnipresent throughout our amazing universe, both in nature, in other human beings, and indeed in our own souls? This may be true, but a special place of focus where people come together in unity creates a special holy ambiance, an association and connection to the Divine. A sacred place removes extraneous distractions in an enclosed space designated for worship. Ramban/Nachmanides suggests that even in messianic times there would be a need for sanctuary, a place where we all come to worship God, where our souls are drawn out in holy space.

Now we must ask ourselves if we are truly doing the work to create a sanctuary within ourselves for God's Presence. Can we become sanctuaries through studying Torah and practicing kindness and respect for our fellow human beings? Can we expand that energy within our groups and communities and into our synagogues? Our houses of worship must not be only showplaces that embody materialistic values, gleaming with radiance that displays material success. A synagogue's resplendence must dignify the honor and the glory of the true holiness of a House of God. We ask ourselves if we are creating our synagogues (our modern-day sanctuaries) as spaces where we truly meet God and open our hearts with fervor and gratitude as we feel the Presence of the *Shechinah*.

The community that worships Hashem with intensity has an impact on each of its members. Our liturgy reflects this: the words of the blessings in the Amidah are all in the plural, noting the interconnections and caring we have with and for each other. During Covid, we missed the smiling faces, warm greetings, and communal intimacy of a real-life shul experience, where the ecstatic and contemplative modes of the service are accessible to all of us. We are blessed to be able to pray together once more, in love and respect.

On this Shabbat, we also read Parshat *Zachor*/Remember. We fight against Amalek in every generation because Amalek's radical evil energy remains alive and well in our world. Our Torah teaches that this must not be ignored. We are to fight against Amalek/Radical Evil in every generation lest this negative energy increase and imperil our world (Ex. 17:16).

It is a mitzvah, one that is necessary. Love does not mean accepting everything that another person does. Truly loving means caring enough to correct that which is destructive and harmful to others. And we must do it responsibly. As the Talmud says, "Hate the sin and not the sinner." Everyone may be worthy of redemption, but evil acts are not to be tolerated. If they are ignored, they will increase and destroy our world.

As mentioned in a previous parsha, the shame and rejection the woman Timnah suffered at the hands of Jacob's family remained a deep wound passed on to her son, Amalek, and hence it went from generation to generation. The painful reality of our intolerance, rejection, and treating others disrespectfully can lead to dire and egregious consequences. Insensitivity can create very deep wounds that lead to destructive anger and tragedy. One way to obviate the hostile, incorrigible actions of Amalek is to bring warmth, acceptance, and friendship to those we meet from all walks of life, so that the seeds of Amalek are rendered infertile, and the seeds of goodness and decency can germinate. As Rav Avraham Yitzchak Hacohen Kook famously said, "The way to obviate endless hatred is through endless Love."

Our community is now bifurcated. Very few of us know "the other," and we create caricatures based on fear and the insecurity of our own positions. We must realize that we must become a loving community for the *Shechinah* to dwell with us again. The Chassidim suggest that perhaps our homes today can become the equivalent of the Holy Temple; our Shabbat tables should be imbued with hospitality and love for our guests, to become the Temples of our day to promote unity and knowledge of each other. They point out that in *gematria*, the numerological sum of the word *bayit*/home is 412; and the numerological sum of the word *mikdash*/temple) is 444. The numerological sum of the word *lev*/heart is 32. Thus, if you put your heart into your home, you create a Temple!

May we all yearn with great desire for the Presence of the Lord and be blessed to turn our homes into sanctuaries to create peace and love in our world. May we learn to express love to each other as human beings created in the image of God. May we be worthy to truly create a world where God's Glory can comfortably dwell in it and in us! May we be blessed to make it so. Amen.

Tetzaveh / Purim

There's a medieval English quote, "Clothes make the man," and Parshat Tetzaveh describes this phenomenon as one of the reasons for the opulent clothing worn by the high priest.

Why is this important? The condition and cut of one's clothing marks the wearer's status in his community. On the one hand, it affirms the importance of the wearer and one's office; on the other, the clothing supports the quest to live up to the obligations of the office holder, reminding us to do God's work. When we wear the "right" clothing—clothing appropriate to the settings we are in, we become bearers of God's candle, "Ner Hashem nishmat adam/The light of the Lord is the soul of man" (Proverbs 20:27).

In the Garden of Eden, God clothed Adam and Eve when they realized they were naked. A garment is called levush in Hebrew, which means Lo yibosh/Do not be ashamed! Be proud you are created in the image of God. The human body is a miraculous wonder; its architecture is sublimely and Divinely engineered. But the shame the two of them felt came from self-awareness and the realization that they did not obey Hashem and from not taking responsibility for their act of disobedience.

Many people wear expensive designer clothes to make themselves feel better about themselves, looking to others for approval and validation. We permit others to determine how much we matter and our "style" sends them a superficial message of who we are. How much we value ourselves affects our ability to learn and grow, our choice of careers, companions, and mates, and our likelihood of succeeding in our chosen vocation. It is our inner style we should be concerned with. We must never allow our wardrobes to lead us to hubris.

In telling the story of the high priest's garments, the Torah teaches us the quality of gratitude, interconnection, and humility that are possible even when wearing exalted clothing. One must wear outer garments to support one's high purpose yet remain humble—while remaining connected to all those who supported us throughout our lives. We learn this from the high priest Aaron, Moshe's brother. Despite the jewel-encrusted apparel made of the finest cloth he wore as part of his duties to God and the Israelites, Aaron was a man of great humility, a model of dignity, and *not* an authoritarian. He was a compassionate, forgiving soul who was very close to the people of Israel. When he died, the Israelites mourned him longer than they did Moshe.

The parsha also tells us that Moshe made Aaron's clothes (Ex. 28:2), and clothed him (Ex. 28:41). Aaron was grateful and humble, for he realized his office and stature were dependent on others and on the kindness and support of Moshe. We are taught by the Torah that even when you are given vestments of grandeur (titles and honors), it is the giver who clothed you and empowered you, and you did not reach that level of success by yourself. Each of the garments of the high priest had a purpose and wisdom attached to it. For example, one of the unique garments of the high priest was the robe (Ex. 28:31) decorated on its hem with little golden bells and pomegranates (Ex. 28:35). This was done so the tinkling of the bells would signal the *Kohen's* approach and departure to and from the Sanctuary. This suggested courtesy and respect, by establishing the notice of his comings and goings. One is not supposed to enter a place unexpectedly, for this might disturb another's privacy. Announcing oneself before entering a room suggests sensitivity and humility. Not abusing the privilege of one's clothing is important. Hence, one must respect boundaries and not enter another's space without first being welcomed in. Moreover, the priests were wise and humble enough to remove their special clothes and wear street clothes when they left the sanctuary so as not to abuse their power.

Why was Aaron chosen for the priesthood and not Moshe? Because Aaron's closeness to the people made him better able to offer their prayers to Hashem. Moshe was the bestower of the law to the people which required discipline and sacrifice from the people as they acquiesced to the law. Aaron was soft, pleasant, tolerant, forgiving, and unable to see any wrong in his children. As we have seen, Moshe at times readily expressed his anger with his people. This difference of character came across in the episode of The golden calf (Ex. 32:1-24) and the incident involving Korach and his followers. Aaron protected the people and stopped the plague (Numbers 25:8-26:1). He was an *oheiv shalom*, a lover of peace and a pursuer of peace (Pirkei Avot 1:12). The people recognized they needed both the compassion of Aaron and the law-giving of Moshe. Both were necessary to maintain the balance needed in a successful community, but Aaron was especially beloved to them. After his death, the Israelites' deep appreciation of him was confirmed by the large funeral held in his honor.

Finally, a word about the menorah (Ex. 25:31) referred to as *Edut*/Testimony; a term which usually refers to the Tablets, but here refers to the menorah (Ex. 27:21). Why? Because a miracle was associated with it! Every evening the *Kohen* lit all seven lamps with an equal amount of oil. Six would burn until morning, and the seventh, the *ner tamid*/the *ner ma'arav* closest to the Holy of Holies, would burn until the next evening to show that God's Light is always burning (Shabbat 22b) and that the *Shechinah* is always present. The light was not needed in the morning when the priest came in to light the incense. It was there only to testify to God's Presence. This one candle burned even in the morning light—when it was not needed!

This miracle recurred throughout the Second Temple period until the death of Shimon the Just (Pirkei Avot 1:2), when the Jews were no longer worthy of this miracle and experienced a diminution of this Light.

May we be capable of both love for ourselves as candles of the Lord; may we be humble and thankful for all the gifts we receive from others and from God that make our Holy goals possible.

Friends, at this time the month of Adar appears! *Mi she nichnas Adar marbim be simcha*! When the month of Adar begins, joy is multiplied. It is the month of Purim, one of the most joyous days in our Jewish calendar. Our Sages declare it is even more special than Yom Kippur, for it is filled with joy rather than awe. They declare it to be the only holiday we will celebrate in the messianic era, for it reveals the Light becoming manifest when evil is overcome by the forces of good. It enables the Holy Light to be revealed when human beings choose to recognize the Light of God that has always been hidden by evil but now is revealed in the victory over Haman/Amalek. There is even a custom to get so drunk on Purim that one does not know the difference between blessing Mordechai and cursing Haman—the difference "between good and evil," for a state of blending of "opposites" occurs when one is inebriated, just as the mixture of good and evil occurs when Amalek is defeated. This is the reality manifest during the messianic era when all will be unified and evil will not be a separate reality.

There are the beautiful Purim customs of *mishloach manot* (sharing food with others), *matanot l'evyonim* (giving gifts of sustenance to those in need), eating a Purim meal together, thus enhancing friendship (*seudat Purim*) and listening to the Megillah, the Purim story describing overcoming our enemies through the courageous gallantry of our heroes Esther and Mordechai. All these customs promote unity. And the Megillah teaches us that turning the tables on evil can happen in a rapid, surprising "blink of the eye" moment (v'nehapich hu), when tzaddikim such as Mordechai and Esther stand up in faith and oppose forces seemingly greater than theirs. Overcoming despair and darkness with faith in God is a relevant message for us today as well, as we confront the forces of darkness running rampant in our world.

Where did Mordechai and Esther get the strength to confront evil as they did? What is the source of strength and definition of someone who merits the term tzaddik (the righteous one)? Our Sages teach that a tzaddik is defined by three qualities: one who has the capacity to sacrifice their money (mamono), their very body (gufo), and their very soul (nafsho) and derives joy and fulfillment in this very sacrifice.

What does this mean? And why is the tzaddik defined as one who embodies joy? A tzaddik often gives money to a special cause or person because it is needed and feels great joy when the recipient appreciates the gift, and when because of this gift the person or cause reaches its potential. And when thanks are given, when there is an expression of gratitude, invariably the giver feels greater joy than the recipient. Secondly, there are times when the tzaddik gives of their body, time, and talents to another, and this devotion leads to interactions that are uplifting and joyful. They are among the most meaningful and memorable moments of their life. Finally, there are times when the tzaddik sacrifices their very soul for another, for this is what they feel called upon to do. They are willing to put the needs of others, of the community, or humanity ahead of their personal needs because ultimately this "soul calling" gives them meaning and thus great joy. This is the great joy of the tzaddik born out of "soul giving" ("to give is to live") as one's very purpose and meaning is edified.

Our Sages teach that every human being can be a tzaddik. Therefore, it behooves each of us to go out and give of our money, our time, and talents, and yes, even our very souls, to that which calls us today.

May we have the courage, the wisdom, and the opportunity to meet this moment with our generous souls and be rewarded with the fulfillment of what it means to be a tzaddik in our day. Let's show support for all organizations that work to overturn injustice in our communities. In the spirit of Purim, where we celebrate our blessings, let us remember to show up for those who suffer from various forms of oppression.

May we all merit the ability to be of help to others, to revel in the spirit of Purim, and never to forget our obligations to those who depend upon our voices and actions to redeem them from suffering. Amen.

Ki Tisa

Parshat Ki Tisa presents us with the challenges, demands, struggles, conflicts, moral dilemmas, and miracles in the desert as the Israelites face the task of attaining freedom in the Exodus from Egypt.

The story of the liberation from slavery in Egypt describes a very complicated process and the text can be read in a myriad of ways. It is a story of a gradual awakening, one that raises the notion that sometimes a purge is necessary when behaviors threaten the hard-won progress made toward realizing freedom. There are "opposites" that abide; different energies appear at the same and different times, and the journey proceeds despite the impact of these innumerable forces. There are problems, struggles, and resolutions in this story.

Once the Israelites crossed the Red Sea, through their procession and regression in the desert, we learn much about human and group behavior, its complexity and variability on the long trek to the Promised Land. We see that journeying through the desert toward wholeness and true liberation is a complicated process, with moral and psychological challenges. It is clear from this "Journey toward Wholeness" that liberation does not guarantee liberty.

We know the bulk of what the slaves learned in Egypt was servitude and slavishness as they endured the moral and psychological effects of oppression. The slavishness of the Israelites is used to explain their struggles in the desert, their desire to return to Egypt, and the deep challenge of finding true liberation. In addition, some commentators feel that since the elders were afraid of their masters, unwilling to challenge Pharaoh and overawed by the size of his army, the older generation needed to die out, and a new liberated generation needed to form.

Though they left Egypt, the Israelites were still weighed down by oppression. Interestingly, in the wilderness we find a people who do not complain about their slavery in Egypt but do complain endlessly about their liberation. They complain about the manna and have nostalgia for the meat in the house of bondage. In Egypt, they were subservient, despondent, and unwilling to revolt, since slaves internalized their own crushed identity. In this parsha we read about internal fighting in the desert between different factions with different proclivities. We find them marching ahead but complaining along the way. Some were faithful and willing to undertake the trial of the wilderness, and some were impatient and wanted to return to Egypt.

The impatience of some of them led to the construction of the golden calf and yet others understood that progression takes time. This story also served to implant in us the quality of kindness and empathy for others who suffered as our ancestors did. But the experience of bondage did not implant in them the qualities of initiative, self-respect, anger at oppression, and militancy.

Freedom demands effort and responsibility. It demands choice and decision. Perhaps in some way, being told what to do in bondage is preferable and less strenuous. Perhaps, paradoxically, in the desert they were also rebelling against a new world of laws—the whole legal system founded by Moshe (kashrut, Shabbat, rules about the manna)—so Egypt appeared in their psyches as a place of greater freedom. In fact, there is a kind of freedom in bondage—the freedom of not having to make decisions, and a kind of bondage in freedom—the bondage of law, obligation, and responsibility. They did accept the Sinai covenant, but they also resented its standards and feared the responsibilities it entailed. And so, the wilderness had to be a new "School of the Soul."

The march toward this new "School of the Soul" moved through organized education, and included periods of violence and purging, as counter-groups emerged to object to the challenges facing them. Karl Marx posited that the old world must go under to make room for people to cope with a new world. Thus, in the wilderness, we find that there is violence, not only marching and murmuring but fighting too, internal war and Divine punishment. With the golden calf, the murmuring of the people turned into something like a counterrevolution, to which Moshe did not respond with patience and understanding or by acknowledging the difficulties of slavery. When Moshe saw the golden calf, he forgot that progress takes time.

Our ancestors seem to move through three stages on their journey from Egypt to *Eretz Yisrael*.

Stage One: Slavery—the Israelites felt weak, restricted from within and without—*Mitzrayim*. Stage Two: Freedom—they felt more powerful but had to move through the many challenges holding them back and inhibiting true freedom—wilderness. Stage Three: Covenantal Freedom—they used their power responsibly—the Promised Land.

Going through these stages enabled them to live in consonance with the higher soul values of our tradition. The way to the Promised Land is through the wilderness, and there is no way to get from here to there except by joining together in this taxing process and marching forward. On the journey, we learn that "Liberation is not a guarantee of liberty." For wherever we live, it is probably still Egypt. And there is probably a better place, a world more attractive, a promised land where we can go, but we have to make it through the wilderness first (Edinger, *The Bible and the Psyche*).

The internalized slave mentality of the elders, their struggles in the desert, and their desire to return to Egypt are cited by many thinkers as evidence of the challenges faced by any group facing change and obstacles along the way. The text tells us the elders joined Moshe to dialogue with Pharaoh and then relates how the elders slowly slipped away, ultimately leaving just Moshe and Aaron to confront Pharaoh. In Exodus 5:1, we read, "The elders slipped away." Rashi says it is "Because they were afraid." The elders, like the people as a whole, were afraid of their masters, unwilling to challenge Pharaoh in his palace, and were frightened by the size of his army (Ex. 14:10). According to the Torah there were 600,000 Hebrews who marched out from Egypt, so why should they have been afraid? Ibn Ezra asks (Ex. 13:14), why didn't they turn and fight? He answered his own question, "They were psychologically incapable; they suffered from a slave mentality, because for centuries they had not defended themselves—at least, not by fighting."

Theorists of revolution and writers about the Exodus can be divided into two groups. There are those who believe that the liberation of the oppressed will always be a gift from God, and others who believe that liberation must, to some degree at least, be the work of the oppressed themselves.

God and Moshe take the long view. They see the Promised Land ahead and think no hardship is too great to endure for the sake of such an end. But many of the people were unsure of the end and remembered the bread and meat they ate in Egypt. The conflict was one between the fears of the people and the idealism of their leaders, between the demands of the present moment and the promise of the future.

Some commentators suggest that the people's complaint was not because the desert was a place of austerity, but because of the laws of the Torah. The whole legal system founded by Moshe, including kashrut, Shabbat, and manna felt oppressive to them, so they rebelled, remembering Egypt as a "house of freedom." But Moshe made them free by breaking their chains and by organizing them into a society, by giving them laws. He brought them into what we may call positive freedom—a way of life and regulation to which they could and did agree. They accepted a common standard: the Sinai covenant. But they also resented the standard and feared the responsibility it entailed. And so the wilderness had to be a new School of the Soul.

The incident of the golden calf is the great crisis of the Exodus. The question is whether the response should have been a response of gradualism or purging. Purging is what actually took place (Walzer, *Exodus and Revolution*). Revolutions produce hard men and hard women. When slavish people are incapable of liberating themselves, incapable of imagining what liberation might be like by themselves, a revolutionary leader may step up. It is usually one who comes from the outside. The revolutionary leader who comes from the outside, such as Moshe, whose life experience was entirely different from that of the oppressed men and women he led, has the capacity to take charge as he sees it. He senses that unless this group of rebels revealed by the incident of the golden calf are reined in (purged), all hopes for a better future and all that they worked for will be destroyed. Is that rationale sufficient to perpetuate an act of violence to save the masses and the great idea? Do not the Ten Commandments clearly state, "Thou shalt not murder"? How can God condone the murder of the rebels? And yet Moshe is not chastised by God for purging the idolaters from the people.

The argument that supports gradualism states that any movement from oppression to freedom must endure progress and regress; there must be an acceptance of gradualism and education along the way and eventually progress will be made, faith firmed up. Oppression is an experience with predictable consequences and thus necessitates patience. Physically, the escape from Egypt is sudden, glorious, complete. Spiritually, it is very slow—a matter of two steps forward, one step back. Education, it would seem, should have been the response to the crisis.

But because of Moshe's absence for 40 days, at the foot of Mount Sinai there was chaos, revolt, rebelliousness, and recklessness. When he came down from the mountain, he broke the Tablets of the Law in his rage. Moshe then mobilized the Levites and had the idol worshippers killed (3,000 out of the population of 600,000 Jews). He felt it was crucial to take this drastic step, since allowing the raging insurrection to continue would destroy the progress of this most difficult journey. This purged the nation of those who threatened to extinguish the cherished goal of God's promise.

Interestingly, Moshe proclaimed, "Thus Saith the Lord, 'Let every Levite take his sword and slay the rebels'" (Ex. 32:27). But nowhere in the text does God order the killing of the idol worshipers! Did Moshe invent this command? Perhaps it was easier to do what in any case had to be done for the leader to claim Divine authority. Moshe saw the rebels as a threat to be removed if the march forward was to succeed. He felt this sub-group, if left to survive, would grow in power and sabotage the whole enterprise. It had to be prevented at all costs for the promising new world to be born. So this rule of force, this purge, though the enemy of patient gradualism, must be implemented as an emergency necessity or else all would be lost.

As people who pursue peace and express compassion, can we imagine a moment when violence is valid to prevent a greater tragedy? Can we institute a rule for when it is valid and when it is not, and consider, perhaps, that both violence and gradualism are necessary at different times? This is a most challenging question that has to be addressed when a terrifying threat faces us

Radical revolutionaries note that even "meek" Moshe had to be "a "man of blood" at times. Moshe's only way to bring them to *Eretz Yisrael* was to overwhelm the opponents of their journey and then drive on with his reluctant marchers. Moshe, against his natural compassion, had to call upon *gevurah*/strength to cope with this extremely dangerous crisis.

Three thousand of the 600,000 Israelites were murdered! Michael Walzer points out, in *Exodus and Revolution*, that in every revolution there is a moment when a group of people want to return and abandon the journey forward (the counterrevolutionaries) and the success of the original mission depends on that very moment. The leaders must stand up to the counterrevolutionaries and not allow them to take over and derail the proclaimed cherished goals, or all progress is lost. It is the moment when a purge is necessary, when we despair of further education because of their threatening impact on our march forward to that which is beneficial for all humanity. Moshe realized this and purged the rebels by commanding the Levites to slaughter the insurrectionists—with no warning and without pursuing judgment. This was the crucial moment that saved the transition from going from the House of Bondage to the March to the Promised Land. *Eit la'asot l'Hashem*/A time to do for the Lord (Psalm 119:126).

Buber interestingly says the Exodus was the kind of revolution that could not be organized by anyone raised as a slave. Moshe was separated from the people in his early life and later separated himself from the people again. Immediately after the incident of the golden calf, Moshe took the *Mishkan* and pitched it far off from the cam

p (Ex. 33:7). Moshe (brokenhearted for what he had done) could not dwell among the people whose brothers, companions, and neighbors he had ordered to be killed.

Another lesson from the Exodus/Wilderness journey is that perhaps it is only a new generation with a different experience that is capable of liberation. The elders with memory and fears of slavery had to raise a generation of freeborn children, for they could not completely overcome their own earlier experiences of oppression in Egypt. Moshe educated this new generation to the laws and rituals of Israel's new religion, and the result was that the Israelites at the Jordan were very different from the Israelites at the Red Sea. They were faithful and courageous. They were committed to one another and to the covenant that bound them together. This was the achievement of four decades in the wilderness.

But we have not answered the original question. Was it the purging or the teaching that made the decisive difference? Our text is telling us that at some point the counterrevolutionaries had to be defeated if Egyptian bondage was ever to be left behind. Would the Israelites have survived to accomplish this great task, this transformation, without the purging that could have plunged them back to enslavement? This may have been a crisis moment when a purge, though an anomaly, was necessary to prevent a regression to a lower consciousness. Some want to use this text as justification to coerce and kill their enemies. They are convinced that at some point the counterrevolutionaries must be defeated if Egyptian bondage is ever to be left behind. But it is more likely that patient teaching over 40 years created the new reality. There is also the preferred possibility of intervening in the subgroup, creating dialogue that may obviate the insurrection. Or, if possible, removing the group without violence because of the disparity of views that are incompatible and unbridgeable.

This incident raises an excruciating, tormenting moral dilemma. There are some radical commentators who favor this violence (the murder of the rebels) as a necessary exception in a time of great crisis (preventing a greater evil), and most who condemn it as unjust and murderous. There are some who distinguish between when purging is valid and when it is not (it may be valid to save your own life or the life of another), and some who acknowledge that both violence and gradualism are necessary at different times. (When can the sword be rightly used? And by whom can it be rightly used?)

We must ask: Is violence ever justified even to protect others? Can it not be abused all too easily by those who possess power? Is the motive of the welfare of the people the justification, or is the taking of even one life seen as if you have destroyed the whole world? Is violence justified to quell the dangers and destruction of the radicals, the rebels?

At such critical moments, it is expected, though agonizing, for people to stand up with courage to defend their ideals. We must confront those who wish to maintain the status quo due to their fear of change and loss of power. We must not allow the naysayers, or minority opinions shouted louder than anyone else's, to deter us from goals that will benefit the larger society, one yearning for justice and kindness for all. We must confront the Egypt within us, overcome our fears, and choose *derech hayashar*/the direct path, which we are commanded to do.

The text makes clear that the counterrevolutionaries, who are not fully committed to the higher goals, cannot be defeated by force alone. It took a generation of gradual education to transform their consciousness. It took 40 years of living through trials and tribulations to embrace the path of faith and higher consciousness.

It takes a long process in the desert, an educational process, where people work and struggle to grow and take on the higher, noble ideals that God has "called" us to uphold. Sometimes they had the courage of their vision and were able to commit themselves to the Covenant at Sinai (*Na'aseh v'nishma*) and sometimes not. Sometimes it takes a whole new generation, and sometimes with patience, persistence, and prayer, God's blessing will bring us to the Promised Land "on the wings of an eagle" (Ex. 19:4).

So, while purging might be necessary and acceptable at moments of great and certain danger, it is an anomaly in the sublime teachings of holiness, ethics, and virtuous living found in our Torah and it is not the way of the covenant. The way toward change and marching to the Holy Land is a gradual process that must be lived in our personal wilderness, with patience and expectations of failure, as the dark side in us is always present. But one day, after the long journey, we will reach the blessed Promised Land found within and without.

Moshe eventually successfully teaches this new generation the laws of the Torah, this new religion. He becomes *Moshe rabbeinu*, Moshe our teacher! The people have matured, and they are ready to commit to the covenant and to one another. This is the achievement of four decades in the wilderness.

May we all find the strength to stand up for the exalted goals that we are "chosen" to uphold, oppose those who would deter us from these goals, and continue to educate ourselves and others with patience, love, and respect as we grow on our journey toward wholeness. Shabbat Shalom!

Vayakhel

…A time to love, a time to hate. A time for war, a time for peace.
—Ecclesiastes 3:8

Our parsha continues with the details of building the *Mishkan* and introduces us to its builder, Bezalel. Who was Bezalel and why is he mentioned again as the person chosen to build the *Mishkan?* One reason is that by the time he was 13, he was acknowledged as being a great artist. A mystical reason is also found in his name, Bezalel, which means dwelling "in the shadow of the Lord," and our tradition says there is destiny in a name. The Talmud notes an even deeper reason for why he was chosen, and it relates to his grandfather and family history. His grandfather Chur is mentioned in his lineage, and it was unusual to identify a person by anyone other than his father. Bezalel is identified as the son of Uri, and grandson of Chur (Ex. 38:22) because hidden in this story is an important lesson about forgiveness.

Chur, Bezalel's grandfather, was the person who stood up to the crazed mob who built the golden calf and was murdered by them. (Sanhedrin 7a). Chur was Miriam's son, a nephew of Moshe and Aaron. He had willpower and courage and was artistic. His grandson, Bezalel, was chosen to build the *Mishkan* because he was a great artist, and had an evolved, sublime character; he was a person with the same great courage and willpower as his grandfather.

Moshe singled him out, saying to the Jewish people that Hashem proclaimed him by name as the person to design the *Mishkan*: Bezalel, son of Uri, grandson of Chur of the tribe of Judah. He added that God filled him with wisdom, insight, and knowledge of every craft in order to build it (Ex. 35:30-31).

Moshe recognized Bezalel had an enormous depth of soul to overcome the understandable and justifiable proclivity to fulfill his need for revenge. Instead, he chose to forgive! One would think he would have felt some hatred toward B'nai Yisrael for the slaying of his grandfather, and this would interfere with his ability to act on their behalf with the level of purity of intention necessary. But he chose to emulate the refined character traits of his grandfather Chur!

How was he able to reach this level? It is easy to think Bezalel would be justified in resenting the people who murdered his grandfather. Although revenge may be our only comfort for the anger we feel toward those who wronged us, we are also endowed with the capacity to meet that challenge. Many of us face this when chastised by our people. The love of brothers and sisters, the capacity to overcome taking revenge, is precisely what is needed to bring peace and harmony to our world. We must and can follow the courageous example of Bezalel if peace and harmony are to be restored in our world. Asking Bezalel to build the House of the Lord, the atonement for the sin of the golden calf, was asking him to do something extraordinary. You would think his grandfather's murder would interfere with his ability to act on the people's behalf with the necessary level of purity of intention.

But Bezalel disdained the satisfaction of revenge and instead forgave the very same mobsters who brought such pain upon him! How was he able to reach this level? He shared Chur's love of the people, a love that compelled him to risk his life to try to stop them from sinning. This loving trait was inherited by Bezalel and made him uniquely suited to build the *Mishkan*. He mobilized the great capacity—one inherent in each of us—to overcome our instincts and fears.

You might say, "But Rabbi, how can you even think of forgiveness at a time like this, when an evildoer is using his army to overrun another country's property and slaughter masses of people in the process? Aren't we supposed to stand against evil and fight with all our might to overturn the evildoer to save the world from destruction and uplift our world to the beauty and justice that was meant to be?"

And I would answer, "You are absolutely correct! When an arch-evil, beastly person, an Amalek—whether it is Hamas, Putin, or another tyrant—arises to destroy us and/or others, we, as the Jewish people, must be the first to oppose this behavior, to save the innocent, and fulfill the mandate of our tradition—to fight against Amalek in every generation. As the verses state, "The Lord said to Moshe, 'Write this as a remembrance in the book and recite it in the ears of Joshua, that I shall surely erase the memory of Amalek from under heaven….' Thus, you shall maintain a war against Amalek from generation to generation." (Ex. 17:14-16). God swore God's name and throne would not be complete until Amalek was destroyed. In every generation we must fight against the archetypal enemy so that God's glory will be able to inhabit our world.

The Torah lists two mitzvot regarding Amalek: to obliterate the nation of Amalek (*timcheh et zecher Amalek*, Ex. 17:14), and to never forget his evil deeds (*zachor, al tishkach*, Deut. 25:17-19).

May we all be strengthened to achieve the capacity to fight radical evil in our world. But there is a justified time and an obligation to uproot evil when it raises its destructive fangs. There is a time to fight and a time to forgive. May Hashem aid us to respond appropriately in each case, so that each of our responses will contribute to creating yearned-for peace in our world.

We must fight against Amalek, but we must also understand the roots of the hatred and denial of morality that permeates the energy of Amalek and his inheritors. While fighting against Amalek is a mitzvah, we should also never forget the example that Bezalel provides for us in choosing a path filled with forgiveness instead of vengeance, overcoming our hatred, and creating harmony in our world. We must not neglect our capacities to forgive, to reach out to others, and recognize that we have the same ability as the noble Bezalel to see the greater picture and that we are here to be loving to others, even to those who have hurt and angered us.

Bezalel's path was to be suprarationally good, calling forth the inner connection to God residing in his soul, and connecting to that Divine spark within. This connection is beyond logic. One might call it foolish or irrational—or blind faith—but our tradition teaches that even Amalek cannot defeat such a deep, abiding faith and so the enemy loses his brazen power, and good triumphs.

Bezalel teaches us that doing good shatters the armor of evil, and elevates God's name and the power of good on earth. That is how the memory of that evil nation is obliterated. "Not by might and not by power, but by My Spirit alone," says the Lord of Hosts (Zechariah 4:6).

May we be capable of love for ourselves as a candle of the Lord and be humble and thankful for all the gifts from God—who makes our holy goals possible. May we find forgiveness in our hearts for those who have wronged us in the past! Let us not forget to provide necessary aid to those who suffer the devastating, cruel pangs of war. Let us work and do our duty to make it so. May the cherished qualities of kindness and compassion aid us in bringing peace to our world, and let us say Amen!

Pikudei

Let us study the uplifting, comforting jewel of Torah found in our parsha this week. Our parsha begins with the words, "These are the accounts of the *Mishkan*..." (Ex. 38:21). We continue the story of the building of the *Mishkan* and repeat instructions already mentioned regarding the counting of the furnishings, the appointment of Bezalel as the architect of the *Mishkan*, and the details of priestly garb. Why was the repetition necessary? Perhaps it is in the important lessons we can learn from each of these themes, but we will concentrate on the counting of the items.

Pekudei/Accounts can also mean "to be missing," for in counting there is limitation, and therefore the Gemara says, "Blessing is never found in that which is counted." There are many warnings about counting. Counting has the potential to attract the *Ayin Hara*/Evil Eye, the eye of jealousy. The Torah prohibits taking a census, or even counting a minyan. In our Scripture we read of punishment by plague associated with the census in Ki Tisa and the plague during the reign of King David (which we recall during the weekday *Tachanun* prayer). And when we need a minyan (a quorum of 10 people for a prayer service), rather than counting with numbers, the custom is to use a Hebrew verse containing ten words to identify the minyan.

There is a tradition that when one hears praise and is singled out, one says "*B'li Ayin Hara*/May this praise not attract the Evil Eye." There was even a custom in Europe to cover up one's baby in the baby carriage to protect the baby from praise, just to prevent an *Ayin Hara*. (Other customs to ward off the Evil Eye include the tying of a red ribbon or string on a child or adult, or spitting three times—the "pooh, pooh, pooh" grandmothers use to chase it away from their adorable tykes.)

The command to count the gold, silver, and copper in the Sanctuary runs counter to the axiom of the rabbis in Ta'anit 8b, "*Ein habracha matzui ela b'davar hasomui min ha'ayin*/Blessings exist only in something that is concealed from the eye, and not in something that has been measured and counted." So, how could this counting be legitimately carried out? Why were the Jews commanded to count all the items in the *Mishkan*? After all, the Israelites suffered plagues after the census during the time of Joshua. And Balaam was chastised by our commentators for his selfish personality—for as soon as he saw something, he counted it for himself. So how was it permitted?

This is the answer: The Zohar says, "There are two types of counting, counting from the left and counting from the right" (Zohar Shmot 221b). One is permitted and one is forbidden.

Here's the definition of "counting from the right." It is a counting that recognizes that that which one is counting as a gift from Hashem. It is a counting of gratitude, of recognition of the bounties that God bestows upon us in this world. So it is permissible and laudatory to count from the right and connect to the source of all blessings; Divine Light was in everything used for the *Mishkan*, and every object reflected God's blessings. It is this spirit in counting, this way of seeing things, that brings harmony and gratitude to our world. But if counting is done only for one's private goals and greed, it severs the link to the Holy One and is called "counting from the left."

What is counting from the "left?" The Talmud points out the limitations and dangers of "counting, of taking accounts." Counting from the left is an indication of a temperament that can lead to greed and acquisitiveness as a way of life, and to forgetting the source of one's bounty. It is a temperament that is never satisfied, and always looks for more for his satisfaction. Hence, it develops the character of one who lives for material gain, one who is insecure because material gains are ever-changing. It may lead one to look at one's neighbor who has more than he and therefore feel jealous.

As we read in Pirkei Avot 4:1, "Who is happy? One who is satisfied with one's lot in life." This teaching is a teaching from the "right." It is a feeling of appreciation for all that one has as a gift from God. It is a movement from habitual wanting to habitual having. Moreover, the habit of singling out people—counting them—can create a feeling of jealousy in others toward individuals who are being recognized. Additionally, bringing special recognition to them may conjure up the evil eye (*ayin hara*).

"Counting from the right," on the other hand, recognizes and brings forth gratitude to the source of the blessing and this is permissible. The "right" counting stems from the side of holiness, and creates a positive feeling of blessing that brings joy to the universe—like when we generously give charity as a sacred counting, and therefore blessing resides in it. That was the way the materials in the *Mishkan* were counted.

Zohar Shemot 223a reiterates that it was a sacred counting. Everything was counted for the sake of dedicating it to God, and so it intensified the Divine Presence within each item. Everything is good when counted and used for the purpose for which it was created—as is God's gift to us. This, as the Zohar says, is "different from all other counting done for private ends and which sever the link to the Divine."

"Right" counting restores that link. It teaches us how to see. A jealous, critical eye (ayin hara) conceals the connection with the Divine, a benign eye (ayin tov) sees the link between every aspect of creation and the Divine store of bounty. This way of seeing casts blessings and lifts the spirits of everything seen in that way. What is "right" counted is not the sum total of individual greed, but the sum total of communal sharing. In this there is no envy, only great appreciation.

The Zohar also points out that the first word in our parsha (Ex. 38:21), Aileh/These, singles out the uniqueness of this counting. It states, "This was a counting that canceled all other countings" (Zohar Shemot 221b, 223a).

The Kedushaht Levi points out that when Moshe counted the materials, it was the same Moshe who blessed them (Ex. 39:43), and he did it with a beneficent eye (ayin tov), for Moshe saw the Divine Light in everything! This is different from one who counts just for the sake of accruing something, coveting it for themself (ego), and neglecting the source of the blessing. This is very different from people like Ba'alam and Korach, who are "takers." Everything that they set their eyes on, they counted for themselves, and were blinded by their selfish motives (ayin hara).

But when one sees objects as reflecting the Divine blessing, this way of experiencing the cosmos brings blessing to the world. Our Sages tell us that the various vessels and draperies of the Mishkan were chosen to represent different parts of the universe. If one is mindful of the fact that we are building God's world, the Shechinah will constantly be with us, for the Mishkan represents the Holy Presence dwelling in our midst as we engage in the work. It is the restorative that brings peace and harmony to each person blessed with the giving power of a benevolent heart and benevolent eye.

This way of seeing the world and those who inhabit it brings blessing and warm encouragement to all who experience our love. This energy, projected outward, makes everyone feel better after experiencing it. By "right counting" we make our hearts into God's dwelling place, to be "lit candles," and can see the good bestowed upon us every day. The Eternal Light is already within us if we are open to it, if we embody an ayin tov.

Some commentators also attribute the necessity of counting the articles of the Mishkan to teach us of the importance of accountability to those handling public funds. Our rabbis suggest the exact accounting of all the articles donated to the *Mishkan* was to protect the reputation of those handling public funds. All the gold and silver donated for the Ark was listed to prevent any slander about public officials who might be vulnerable. Even the most trustworthy, even Moshe, the builder Bezalel, and craftsman Oholiav, were held accountable. Since there is a tendency to envy, slander, and project hostility on those in power, Midrash Tanchuma noted that Moshe was a target and the people said, "Look how fat he is getting, he probably is using our donations for his benefit." And Moshe replied, "When the *Mishkan* is finished I will give them an accounting."

The halakha develops this notion. The Mishnah (Shekalim) tells us that three times per year, the *kohanim*/priests came to take money from the shekel chamber where the annual shekel tax was deposited—a half month before Sukkot, Pesach, and Shavuot. To be above suspicion, we are told, the *kohanim*/priests did not wear sleeved cloaks, sandals, or shoes when they collected the tax. Also, charity collectors must come in pairs and cannot separate from one another while collecting or giving change from their own money. Surplus funds must be invested with others so no personal profit can be derived from the investment (Bava Batra 8b; Mishnah Peah 8:7; Rambam; Mishnah Torah: Matanot Aniyim 9:8-9).

May we "right count" every human being as a precious, unique creation, meant to bring something special to our world, and consider them souls who deserve our honor. May we "see" them with a benign eye. This is the enlightened way of being and the way to bring peace to our world. May love triumph over hatred. May each of us feel as special as God sees us; precious, cherished, and majestic. And may this be the antidote to cruelty and vicious wars in our world. Amen.

VAYIKRA
Leviticus

Vayikra

In Megillat Esther, Mordechai said to Esther—as he implored her to use her position to intervene on behalf of the Jewish people—"If you are silent and do nothing at this time, help will come to the Jewish people from another source.... And who knows whether it was not for such a time as this that you came into royalty?" Knowing she was risking her life, she courageously replied, "Then I will go to the King, though it is against the law. And if I perish, I perish" (Scroll of Esther 4:14-16). Because she answered the call, she saved the Jewish people from destruction by Haman. She took a stand for justice, even though her life was at stake.

Sometimes we feel helpless and do not think we can do anything that would have a powerful impact on whatever issue is before us, so we remain inert—though filled with pain and regret. But in Pirkei Avot we are taught, "It is not up to us to complete the work nor are we free to desist from beginning it" (Pirkei Avot 2:21). Every little bit of action helps, whether we donate our funds to organizations helping on the front lines, or influencing those in power to take action to overcome Amalek and create the peace in the world for which we all yearn.

The Chasidic masters and our Sages in Pirkei Avot teach us that we each have a unique contribution to make to our world when we are called. Each of us has experienced such a moment, and we know, like Esther did, when that moment has come (Pirkei Avot 4:3-4)—and as Moshe does in this week's parsha.

Our parsha teaches us that it is often the humblest of people who are chosen for the call because they are open to the Divine beckoning, as was Moshe.

The first word in our parsha is *Vayikra*/And God called Moshe. It is spelled with a small *aleph* at the end of the word. God called Moshe by his name to show love for Moshe. It is nice to be called by one's name, to be known, instead of being greeted by a basic Hello or Hey You. And who deserves to be called by Hashem? Those who are modest and open like Moshe. It says Hashem spoke in a loud voice from the Tent of Meeting (*Ohel Moed*), but only Moshe heard. He was not "full of himself" and oblivious to the sounds surrounding him. Rashi says it was an affectionate call to participate in a loving relationship.

When we are genuinely called, we feel the power and are drawn into the soul-call. It is a holy blessing. The Zohar poetically declares, "Moshe was being called to the nuptial chamber by his bride—the *Shechinah*/the Feminine Divine Presence" (Zohar III, 4b). How beautiful to be called to the experience of intimacy!

So why a small *aleph* here?

Our Sages teach that Moshe, in his deep humility, did not want the aleph at all. He wanted the word *vayikar* which means "and it happened." It just happened that God met Moshe, just as the verse says in connection with Ba'alam (Num. 23:4). *Vayikar* is not the language of love. Rather, *Vayikar* suggests a casual and temporary meeting.

However, God wanted to show love for Moshe, and call him, so the small aleph is the result of compromise. Moshe didn't feel it proper to state that the One God, the awesome Hashem, called on a mere mortal like himself, to bring the Israelites to *Matan Torah*, to receive the law. So, when he transcribed the Torah, he purposely made the aleph in the word *Vayikra* very small, so that it would read like *Vayikar*—meaning God met Moshe by accident, which would downplay his (Moshe's) importance. The greater the person is, the more aware they are of their failings. Every minute blemish becomes noticeable, which makes one humble despite one's greatness.

What is the Torah's definition of humility? Rabbenu Yonah explains the concept of haughtiness, and through this we understand its converse—humility. He asserts that often a person who feels themself to be lacking in knowledge, or a certain quality, compensates for this inferiority complex, small as it may be, by denigrating their peers to make oneself feel better in one's own eyes. This process may take place on an unconscious level or may be manifested outwardly.

In other words, haughtiness and pride are derived from their opposite feelings: inferiority, insignificance, and shame. One who feels confident does not need to deprecate others or represent themselves as something other than what they truly are. One accepts the complex inner energies that contain contradictory qualities, and does not deny the imperfections of their being. One feels the abundant love of God, who loves us with all the flaws and speckles that may be mixed into our beings.

From R. Yonah we see that humility comes with the realistic understanding of one's own worth. The negative traits Moshe was able to feel and own within himself came from knowing his unique value—despite his inadequacies. He viewed the latter as opportunities from which to grow. He did not underestimate himself and did not need to overestimate himself. He knew each of us is created in the image of God, with our own unique talents.

With this understanding of ourselves in hand, we can now face the difficult task of admitting our shortcomings and thereby show our inner strength. Many of us have the misconception that admitting imperfection is a weakness—especially if we are community leaders and clergy who want to bask in the adoration of the elevated status projected upon us and rely on such praise for our sustenance/ego gratification. The Torah tells us the opposite is true. If we understand our potential as humans, we can then feel the self-confidence necessary to be humble—and not get caught up in our egos. This will enable us to continue to grow to fulfill the unique destinies with which we have been blessed.

May our humility, based on inner confidence and faith in God, enable us to face our calls with courage, compassion, and clarity. May we join together with others to move through our current crises and be among those who create the world that God's Love calls us to create. May we each feel called to our duty, to the voice heard in our inner hearts, and follow the call of love, that powerful energy that can triumph over all darkness. I wish for each of you a time to pray for peace, for a moment of respite, and to recharge the energy to meet the call that awaits. We are all strengthened and sustained by the goodness of each other to come to the aid of our brothers and sisters throughout the world. May the Lord sustain our efforts and bring the constant wars to an end swiftly, and let us say Amen.

Vayikra is also concerned with the laws regulating the sacrifices offered in the *Mishkan* and later in the Holy Temple in Jerusalem. Some think the system is out of date and yet, traditionally, Vayikra is the first book of Torah taught to children.

In this same book, we find the classic command, "Love your neighbor as yourself" (Lev. 19:18), so Vayikra is more than just a book about the priestly code. Many people skip Vayikra and are not aware that "Love your neighbor" is in the Torah—Christian Scripture repeats it but it is found earlier in Hebrew Scripture.

Apart from ethical dicta, Vayikra is worthy of attention for its descriptions of the sacrificial system. Part of the reason our generation tends to show contempt for the sacrificial system is because of the incorrect way we perceive ancient life. We criticize institutions from 3,000 years ago in the light of 21st-century ideas, which results in a distorted conception of the past. We think of sacrifices as a relic of barbarism and savagery and fail to understand the principles on which they are grounded and the motivation behind them. What we denounce as pagan or archaic was a brilliant means of inculcating principles essential for the development of the young community. The form it assumed was the one best suited for that purpose at that time.

What were the main features of the sacrificial system? The offerings fell into two main classes: First were public, or communal, sacrifices; second were private sacrifices. The "public" act of worship immediately suggests the idea of unity and close interrelationships. Every member of the congregation of Israel felt that they had their personal share in sacrifices at the side of their brothers or sisters in faith. The central sanctuary with its communal sacrifices was an experience of the ideal of communal solidarity. Without it, the tribes would have drifted apart. With it, they were cemented into one homogeneous group. The *Mishkan* and the *korbanot* (ritual sacrifices) were a vital part of maintaining a united community.

Of the "private" sacrifices, there were two types: voluntary and compulsory. The voluntary ones were brought from a feeling of gratitude, or in fulfillment of a vow. The compulsory ones were for expiation of a wrong that was committed.

As tillers of soil who depended on what they produced for the necessities of existence, our ancients looked upon the harvest and flocks and an urge arose in one's heart to express gratitude to the Power that sent the rain in due season, without which the land would have been barren and animals would have perished. How was one to do this? Customarily, it was done by sacrificing part of one's increase as a token of thankfulness. Was this sense of gratitude barbaric? Most of us today have a tendency to take things for granted and leave God out of our lives. Maybe we can learn an important value from the "barbarity" of the ancients who longed to thank God for what was provided. Of course, we cannot use the ancient method of doing so; but the memory of the sacrifices of old can act as a reminder of our duty.

Our prophets, such as Amos, Hosea, Micah, and others do criticize the incorrect motivation of those who perform some of these rituals. Amos says, "Yea though you offer me burnt offerings and meal offerings, I will not accept them. . . . but let justice well up as waters and righteousness as a mighty stream" (Amos 5:21-27). Hosea says, "For I desire mercy, and not sacrifice, and the knowledge of God rather than burnt offerings" (Hosea 6:6). Micah says, "Shall I come before the Lord with burnt offerings? What the Lord requires of you is only to do justly, and to love mercy, and to walk humbly with thy God" (Micah 6:6-8). Maimonides, in his *Guide for the Perplexed* (3:32), suggests sacrifices were ordained only as a means of turning the Israelites away from idol worship and human sacrifices at that time.

One may ask why God needed physical sacrifices and why the compulsory ones could erase sin. Why should we believe sins can be forgiven by paying a "ransom" with sacrifices? Does slaughtering an animal forgive our sins? Does it make the sin disappear? How can one endure this cruelty to animals? What sense do our Sages make out of this ancient practice?

Our Sages were not satisfied with the abstract "So sorry" sense of remorse, which quickly evaporates. For how do sacrifices of animals expiate a person of their sin? The simple answer is that they do not. The purpose of the rite was to intensify feelings of repentance by the sinner and modify behavior toward the positive. For that reason, the purpose of sacrifice was reinforced by publicly connecting the sinner with an open confession and by compensating the victim. This was a profound insight into human behavior. It is not sufficient to merely say "I am sorry" when one does something wrong. If one is truly sorry for what one has done, they must demonstrate regret, and mean it.

R. Yochanan says in the Midrash, "A man who sacrifices an animal for his sins has to be present when the sacrifice is made, and he should say: 'I have sinned, and I did wrong. I pray that God may help me, so that the sacrifice that I am bringing will make me understand how my sins have changed my personality, and how much evil I have created around me. However, God is not interested in punishing me physically. God only wants to teach me, so that I shall undertake this minute never to repeat what I have done.'" The sinner says this publicly, in the presence of the priests and the people, which means the sacrifice represents an important step toward his rehabilitation.

The sacrificial system was a safeguard against superficiality because it necessitated action and reconnection. It helped attenuate the sinner's ongoing guilt and promoted true reconciliation with God and the community. We all make mistakes and must find a way to reconnect with those we may have harmed, taken for granted, or ignored, whether other human beings or God. These *korbanot* made that possible.

The values of authenticity, true connection to others, and the ability to move from judgment to compassion are too often ignored today. We may have outgrown the forms of repentance used in the ancient world, but we certainly have not outgrown the need for its teachings. Too often, we run around with all our tasks and distractions and forget the authentic value of deep connections; the goal of sacrifices was to instill in our psyches and hearts Torah values—and open us to ethical and loving behaviors toward others and God.

To move beyond superficiality, to atone for our mistakes, to wake up in the morning with gratitude and eagerness for a new blessed day, are all essential practices for all time. May our homes be as Holy Temples! May our dining tables be altars for sharing our food with others. May we appreciate our bounty, our daily gifts, and share them, while moving closer to God and our community with sincerity, with the desire for closeness and harmony. May it be so, Amen!

And do not worry!! When the Third Temple is rebuilt in our time, Rav Avraham Yitzchak Hacohen Kook teaches us that the only sacrificial offering that will be required will be the meal offering (no animal sacrifice) accompanied by incense, music, and uplifting sincere prayer! Hallelujah!

Tzav

The nature of *korbanot* (sacrifices) and the purpose of the sacrificial system were explained at great length in the previous parsha, and are repeated in this parsha as well. In Tzav we also learn of the unusual language the Torah uses regarding the *korban mincha* (a meal offering consisting of flour). The verse states: *Nefesh ki takriv*/the soul who will offer a *korban* (Lev. 2:1).

Would it not make more sense to state, "*V'Adam ki takriv*," when a person (not a soul) will offer a *korban*? The Sages explain a *korban mincha* is ordinarily offered by a poverty-stricken individual. It is not easy for such an individual to offer a *korban*. Yet that person sacrifices personal needs, scrounges and saves to make the offering of thanks to God. Such a sacrifice is worthy as if the very soul of the person is sacrificed. This is the essence of offering a *korban*, or giving charity—to make sacrifices is a way of offering our own souls in gratitude for our blessings.

We see that idea in the very first verse of our parsha. This verse is puzzling because it says, "If any person of yourselves brings a sacrifice unto the Lord" (Lev. 1:2). It does not say "If any person of you brings" but instead it says if anyone of yourselves brings an offering. So, the implication here is that the sacrifice must be part of yourselves. The Sages teach that it must rightfully belong to you and you must see it as if you yourself were vicariously offered on the altar. You should feel as if you brought yourself as the offering.

Thus, the ability to bring a *korban* comes from the impulse of giving and sacrificing. It takes these two energies at the very core of life to do so. In the sphere of *korbanot*, the willing sacrifice is the overflow of an abundant spirit, seeking to give from one's joy and fullness. It is the very opposite of the sensation of needing, or of covetousness, or mental acquisitiveness. Therefore, a stolen animal is eliminated from the possibility of serving as a *korban*.

A question often asked is why does the Torah even include these sacrifices instead of moving to a more palatable ritual that would be acceptable to the modern temperament. Maimonides explains that since animal sacrifices were the common form of Divine worship in the ancient Near East, our ancestors were enamored of it and connected to this form of worship. And he notes it is impossible, in terms of human nature, for people to leave all that they are accustomed to all at once. People form powerful emotional bonds to their favorite rituals. Asking them to give up those rituals might overwhelm their ability to adapt, and would ultimately fail.

In other words, our ancestors were attached to a pagan ritual for which the Torah had no use, but which it could not abolish. What it did instead was to leave sacrifices in place, but use them for its own purposes. The way the Torah used sacrifices for noble cause was to direct them to God while prohibiting offerings to pagan deities. The result was that a deeply entrenched idolatrous practice was converted to Divine service.

The Torah legislated a whole host of limitations to curb the practice of sacrifices and wean the people away from the sacrificial cult. For example, the sacrifices could only be brought in one place, the Temple (Deut. 12:13-14), and only in the specified manner described in the Torah. The rationale, according to Maimonides, is the idea that the Torah creates a willingness to accept progress in small steps. The Torah took into account what our ancestors could and could not do in terms of human nature, and it legislated accordingly. It did not ask them to do what they could not do.

Instead of immediately abolishing the practice because of the understanding of human resistance to radical change, Sefer Vayikra sought to wean the Israelites away from idol worship by incremental steps. Change begins with God's accommodation to the rituals our ancestors were attached to. It then proceeds to God's agenda, when we are called to embrace the call to "Holiness" and the ethical and spiritual principles in Parshat Kedoshim/ The Holiness Code.

Let us practice the principles of giving and sacrifice that are the foundation of the sacrificial system in our modern era, using prayer, Torah study, and good deeds for the unification of all human beings and the honoring of God's world.

Pesach I

Once again, we are retelling the story of Pesach. Despite the sorry state of the world, it is in the telling and the retelling of the story of our redemption that potential healing emerges, and this telling is the spiritual task of the holiday of Pesach.

Our Rabbis note that the Jews' experience of slavery in Egypt became reality because of evil speech and gossip/*lashon hara* brought about by Joseph and his brothers and his subsequent exile to Egypt. So, the spiritual task of Pesach is the purification of speech through telling. It is this holy work that leads us from slavery to freedom. Of course, evil speech is merely a symptom of inner discord. We must expose the symptom, trace its roots, and discover its underlying influence on our behavior. For us to be free, we must go back to our earliest roots (*Arami Oveid Avi*) and understand their influence upon us. If we do not, we remain unknowingly enslaved by these unconscious forces. The repressed memories control us and only our awareness of their undue influence can liberate us.

By reciting the Haggadah, we spend a whole night retelling the story of our past; and the more we retell it, say the Sages, the more we are praised. This is because unpacking our histories, unveiling the symptom of degrading speech, and understanding the underlying energies that propel this behavior, take time and work. To purify our speech, we talk (*peh sach*—the mouth speaks) and we unveil our own proclivity to gossip and its consequences. We discuss the evil speech of Pharaoh (*peh rah*—the evil mouth) and its destructive impact on our people. Pharaoh revealed his unwillingness to change, even in the face of the suffering caused by the plagues (*kaved*—his heart was hardened and he strongly resisted changing his behavior).

It takes great strength and persistence to give up deeply rooted behaviors. It is through the telling of our stories that we can gain clarity to find the true path to freedom. We realize how we may have left the path of our souls, how we have become distracted by ego satisfactions, and thereby are enslaved by our ego's needs instead of achieving true freedom. As our Rabbis point out, we are never fully free from *Mitzrayim* (the place of constriction) and we must vigilantly work every day toward greater freedom. One of the six daily commandments to remember is to "Remember that we were liberated from our enslavement in Egypt," and therefore must work to remain free and help others to become free.

The holiday of Pesach and the symbols of the Seder enable and support this spiritual task. To become free, we address the sources of our oppression both outwardly and inwardly. Outwardly, we are asked to overthrow cruel oppression and free those who are terrorized by despots. We are to remove *lashon hara* from our political discourse. We must obviate mendacity, propaganda, and false advertising. We are asked to distribute our wealth to others who are in need. We must create justice for orphans and widows and we are commanded to own honest weights and not cheat and lie.

Inwardly, we are to move from the realm of *chametz* to the realm of *matzah*. *Chametz* is bread that rises, and represents the bloated ego that creates our enslavement. *Chametz* represents our wounds, our jealousies, our anger and reactivity, our self-centeredness and stubbornness. *Matzah* does not rise; it represents humility and soulfulness. The path to freedom is the movement from ego-centeredness to the path of openness to others. Both *matzah* and *chametz* have the same Hebrew letters except *chametz* contains the letter *chet*, and *matzah* contains the letter *heh*. The shape of *heh* is open and the shape of *chet* is closed. The path to freedom is one that is open to change, to friendship with others, and to the energies of God's Grace as the openness of the letter *heh*, (one of the letters of God's name) suggests. It is the movement from the place of restriction, *Mitzrayim*, to the place of promise, *Eretz Yisrael*.

The Haggadah also introduces us to the different types of children, different archetypes: the *chacham*, the wise one; the *rasha*, the wicked one; the *tam*, the simple one, and the *sheaino yodeah lishol*, the one who does not know how to ask the questions. In contemporary times, Rabbi Yitz Greenberg added the child who is not here to ask because it did not survive the violence of persecution or the ravages of disease. It gives us a chance to experience multiple ways of seeing things, and to listen to others who see things in unique ways.

We are then blessed to expand our consciousness and the consciousness of those who listen to our telling (*maggid*). Freedom from our unconscious patterns revealed through this dialogue takes time and effort, so we are praised if we take a whole night to carry out this task. A slave who has lost hope, who has been deprived of the power of speech and expression—those things which make us most human—regains these powers on Seder night. On that night we celebrate our ability to speak freely through the proper use of our mouths—by eating, singing, and conversing with gratitude and praise at the Seder, the service designed to help us tell the story.

In our night journey, we also become aware that *lashon hara*, critical, mean-spirited speech, may also be directed at our own selves. The constant self-judgment, the self-criticism of our lack of perfection, can be constant chatter in our psyches that tears us down—and we are unaware of it until we undertake the journey from *chametz* to *matzah*, the painstaking and glorious journey out of our own *Mitzrayims*. It is *zman cheiruteinu*, our time to create our freedom, of creating a messianic world imbued with lofty, loving elevated speech.

There is, however, one paragraph in the Haggadah that is disturbing to many, and that paragraph is: "Pour Thy wrath upon the nations." It is important to know that this prayer entered the Haggadah in 12th-century Europe because of pogroms and antisemitism. It was foreign to the Haggadah of the Talmudic Sages. It does not appear in the 16th-century Aleppo Haggadah; the text there goes straight from the saying of Grace After Meals to the completion of *Hallel* (Praises to God).

Thus, the paragraph is an anomaly not fitting in with the lofty spirit of the Haggadah. Every year I am so impressed by the sublime, creative commentaries of our contemporary Haggadot that alert us to the salient issues of our time, that demand our time and effort, our mandate to move our world to the liberation of all. That paragraph is there to remind us that it is God's job to take revenge on our enemies, not ours.

The spirit of the Haggadah is filled with gratitude, and the hope for a better, more loving and just world. Our Sages suggest that the messianic world will be ushered in at the conclusion of Pesach. We will be free people—all joined together in our integrated humanity; thankful for the blessings of life; exhilarated by the beauty and generosity of God's creation; and committed to continue the messianic spirit all the days of our lives. And let us say Amen!

Pesach II

*The Foundational essence of freedom is that elevated spirit by
which a human being and a nation rises to be loyal to their
inner being—the Divine Image within.*
—*Rav Avraham Yitzchak Hacohen Kook*

It is challenging to celebrate Pesach, a time of liberation, when much of the world is still enslaved, suffering from vicious wars, and violence on our streets and the streets and kibbutzim of Israel. It is painful to watch the devastating loss of lives in Ukraine, in Myanmar, in Yemen, in so many places on this small planet. Our heroic, uprooted brothers and sisters are fleeing with nowhere safe to go. It is painful to watch the death, suffering, and carnage, less than 85 years after the Holocaust and many other genocides. There is homelessness, racism, antisemitism, poverty, and climate devastation. We must find a way to bring our faith and our strength to the task of overcoming this darkness with the force of love and vigor. It is part of the journey as we continue our journey to leave *Mitzrayim* and create a world of peace, love, and justice in our time.

The telling of the story of the Exodus from Egypt is one of the most important parts of the Seder. Our Sages tell us that it is an obligation for every person to tell the story of leaving Egypt with praise and is a mitzvah that applies for all time. Says the Zohar, "Whoever tells the story of the Exodus from Egypt, and rejoices happily in the telling of it, will be invited in the future to rejoice with the *Shechinah*." By remembering and internalizing its message we will fulfill our mandate to bring unity, compassion, and justice to our world. We will remember what it was like to be slaves in Egypt and thus remove slavery from our world. We must live in gratitude and faith in God's power to aid us in creating this salvation. We will be rewarded by having the season of joy in the future and be part of the ultimate redemption.

The telling of the story also fulfills another mandate of our tradition and that is to purify and uplift our speech, the words that come out of our mouths. For after all, our Rabbis remind us that the reason that the Jews descended to Egypt in the first place was due to the "evil speech" and gossip (*lashon hara*) uttered by Joseph against his brothers. This caused jealousy and hatred toward Joseph, and his brothers sold him to traders traveling to Egypt. He was subsequently imprisoned there before ascending to the house of Pharoah. Due to famine, the Jewish people followed Jacob's family there, and Pharaoh enslaved them, as he perceived them as threatening foreign intruders. Thus, the Rabbis exhort us to use this holiday to cleanse the cause of our slavery: our evil speech. The word Pesach in Hebrew means the mouth speaks—*peh sach*. Thus we are to use the power of speech to obviate the evil speech that brought us down to Egypt. This is the speech embodied by Pharoah. His name, in Hebrew, means *peh ra*—evil speech! We must use the whole night of the Seder to speak to each other with words of kindness and rectify the sin of evil speech (*lashon hara*). We eat *matzah*, bread that does not rise, hence bread of humility as opposed to *chametz*, bread that rises (hubris, arrogance), that leads to derogative speech. We are to use our mouths the whole night in dialogue that leads to liberation and freedom—within and without—and through our listening to others and responding respectfully we bring about redemption. We include four archetypes and learn to accept difference. And we speak holy words all the way till the morning, for this dialogue takes effort to repair our proclivity toward *lashon hara*, a habit that the Talmud says is the most common sin of all.

We also tell the story as if we, too, were freed in the original Exodus. This custom reawakens the original joy and ingrained faith always present deep within the roots of our souls. Thus, we rejoice in the telling of the story of the Exodus in a joyous manner, even in the darkest of times. Even as the Jews in the Warsaw Ghetto did, and even in the earlier torturous times of suffering in our pogrom-stained and vicious antisemitic history. By retelling and recalling these miraculous events, we connect to their original power; we know that this power of redemption/liberation can be called upon, and is truly within our reach. We are aware of our particular charge of healing our world with conscious words of kindness, respect, and encouragement of the other and we fulfill our charge.

We can activate our strong spirit ("Not by might, not by power, but by my spirit alone, saith the Lord"—(Zechariah 4:6), even in our current broken world. We can create justice and joy for all people in a world where justice and equality are the norms and where love shines and liberation is achieved for all people. Let us conjure up our faith in this season of Pesach, in this our season of joy and liberation to create this redemptive, messianic world. Our tradition tells us that it is on Pesach, with its unique story and ensuing energy, that this is possible. Rabbi Tarfon declares in the Talmud that we pour a fifth cup of wine to celebrate universal hope. Remember the Exodus and God's outstretched hand! And be awakened to the miracles that we encounter every day!

Every year a new Haggadah is created relating to our contemporary struggles for freedom and justice. Seeing the catastrophic unnecessary loss of life all around us, we must remember that we are all interconnected in this, our world, and we are taught, "Do not stand idly by while your neighbor's blood is shed" (Lev. 19:16).

The journey through the celebration of Pesach has also given us the opportunity to look inward and do the work of conscious inner exploration. It bestows upon us the opportunity to free ourselves from inner discord and move toward greater harmony, faith, and gratitude for the gift of life. We must do this despite the daily darkness that emerges, even if this darkness reduces our enthusiasm.

The seventh day of Pesach is special because it is the day the Sea of Reeds was split when all seemed lost as the Egyptian army pursued the Jewish people. Our Sages teach that it was the people's courage to proceed, following Nachshon's jump into the water, that called forth the great miracle. This is a message that lets us know that miracles are a result of, first and foremost, extreme effort and strong faith. When this is present, the most extraordinary, serendipitous manifestations may occur. We are taught to light a candle rather than curse the darkness or deny its presence. Acknowledging the darkness and making the right effort to transform it is the message of our holiday. This is how we bring in redemption.

The Baal Shem Tov added that the seventh day of Pesach, in addition to being a shining ray of our redemption from Egypt, is also a precursor of the future messianic redemption. He instituted a special meal to be held during the evening of that day. The Chabad Chasidim maintain this custom to this day. They call it the "Meal of Moshiach," and drink four cups of wine during the meal, mirroring the Seder held on the first two nights of Pesach (two nights outside of Israel; one night in Israel). Some friends in our own community have taken on the custom of the "Meal of Moshiach," anticipating and committing themselves to the ushering in of the beginning of a new era, a messianic world where Light and Love are palpable and actualized.

There are certainly reasons to feel despair in these challenging days. But we should raise a cup of optimism at the end of the seder to acknowledge that we have the power and God's promise to turn darkness into joy during these very days. Let us do our utmost to turn blood into water of sustenance and joy. With the help of God, we will create this elevated world of our dreams.

It is not accidental that Pesach (and Easter) take place in the season when the earth moves from darkness to the splendorous colors of Spring. With the renewal of nature, faith is reborn. We are reawakened to God's Presence and feel gratitude for our gift of life. The chirping birds, the flowers in bloom, the shining sun all rekindle hope for a more peaceful, vibrant world of equality and joy.

We remember in this season to acknowledge our gratitude for the blessing of freedom from bondage, but also how we must ensure freedom for others. There is so much we can commit ourselves to do at the Seder table. Even one commitment will be fulfilling the mitzvah of our season. God heard the groaning of the slaves and sent us as a people of messengers to remind the world of the sin and pain of servitude and the charge for all of us to be free, for we remember what it was like to be slaves in Egypt.

The first commandment of the Decalogue is, "I am the Lord your God who brought you out of the land of Egypt, out of the house of bondage." Thus, God is the God of freedom, and it is up to us to take on this charge in the world. Pesach awakens us to our determination to work for the day when we will all be free. "Nation will not lift up sword against nation, neither shall they learn war anymore" (Isaiah 2:4).

Israel Zangwill once said, "On Pesach, the Jew eats history." The food, this bread of affliction, the *matzah*, becomes the bread of our salvation. It nourishes our hunger to work for freedom and justice for all, to take pride in our people's history as representatives of this mission, to join with all humanity in the glorious future we are charged to create, and to ingest the joy that such a life of service and meaning creates.

Pesach charges us to discipline ourselves, to take control of our inner slavery, and then work to remove the bondage of our fellow human beings in our current world. During these days we continue our journey of liberation by counting the *Omer* every evening for 49 days, from the beginning of Pesach until the holiday of Shavuot. During this time, we prepare ourselves to attain the communal unity and love that Jews attained when they became worthy of receiving the Torah at Mount Sinai. This counting is a further attempt to move from the realm of discord to the realm of harmony, creating vessels worthy of receiving and implementing the sublime teachings of the Torah. Each day we concentrate on a specific spiritual trait, brought to us from the Kabbalistic doctrine of the Sefirot.

As we count the days of the *Omer*, we focus our energies on absorbing and embodying the energy of the *malchut* of *chesed*/the nobility of lovingkindness. We try to strengthen our capacity to bestow our love upon others, to understand that love is something we can and must initiate for it to flourish and spread in our world. We are not to wait for love from others before we shine our light. We have the capacity to bring love to our world and this is our nobility. This is the power that we all contain, created in God's image. So, it is up to us to feel this, to own this, and to express it in our world.

Happy Pesach to all, to our fellow Jews, to our Christian brothers and sisters who celebrate Easter at this time, to our Muslim brothers and sisters who celebrate their holy month of Ramadan, to all worshippers of their historic religions, and to all human beings sharing and caring for our planet. We include secular, agnostic, atheist, and all beloved members of our human family who celebrate the majestic glory of the season of renewal. May all the wishes of your heart come true, and may we create a world of peace, truth, justice, and love together.

May we all be blessed with the nobility of lovingkindness and may our communal energy of love and fellowship bring the messianic era speedily in our days. May we leave *Mitzrayim* and reach the promised land which exists wherever we bring our love, and may we meet at Mount Sinai, whole and beautiful within and without. Amen!

Shemini

One of the events in this week's parsha, Shemini, is the incident of Nadav and Avihu, the sons of the high priest Aaron, who brought "strange fire" to the *Mishkan* (Lev. 10:1). They brought up the incense offering with this "strange fire" and were consumed. The Rabbis offer a variety of reasons for why they perished while doing so. There are two seemingly contradictory explanations. In the Talmud, Eruvin states they committed a grave sin. One sin was that they could not wait for the old leaders, Aaron and Moshe, to die. But in Zevachim, a more benign opinion says their death was not because of sin, but from the sanctification of God's name, *Al Kiddush Hashem*. The Midrash says that Moshe said to Aaron, "Your sons were closer to God than we were, they attached 'fire to fire,' and everything they did was out of concern for the Jewish people."

Nadav and Avihu felt the people were too dependent on Moshe and Aaron, which is why the people built the golden calf—to have someone to look after them in Moshe's absence. Aaron's sons felt they had to teach the Jewish people that they would have capable leaders even after Moshe and Aaron die. They acted, but erred by not distinguishing between the holy and unholy wine and unauthorized fire. They also taught the people in the presence of Moshe, contrary to Jewish law. Though their intentions were good, their means were wrong.

The *kohanim* (priests) were supposed to be very careful in their rituals. They were to be holy examples to their people, acting with discipline and generosity. They even acted as guides for those who came to Jerusalem, giving them hospitality and thereby creating unity. Some of the Sages' explanations for Nadav and Avihu's behavior have no foundation in the biblical text. It seems the Rabbis were not so concerned about solving the mysterious episode as they were with indicating important lessons to the Jews of their own time with explanations that may have relevance for us today.

One lesson involves the arrogance attributed to Nadav and Avihu for offering a sacrificial practice that was not the norm. The brothers identified themselves as part of the aristocracy. They said, "Our father Aaron is the high priest, our uncle Moshe is the king/ruler, our Mother's brother is a prince, and we are priests."

Because of their conceit, they never married since they thought no one was worthy of them. Another explanation is that they offered a sacrifice that they had not been commanded to bring, another symptom of arrogance by breaking accepted, defined boundaries. Some say the reason they were waiting for Moshe and Aaron to die was so that they could take over the leadership. Their impatience and disrespect broke new ground, and manifested a way of worshiping God that cost them their lives.

A more text-based explanation comes from the Sages, who state the brothers' sin was that they were drunk when they brought their sacrifice, having imbibed an abundance of wine before carrying out the sacrifice. Verse 10:8 states, "Do not drink intoxicating wine, you and your children with you, when you come to the Tent of Meeting, so that you do not die. This is an eternal decree for all generations." Being drunk means abandoning one's intellectual faculties to react on a totally emotional level in a state of euphoria. But acting out emotions cannot dictate the way we serve God, nor can artificial highs.

There is another explanation from the mystical tradition which states their death was not a punishment at all, but a blessing. As the verse reads, "I will be sanctified through those who are nearest to me," and thus Aaron did not mourn, but was silent when he learned of their deaths (Lev. 10:3). Sifra says, "They saw a flame coming down from heaven and wanted to "add love to love." Thus, they were taken by *mitat neshika*/a "kiss from heaven." They went beyond what they were required to do, and such a lofty action draws the soul from the body to its Creator. When the Torah was given to the Jewish people at Mount Sinai, there was such a love connection. There was so much soul elevation that Moshe had to ask God to cease speaking, and Moshe himself had to continue to speak after the first commandment because people were dying in the Presence of God.

The Rabbis here teach that even though the righteous may leave their physical reality during worship, they must return to their bodies afterward. But Nadav and Avihu did not realize the importance of physical reality and that they must not leave this world. The fact that they did not take wives and have children showed they were fatally drawn to the upper world.

The Talmud, in Moed Katan 25b, says, "The *Shechinah* who rides in the Heavens jubilates and rejoices when the soul of one pure and righteous ascends to the upper world." Sometimes that soul is needed in Heaven. The rabbis tell us regarding the passing of Rabbi Yehuda Hanasi in Ketubot 104a, "There is great joy Hashem experiences when He gathers a holy soul to the light." Thus, Aaron's silence was an indication of consolation and indicated that he participated, as it were, in Hashem's joy—for Nadav and Avihu investigated the hidden depths, and wanted to stand close to God.

Their hearts burned with such passion, with such an intense love of God, that they gave their very lives, increasing the good God did not command, bringing fire to fire. They removed all borders, were drunk, and did not even wear the required proper priestly garments during their worship. They did not wear the *me'el*/coat made entirely of sky-blue wool (*techeilet*), teaching the intense fear of God; nor did they wear the bells which teach humility. The smoke from the incense rose up to connect heaven and earth, and as the holy Zohar says, "What is *ketoret*/incense? It is the connection/*ketira* of everything (Zohar II 218b-219a, Zohar III 151a).

The danger of this kind of worship through intoxication is that it is a holiness so intense that it negates everything in this world. Reality can be seen as limited and deceptive. It may lead one to feel that there is something greater beyond this world's limitations, and that this unredeemed physical world we live in is not good enough. We may feel our existence here does not lead to the ultimate accessibility to God and see God in some other sphere.

The more normative Jewish view is that this world is one in which one can live and find God. In every time and place and through everything, there is significance and the ability to create a better world. This is our challenge and our tikkun! Emotional exaggeration can lead to deleterious ends—such as abandoning creating progress in this world, desperation, skepticism, and escaping to another reality.

The normative Jewish view is that our enthusiasm must be balanced and set by boundaries. Only within these boundaries can we find shelter from our ego's proclivities and discover the Holy One right here on Earth. This is the blessing of Shabbat, where we fully remove ourselves from work and distraction and totally concentrate on the joy of the closeness of God here on earth, the blessings of other people and nature, the glory of the commandments that connect us to God, and the fruits of this world. But when boundaries are neglected and discarded, we remove the possibility to retreat and discover the world beyond our material and egoistic proclivities. We may seek to leave this world through the high of excessive wine and drugs. This is a result of despair rather than joy; traditionally, that is why Nadav and Avihu are seen as sinners and their model is considered dangerous to Jewish continuity.

Shemini is also the parsha where we learn about kashrut, about keeping kosher—mitzvot that should actually be considered *chukim*/laws without logical reasons, done as acts of faith. Our commentators probe the depths of this law to extract some underlying reasons to uplift us. Kashrut resides in the category of Holiness. The act of eating relates us to our Creator as we say blessings before and after eating, to express our gratitude and connection to God by our daily ingestion of food. In every domain, we bring God into our lives, even in the mundane and corporeal aspects of life. In addition, embracing our uniqueness by eating only kosher food reduces our tendency to assimilate and lose our Jewish identity.

There are several themes in the laws of kashrut. First, we are prohibited from eating carnivorous beasts and birds in order to teach kindness and gentleness. We are prohibited from eating a chasida, the righteous bird; a fowl thus called, says Rashi, because it deals kindly with her peers (*chavrose'ha*), and helps them sustain themselves with food. Second, we can only eat mammals that chew their cud, to teach us (as the Rabbis suggest) that we only grow in wisdom if we deliberate and "chew over" what we study.

Rashi points out that, initially, God did not permit Adam and Eve to kill a creature and eat its flesh. "Only every green herb shall they eat together" (Gen. 1:28-30). It was only after the Flood, when violence and instinctual behavior ran rampant, that a change in eating patterns was introduced in the Torah and the eating of meat was permitted (Gen. 9:1-3). According to Rav Avraham Yitzchak Hacohen Kook, this permission was a temporary concession to human weakness, when the people could not resist the temptation to eat meat. He said this will be changed during the messianic era when we will become vegetarian again. "Through general moral and intellectual advancement, the sensitivity to all of God's creatures will be revivified; we will only eat plants again" (*Olat Reiyah* v.1 p.292, Isaiah 11:7).

During this interim period, in deference to moral frailty, and at a time when the power of evolved moral self-control had not yet arrived, it was better for people to fulfill minimal demands rather than become sinful by not being able to realize the higher demand of refraining from eating meat.

At present, kashrut laws remind us that animals are creatures of God and that their deaths cannot be taken lightly. Hence, hunting is forbidden; and we cannot treat animals callously, just as we may not treat human beings callously. Kashrut laws (about the consumption of meat) all gradually lead to the desired spiritual goal of reducing the desire for meat. The permission given to eat meat is contingent upon following specific rules. Only limited species of animals are permitted. In the desert, the Jews could only eat meat as a part of the sacrificial service in the Sanctuary (Lev. 17:3-5), and no "unconsecrated meat" for private consumption was allowed.

Furthermore, the concept of covering the blood of fowl and venison creates a consciousness of shame, which is the beginning of moral improvement. The nature of the principles of ritual slaughter (with their specific rules to reduce pain) creates the atmosphere that one is dealing with a living being, and creates sensitivity. There is a prohibition against eating blood (Gen. 9:4), for the Torah identifies blood with life (Deut. 12:23), so the Talmud elaborates on the process of removing blood from the animal. Perhaps because of the intensive labor required to fulfill the kosher ritual slaughtering procedure, the hope was that our strong and uncontrollable desire for meat would eventually expire (Deut. 12:20-21).

In our contemporary world, it is also important to recognize that raising cattle for mass consumption has a deleterious impact on the environment. Soil depletion due to overgrazing; air and water pollution related to the widespread production and use of pesticides to increase grain to feed the cattle; and the vast amount of water that it takes to bring the animal to slaughter (most of which is used to irrigate land for livestock); and the release of methane gasses, are all devastating to the health of our world. Over fifty percent of all water consumed in America is used for animal agriculture—irrigating land and growing feed for livestock. If this grain were used to directly feed starving children instead of for the preparation of meat, what a great mitzvah that would be! Additionally, the waste products of cattle pollute our waters and create greenhouse gasses that are more than that of all the cars on our planet. If we ate meat only on Shabbat and holidays, we would help save some of those starving on our planet.

We can surely understand the yearning for a messianic reality where ethical food consumption will benefit all of God's creatures. The ingrained habit of meat consumption and the livestock agriculture associated with this consumption causes so much pollution, wastes important resources, treats animals harshly, creates water shortages, and contributes to the scarcity of resources throughout the world. This can only be diminished through our holy commitment and desire to make our entire world and all those who inhabit it respected and protected.

We have the enormous spiritual potential to transform our world. When spiritual growth becomes the goal, the true needs of all humankind will be reached, instead of the illusory needs created by a superficial ethic that benefits the few and causes harm to the majority. As the messianic era approaches, we will one day restore humankind to its true role as caretakers for our planet, as partners with God in actualizing the gift of life bestowed upon each of us.

Moreover, our Torah has always emphasized ethical considerations in our behavior toward raising animals and the expectation to treat them ethically. For example, the Torah prohibits muzzling an ox when it is feeding (Deut. 25:4); it does not allow an ox and a donkey to plow yoked together (Deut. 22:10), since they work at different speeds. We are to feed our animals before we take our food. We are commanded not to inflict unnecessary pain on an animal, and to lessen the pain whenever we can, even if the injury is not through any fault of our own; even if the owner does not do anything to reduce the pain of the animal, one has the obligation to release the animal of its burden. Furthermore, one may not burden the animal with excessive loads, or make it work without rest, or deny it the food it needs (Shulchan Aruch: Choshen Mishpat 272; Or Chaim 305:19-20).

Some of our rabbis today emphasize quite correctly that modern treatment of livestock in preparation for slaughter—such as "shackle and hoist" procedures—are not humane and hence are not kosher. The value of preventing *tzaar baalei chaim*, the suffering of animals, prohibits animal cruelty. Raising animals under cruel conditions, in crowded cells that deny them fresh air, exercise, and clean conditions is not in the spirit of Kashrut. Kosher means fit, or proper. Food should be kosher, and our ethical lives should be kosher as well.

In the 1970s, the Jewish Law Court in Boston ruled that grapes picked by oppressed farm workers were non-kosher. The skins of baby seals clubbed to death were not kosher to wear. R. Israel Salanter said, "Not only is a drop of blood in an egg not kosher, but spilling any kind of blood or embarrassing people (as their blood rises to their face) is not kosher."

It is said that Hasidim who lived as farmers had special sensitivity toward animals. It is said that Rabbi Wolf never shouted at his horse; Reb Moshe Leib gave water to the neglected calves at the market; and Rabbi Susya opened all the bird cages he encountered, for birds were meant to fly and be free wanderers (Elie Weisel, *Souls on Fire*).

The Rambam says that the prohibitions of kashrut have to do with purified speech. For in the future, the Holy One will speak with each person of

Israel, so it is not fitting that the mouth that will speak with God should eat forbidden foods. Keeping kosher is a way of preparing ourselves to receive the word of God, to make us fit receptacles for the Divine Presence. Eating and speaking properly are the guardians at the gateway to our bodies. Though the kashrut laws may seem mysterious, arbitrary, and hard to discern, they encourage us to understand the interrelationship of all living creatures, to sensitize us to the importance of mundane practices as important pathways to God, and to open us up to create a messianic world where each of us honors the blessings of our lives. Chag Sameach!

Tazria/Metzora

One of the main themes of this week's parsha relates to the disease of *tzara'at*, sometimes translated as leprosy. But our Rabbis make clear that *tzara'at* is not a physical disease—it is rather a spiritual disease. Therefore, those inflicted with this disease go to the *kohen*/priest for healing. It is the *kohen*/priest, the spiritual doctor, who provides the correct medicine for the leper. The proofs are found throughout rabbinic literature.

For example, the Torah says to remove utensils from the house before the *kohanim* arrive to examine the home of the *metzora* (the person with leprosy). If the Torah were concerned with contagion, the contents would have been declared unclean. Additionally, the disease was disregarded during the three Pilgrimage festivals, when the people marched together to Jerusalem in large groups. This ignores the public health hazard of people congregating in one place and contracting a contagious disease.

At that time, the lepers marched together with the whole community. The Rabbis explain that *tzara'at* is a spiritual disease related to *lashon hara*/evil speech, not a physical disease. In Exodus 4:1-6, we see Moshe was afflicted because he bad-mouthed the Jewish people when he lost faith in them. Miriam was afflicted when she complained and gossiped about Moshe marrying an *isha kushit* (Ethiopian woman), since Moshe was already married (Num. 12:1-16).

Tzara'at (leprosy) affects a person in three stages, each stage moving the person closer to repentance (*teshuvah*). First, it is found in their house in the mildest form. If the person ignores it and does not repent, then it spreads to their clothing. At first, it will touch our clothes, but eventually, it will reach our souls. Finally, if one still persists in speaking *lashon hara* (gossiping and bad-mouthing others), then Hashem brings it to their body.

According to our Sages, a *metzora* (leper) is *motzi ra*—one who spreads evil. The sin of spreading evil, the sin of slander and malicious gossip, is a loathsome moral disease, a disease to be as strenuously avoided as leprosy. The sin of *lashon hara*, evil speech, spoken about a third party, kills three people: the one who speaks it, the one who accepts it, and the one about whom it is spoken. One Sage says that one who spreads an evil report against another is as guilty as though they had violated all the teachings of the Torah. The confessional on Yom Kippur lists 44 sins; at least 10 are sins of speech. The Talmud says that some sin through stealing, and some through adultery, but everyone sins with the tongue. It is in a wet place; it slips. And it is irretrievable; it takes on a life of its own, creating suspicion and disdain for the other.

In fact, words may burn deeper and last longer than any physical blows we can inflict. Our tradition believes in the power of words, *Baruch sheamar v'haya haolom*/God created the world with words! Yes, we can create and destroy worlds with words. We do not believe that words are cheap. Jews, hearing the vile rants of antisemites, or people of color feeling the wound of curses and belittlement, feel the sting that leaves a permanent imprint on their lives.

Judaism goes beyond these spectacular and dramatic moments. It tells us that at all times and in every circumstance, words are holy. For it is a God-given power to be able to speak, to utter syllables, and to frame them into intelligible means of communication with other people. Three times a day, at the end of each Amidah, we pray, "Oh God, keep my tongue from evil and my lips from speaking deceit."

Any stable society depends upon the relationship between its members. Slander destroys mutual trust. Insinuations and purposeful lies are used to undermine opponents politically. Governments use techniques like propaganda and disinformation. This is so insidious because people believe it even after the truths are revealed. Repeating a lie enough times breaks down defenses of truth, and convinces people to believe lies, which can lead to violence and even murder.

The press and social media are used in this egregious way as well. And the advertising industry preys on people's imagination to sell products in mendacious ways. Flattery too, can be a form of *lashon hara*, for it is based on specious pretense rather than honest feelings. We must be very diligent in exposing those lies that attack the very fiber of our communities. This is why the laws of *lashon hara* are vital for the health of our society and our interpersonal relationships.

Our Sages realize that *lashon hara* is just the symptom, a most dangerous symptom, of inner discord projected upon others; so the rehabilitation process must address the inner core of the individual. A person stricken with *tzara'at* must live outside of the camp for two reasons. One: to give a person a chance to reflect on their behavior and to look inward to identify the source of their discontent. The *kohen* acts as a spiritual therapist to allow the afflicted person to grow through this disease. Two: the leper is placed outside of the camp, not because the disease is contagious, but to make the leper realize what it feels like to be shunned and isolated. Just as they caused a separation in a relationship and isolated another through their speech, just as one's disparagement caused a decrease in friendship, a lowering of self-esteem in another, and a stigmatization of this person, the leper is now separated from the community to see how that feels. They are shunned by others and isolated; this awakens the person to the awful pain they have caused. One can then do *teshuvah*/repent and be rehabilitated.

The Talmud in Nedarim 64b states that one who has *tzara'at* is like a dead person, for one's isolation causes them to lose the ability to give. It is this giving that affords life meaning and purpose. They cannot interact with anyone. *Lashon hara* is punished by removing the factor that defines a person as living—the ability to give.

The Torah consummates the rehabilitation process by having the leper sacrifice two living birds. Rashi comments that leprosy is a punishment for evil speech, for chattering meaningless gossip and slander. It is as if the person were a bird, because birds are "chatterers." The Zohar adds that such afflictions come about both through evil words and even through good words we do not utter when we have the opportunity to speak them. "I was silent of good and my pain was frozen" (Psalms 39:3).

The birds atone for two sins. The slaughtering of one bird, which is forbidden for us to eat, is done so that one will learn to cut himself off from idle chatter and evil speech. The second bird is set free to prepare the mouth and tongue to speak words of beauty and praise, the true essence of the human being (Gen. 2:7, Onkelos).

The Chafetz Chaim suggests that this principle applies to speaking about others and, in fact, it is also prohibited to speak badly about oneself. This includes a negative self-perception in one's mind as well as expressing self-hatred overtly. Rabbi Nachman of Bratzlav asserts that the root of *lashon hara* is hatred of self, and we must learn to love ourselves to obviate the shadowy bitterness that spills out in hatred toward others. Rabbi Nachman cleverly parses the verse "Love your neighbor as yourself" (Lev. 19:18) in a creative way. The word for "your neighbor" in Hebrew is *rayacha*. The root is the same as the Hebrew word *ra* which means evil. So Rav Nachman says we are to also love the "evil" (shadow, dark side) in ourselves in order to love others. For, if we are in denial of qualities that we are ashamed of and refuse to recognize in ourselves, we will often project those qualities onto others and hate others because we have not come to accept those qualities in ourselves. So he suggests that we must recognize the shadow side in ourselves and learn to integrate and come to love that part of ourselves as well.

When one speaks *lashon hara*, what is one actually doing? Disparagement of others leads to a breakdown of friendship—an emotional separation, created from a lack of self-esteem. When one notices this habit, one must isolate oneself, meditate, pray, relate to the priest/therapist, and cultivate the habit of love toward oneself and others; for we are each created in the image of God. We each have the capacity to love others, to give to others, and to create a world of harmony and gratitude, a world of song and praise. The root of *lashon hara* is self-hatred, and the antidote is self-love.

The Talmud says that the Second Temple was destroyed because of the spread of *lashon hara*, which led to the isolation of communities and the hatred of others for no good reason. The antidote is to love others for no good reason! The Talmud tells the story of Kamtza, who, as a result of rejection and being shamed by a fellow Jew, slandered our people to the Roman government, leading the Romans to destroy the Holy Temple (Ta'anit 19b). As Rav Avraham Yitzchak Hacohen Kook teaches, "This hatred for no good reason must be transformed by abundant love for no good reason." We must learn to speak honestly and directly to others about our feelings, so as not to bear grudges that lead to hatred and maligning others. (Lev. 19:17-19).

In our present world, let us be cognizant of the power words have in our world—both those that destroy and those that uplift. We are all God's children and have more power and strength than we realize. When we practice holy speech, we become bearers of God's word and redeem our world that waits for our blessings. Shabbat Shalom!

Acharei Mot

This parsha sets forth the laws of Yom Kippur; offerings in the *Mishkan*; how Jews treat animals for food and for sacrifices; rules regarding animal blood; forbidden sexual practices; and the law against child sacrifice. It also reminds us to judge others carefully; not to hate family members in our hearts; not to take vengeance or bear a grudge; and not to profit from the blood of our fellow Jews or treat them with contempt and disrespect.

After Aaron's sons died, Aaron was instructed to bring a group of specific sacrifices—not just for his sons and himself, but for all Israelites—in the Holy of Holies. Before Aaron entered, he had to purify himself and dress appropriately. One of those sacrifices was a male goat to which the sins of the Israelites were transferred and which was then sent into the wilderness to placate Azazel, the demon associated with Yom Kippur. The kaporah/scapegoat ritual is part and parcel of Yom Kippur rituals until today. (In contemporary life, the ethical way of fulfilling this ritual is not with a goat or chicken, but with money given to charity.)

Yom Kippur is the last day of the Ten Days of Repentance and the end of a cycle that begins with Elul, the previous month, where the shofar/ram's horn is blown daily to call us to pray for forgiveness for our sins—in communal confession and prayer. We pray for all of us. In that month and in those weeks before Yom Kippur (also known as the Day of Atonement or At One-Ment) we bare our souls to God and are One with Holiness. We review our acts toward others and ourselves.

The days flash before us as we ask for forgiveness, compassion, and the chance to live happy, healthy, and prosperous lives. On that day, the holiest day of the year, the Shabbat of Shabbats, God decides if our fates are sealed in the Book of Life—or not. The possible ways of death are listed in the poetic prayer, *Unetaneh Tokef*/We ascribe Holiness to the Day, recited during the service. On the Holy Day it is decided who dies from fire, water, disease, plague, or from a list of other devastating deaths. Our lives flash before our eyes—as people say they would as we lay dying.

But on Yom Kippur, we have the chance to be redeemed, to be inscribed and sealed in the Book of Life. It is like being cleansed and given an opportunity to do better than we did the previous year, the chance to be better people—to live and dance in the Light of God.

Thus, in our Jewish tradition, in *Acharei Mot*/After Death, there is the acknowledgment of resilient rebuilding and the potential for new life as well as a shift in consciousness toward a new reality. We witnessed in our lifetime and the lifetimes of our parents and grandparents the devastating, tragic, demonic evil of the Holocaust and other demoralizing massacres around the world. We also witnessed how heroic people and noble human beings of all faiths have had the strength and fortitude to commit to building a better life, a world of peace and love.

For us to work on building sacred lives, we must think about our value systems. Are we locked into "worshiping" a seemingly secure, materialistic, de-spiritualized reality? Can letting go of this form of idolatry lead to a re-birth of a soul-consciousness, of a life guided by ethics and caring for people and the earth? The Ishbitzer Rebbe (the *Mei Shiloach*) says that to "be Holy is to be always devoted and ready for the moment when the reality of God peers through ordinary reality and enlightens your vision with a higher Light. Imagine that Hashem is constantly present, ready, and waiting to give the moment of Light to you to save you from ordinary negativity. Stand right there and wait and hope that your vision will be enlightened. You don't have to be already holy. But be ready for the moment of Holiness to uplift you. Be in the process—it may occur at any moment. It is experiential and intermittent. It infuses ordinary reality when the moment is right, and you are focused."

At the moment of death, our entire lives unreel before us. We realize that Hashem has been constantly Present, ready, and waiting to give us the moment of Light to save us from habitual negativity, to liberate us from focusing on the confusion of everyday contradictions and disappointments, and to remove us from our dark suffering and inner inadequacy. After death we can realize that the primary vital reason we exist is to love and embrace others, including ourselves; for God loves us and only wants us to connect to the Light, feel this truth, and reduce our burdens.

From that "Aha!" moment, we understand that reaching out to others and accepting love from them is the deepest blessing in our God-created world. For truly, our senses and intellect are attuned to an innate understanding of a higher presence within. Thus, we respond to a new consciousness when we face death, and are blessed to discover where the secret of the joy of life truly resides.

At this critical moment, the line between the "little self" (ego) and the deeper "higher self" is reduced; then meaningful self-adjustment becomes possible. If a person is not paralyzed with fear or frozen in hatred, the soul residing within will rise to the occasion. According to Rav Soloveichik (in *Halakhic Man*), the severing of one's psychic identity with one's previous "I" creates a new "I" possessing a new consciousness; a new heart and spirit with higher goals.

Each of us carries within some kind of burden from the past. One of these is failure, "I was not successful in this endeavor; I was not able to become who I wanted to be, I was mediocre in this and that." Sometimes we repress the memory, and sometimes it haunts us, with a subtle or strong impact. Facing our deaths takes our consciousness to a higher level, releasing this load. We move to a new level with the awareness of a new reality and leave the unconscious memories that controlled and plagued us (when we sought perfection and fled vulnerability). This releases the Light hidden beneath the surface to bring the blissful, fulfilling presence of *Shechinah* to our lives.

Our Torah uplifts us when we follow its mandates and communal connections. The Torah sublimates our instincts, shifting them from extraneous distractions and confusions to the reality of Holiness. When we are enlightened, our whole physical self, our attitudes and desires, change. Our hearts are opened, deepening our compassion, adding to our friendships, appreciating the beauty of nature and the wonder of being part of it.

The strength of our faith is elevated, and we live with greater confidence to meet our challenges with fortitude and equanimity. We are sustained by our prayers, study, and good deeds, and strengthened by our community—from which we draw abiding kinship. We are kind to all people—including those who cannot possibly repay us or be of service. We enthusiastically share our ideas with our students and our neighbors. We know and appreciate the Judaism we are taught, to enter the world of action, the real world, and become as giving and responsible as possible.

There is a story about R. Avihu ben Avima in the Talmud, who embodies this soul-consciousness, this kindness that permeates an awakened soul. It is told that his father was so old, that he spent his days alternately waking and dozing on a couch adjacent to the hall where his son was teaching Torah to his students. One day his elderly father briefly woke up to ask for a drink of water, but by the time Rabbi Avihu came to him with the water, he had already fallen asleep. Instead of returning to his students, Rabbi Avihu stayed next to the couch until his father woke up again. R. Avihu more than fulfilled the commandment to honor his parents. This same commandment did not oblige him to stay and wait for his father to wake up again. He simply regarded it as his human duty to do what he did. This is the way of one who connects to the higher/deeper Light and follows the calling of one's soul.

May we all be rejuvenated in facing our inevitable "death moments," as we emerge with a new life, a new consciousness; more aware of our Creator, who loves us and wants us to use our God-given blessings to uplift our world through the spirit of Love within. Amen.

Kedoshim

We are all children of Hashem and are all, therefore, children of Holiness itself; "For Holy am I, the Lord your God" (Lev. 19:2). It follows that our senses and intellect are attuned to an innate understanding of what Holiness entails. Parshat Kedoshim, Leviticus 19, our parsha this week, contains the "Holiness Code" which instructs us on how to achieve holiness through concrete action in daily practice. It is spelled out in clear dos and don'ts.

The Holiness Code points to another dimension beyond self-fulfillment and personal happiness. It recognizes the ultimate source of life that expects behaviors that necessitate sacrifice for the good of others with whom we are interconnected. There is a recognition of the necessity of courage in the face of inevitable sorrow and pain that life brings us. And this leads us to a higher power, felt and celebrated, even though not fully grasped. Our Torah acknowledges the mystery of existence, along with its blessings and grandeur. Through our relationship with God, we can transcend our own insular needs and follow a path that leads to the building of an enlightened world. It includes responsibilities and sacrifice as well as inner fulfillment. Our faith inspires and motivates us as we reach out to God and to our fellow human beings as we join together on the path of Holiness.

Parshat Kedoshim spells out various ethical behavioral requirements that shape our character. These include respecting one's parents and keeping Shabbat. We are not to become idolaters in any matter (whether of other gods, money, drugs, sex, or other addictions). We are commanded to offer the gleaning of our fields and vineyards to the poor for their sustenance. In the wide array of our social relationships, kedushah/holiness has its daily application. In no uncertain terms, we are enjoined not to steal, to lie, to oppress a neighbor, or to delay payment of a day laborer's wages. It is immoral to curse a deaf person, even though they cannot hear what is said; nor are we to be unrighteous in judgment, though it may never be discovered, because Holiness does not countenance evil motivation.

We climb rung after rung on the ladder of Holiness. We must learn to control our tongues. One must learn to even control one's emotions and not take vengeance on one who has wronged them—or even harbor a grudge. Even more is asked of us. Verses 17-19 state, "You shall not hate your neighbor in your heart, you shall express to your fellow how you feel. You shall not bear a grudge against the members of your people. Love your neighbor as yourself...." It always reminds me of the importance of speaking directly and respectfully to your friend if you feel offended or hurt by them, as they need to hear what you have to say. If you don't, it may lead you to repress your ill feelings, lead you to hate your neighbor, and prevent yourself from loving them as yourself. This is a most wise, deep psychological insight and a directive to create and achieve peace between yourself and your fellows.

The Holiness Code is more than a humanistic declaration affirming the universal right to dignity, respect, and well-being. The code also affirms a transcendental dimension, when it states in the commandment to "Love your neighbor as yourself. . . . for I am the Lord." The humanistic ideal, while rooted in religious tenets, can be removed from its religious moorings in secular society, and emphasizes human self-actualization as the highest value. Therefore, any arbitrary religious interference or restriction imposed upon self-realization must be rejected. Any dimension beyond the empirical reality that we know may be relegated to an inferior position.

Thus, the commandment to love our neighbors as ourselves becomes more than a fulfillment of a social norm, but a way to contact a Holy Presence through our deeds. This is the embodiment of mitzvah, to join through the deed with a higher dimension as the soul is aroused within. When humanism recognizes its source in transcendent roots, it becomes a potential participant in bringing transcendence down to earth to pursue the ethical norms defined in the Holiness Code.

We are urged to practice what Rabbi Akiva calls the great principle of the Torah, namely the commandment above—to love your neighbor as yourself. The Rabbis suggest this may mean, "Make God as beloved to your neighbor as God is to you, or may the name of Heaven become beloved through you." Just as you struggle to bring the love of God into your own heart, you should do the same for your neighbor. Another insight is to translate this verse as "Love your neighbor for they are like you/*kamocha*."

Many years ago, when I served as a Hillel Director at M.I.T., our weekly Bible study group with other religious leaders on campus included members of various Christian denominations as well as Muslim and Buddhist campus ministries. When we read Leviticus 19, my Christian colleagues were surprised to find the verse "Love thy neighbor as thyself" in Hebrew scripture, for they thought it originated in Christianity. It was an illuminating moment that brought us all closer together—Jews, Christians, and Muslims—as we discovered a commonality in our faiths.

Do not do to your neighbor what you do not want done to you! This is not a guilt-inducing maxim—for who can love another as much as one loves oneself? However, this presupposes love of oneself; and if we don't, we must learn how to do that, for loving or not loving ourselves influences our ability to truly love others. As you accept yourself with all your faults and shortcomings, you learn to accept others the same way.

Some of the psychospiritual commentaries on the verses in Leviticus 19 are profound. In 19:17, it says, "Do not hate your neighbor in your heart..." "Correct, correct your neighbor, do not bear sin on your neighbor's account." The commentators say the word "correct" is doubled to indicate that the one who criticizes should be included in the rebuke being offered. One should realize that they too have a part in this misbehavior. That is, "Do not bear sin on your neighbor's account." If you blame the entire sin on your neighbor and absolve yourself, that, too, is sinful.

So, do not cast the entire burden of sin onto the transgressor. Involve yourself in this matter and make amends for your own failings. Your neighbor will surely feel your humility and kind intention and be aroused to repent. Before you chastise others, begin with yourself, and check your motivation. Become conscious of what you are doing; you may wind up feeling the rebuke might be inappropriate, or you might still offer it, but in a gentler manner. Often people angrily yell at others when they are really yelling at themselves, at their own inadequacies, telling themselves how they wish to be.

An example of a commandment in the Holiness Code that has social implications is found in 19:23. "When you come into the land and plant...." Even though the land had many beautiful trees, the Israelites were obligated to plant and provide for others, just as others previously had provided for them. Even if they would not enjoy the fruits of their labor, the next generation would. Our feelings of gratitude and appreciation compel us to give to others what we have been blessed to receive in our lives. We are taught to cultivate and nurture the seeds of an ethical world, to care for its future well-being, to care for our planet, and to provide generous sustaining support for the future welfare of our communities and our world.

The Torah suggests that since we are children of God, we have the capacity to reach this highest level of Holiness, and this is our mandate. Our Sages elaborate that by studying Torah, doing good deeds, experiencing the wonders of nature, being part of a community that practices the goal of attaining Holiness, and observing models of righteous people who radiate humility, kindness, wisdom, and faith, we will grow in our journey toward holiness. The traits that the Torah and Rabbis teach us to emulate and achieve can be assisted by exposure to the holy Sages in our communities who emulate and model the holy attributes of Hashem.

I was blessed as a youngster to witness a community like this and individuals who embodied this trait of Holiness as the radiance of the Light shone from them. One such person was Reb Moshe Feinstein *zt'l*, a giant of his generation, a decisor and interpreter of Jewish law. He was a vessel of God's Light, whose discipline, humility, warmth, smile, and kindness were a constant reminder of Holiness.

Another example was my beloved grandfather, a Torah scholar who every Shabbat, brought me to the synagogue to sit in the first row to experience the humanity of Reb Moshe. Reb Moshe's expression of friendship to a little boy who was the grandson of his cherished friend was heartwarming. My grandfather raised me through his example of kindness, modesty, and brilliance, and dedicated his life to make sure that I was exposed to the depths of Torah and the Sages who honored it and taught it. The Torah spells out the path for doing the mitzvot, doing God's will, that transforms us *l'tzaref et habriot*/into vessels of Holiness. Throughout my wayward journey, I have never forgotten this initial exposure and imprint on my psyche. This opportunity to experience the Holiness of God's children and God's world is open to all of us and it resides in each of our souls.

It is not necessary to isolate ourselves and withdraw from society, thinking that is the only way to avoid the dangers of moral or spiritual decline. We must practice our Holiness within life. It is not a question of what we do with our solitude, but how to live in a way that is compatible with our being a likeness of God; how to conduct ourselves so that our lives can be an answer to all that God wants of us. God wants to be sanctified within life and with our people, as it says, "*V'nikdashti b'toch bnei Yisrael*" (Lev. 22:32). Through our everyday deeds, through our Holiness in our homes, we invite God in.

The concept of Holiness is not a concept of asceticism for its own sake—a general ban on enjoyment—it is a demand for everyone to know oneself and to detect the inclinations that threaten to degrade them, and then to restore their balance. May we all recognize the beauty of the ethical norms of our Torah, share its wisdom as we journey toward the Holiness required of us, and create a world of beauty, peace, and justice for all.

May we each find stories that inspire our lives and become aware that Holiness is imprinted on our souls as we are each created in God's image. May we strengthen our resolve in the radiance of Holiness and use our energy to obviate social and racial injustice, dedicate ourselves to nurturing and healing our wounded planet, actualize our great potential, and deepen our compassion—even with all the darkness and struggles that face us. Let us add to our friendships and remain devoted to truth and integrity. May we each be sustained by our communities, where we find support, acceptance, respect, and understanding. And let us say Amen!

Emor

Parshat Emor tells of the spiritual journey of *Sefirat Ha'omer* (aka *Sefira*), a count that begins on the second night of Pesach with our freedom from slavery in Egypt and culminates with the revelation and receipt of the Torah at Sinai. The 49 days of our counting are a period for spiritual growth, an intense journey toward emotional refinement. Each day corresponds to one aspect of our (7x7) 49 emotional attributes found in the Kabbalistic doctrines. These include mixtures of love, discipline, honesty, assertiveness, endurance, receptivity, and creativity. We focus each day on a different spiritual quality that we want to embrace, based on the Sefirot enumerated in the Kabbalah.

We affirm that we are spiritual beings on a human journey. We are moving through a time frame in which we continue to grow toward liberation from an oppressed slave mentality, liberating ourselves from inner fragmentation to a stage of wholeness worthy of receiving the Torah on Shavuot. Every day of the Omer, those who recognize this tradition adhere to the custom of recognizing and affirming different parts of our inner soul (as symbolized by the qualities and interactions of the ten Sefirot in Kabbalah) toward greater integration and wholeness. Through the journey, our vessels/our bodies become worthy of connecting to God within and without. We move from a realm of dislocation to a newfound resilience, living through a journey of rebellion and acceptance, isolation, and community.

In Parshat Emor we read, "And you shall count for yourselves from the morrow (of the first day of the festival of *Matzot*...)" (Lev. 23:15). Our *sefira* (counting) begins with a *sippur*, a story, a tale of our family's spiritual growth in the desert that culminates in a growth process that prepares our people to be worthy of receiving the Torah at Mount Sinai.

Remember that the Israelite nation is an extended family, with familial memories of origins and how the Israelites came into Egypt as a family of 70 descendants from our ancestor Yaakov/Yisrael. This acknowledges our commonality and noble destiny. To achieve this promised destiny, we are spiritually prepared and adhere to the lofty expectations set forth in the Torah. We are called to actualize our unique gifts as members of our loving family and to participate in our blessed charge to uplift our world. Our

Sages inform us that one of our primary responsibilities is to live ethically in the world, one in which we treat our fellow humans with respect, dignity, and kindness. This way of being elevates our honoring of God in the world, while insensitivity to our fellows and mistreatment of others desecrates and reduces the honor of God's name in the world.

During *Sefira* we also observe a period of semi-mourning for the 24,000 disciples of Rabbi Akiva who died during the count, some 2,000 years ago. The Talmud informs us of why God sent the deadly plague thusly:

"There were 12,000 pairs of disciples of Rabbi Akiva residing between Givas and Antiphras. They all died during this period of 'Counting of the Omer' because they did not accord one another proper respect!" (Yevamot 62b). In Pirkei Avot, *Ethics of the Fathers*, we read, "R. Elazar says: Let the honor of your student be as dear to you as your own; the honor of your colleague as the reverence for your teacher, and the reverence for your teacher as the reverence of Heaven" (Pirkei Avot 4:12).

The Talmud teaches us in Yoma 86a, "A person should study Scripture and Talmud, and deal graciously with their fellow human beings. Then others will say of one, 'Fortunate is his teacher who taught this person Torah. One who studies Torah—how pleasant is this person's behavior and how proper are his deeds, as it says in Isaiah 49:3, "And God said to me, 'You are my servant Israel, in whom I will be glorified."' However, if one studies Scripture and Talmud, but is not honest in his dealings and does not converse pleasantly with people—what do others say of him? 'Woe to his teacher who taught him Torah, how corrupt are his deeds and how ugly is his behavior. To him the verse may be applied, "These are God's people but they have departed from God's ways and land"' (Ezekiel 36:20; Yoma 86a).

Rabbi Moshe Chaim Luzzato proclaims, "It is an honor to God and the Torah when one who devotes oneself to its study is likewise devoted to behaving ethically and kindly to his fellow. To the extent that such refinement is lacking, the study of Torah is disparaged, and this is a disgrace to the name of God who expects us to become holy, humane, uplifted human beings through its study. (Mesilat Yesharim, Ch. 11). The students of Rabbi Akiva died because they did not respect each other; they diminished their stature as students of the Torah, and they should have acted with the greatest amount of compassion and love imaginable to their fellow students and others, all of them containing the Divine Spark and made in God's image. They desecrated God's name. Therefore, during *Sefirah*, we mourn the deaths of R. Akiva's disciples and take to heart the message of the Omer—to live lives of true holiness by elevating the name of God through our benevolent actions and heartfelt kindnesses toward all human beings.

We received the Torah on Shavuot. We accepted it. And we know the goal of the Torah is to refine our character, to transform each of us into a holy vessel capable of bringing love and glory to the blessing of life. By counting the days, and examining ourselves, by promising to do better, we prepare ourselves for Shavuot and "receiving" the Torah again.

Events in our lives should not be able to cause us so much anguish that we abandon this mission to bring Light and healing into our world. We must look for the common root of our pain—which comes from treating others, who are also made in the image of God, badly; by not honoring every human being deserving respect and love. If we cannot and do not recognize our inter-connectedness, we have failed in accomplishing what the Torah has assigned us to do—bringing the Light, peace, and justice to our fellow humans.

On the 33rd day of the Omer, Lag B'Omer, God brought the plague to an end and it became a day of celebration. We also celebrate Lag B'Omer because of Rabbi Shimon Bar Yochai, a disciple of R. Akiva, who died on Lag B'Omer. The Talmud tells us he fled from the Roman tyrants in Jerusalem and spent years hiding in a cave, sustained by only a carob tree and water from a well. In the cave, he studied the deep secrets of the mystical tradition (Kabbalah). He is held in great regard, especially by many Hasidic sects. Lag B'omer is a celebration of his memory, and in Israel hundreds of thousands of Jews make a pilgrimage to his tomb in Meron, to celebrate his life by dancing, singing, and lighting bonfires.

Our daily path over these past weeks, including our Torah readings from Leviticus, points to movement from making mistakes to a healing renewal. An example of this is found in our Torah reading from last week, a double portion. The portion Acharei Mot (After Death) is juxtaposed with the portion Kedoshim (Holiness). Perhaps this suggests that allowing corrupt values to die, to let go of secure, material, de-spiritualized reality, can lead to a rebirth of a soul-consciousness and to a life guided by ethics and caring for people and the earth. The first method of the Omer period is by meditation and introspection. The second method is through action. These are our challenges in the journey to become a holy nation, and the counting of the Omer reminds us of our responsibilities to achieve this noble goal.

Though Lag B'Omer is a day of both rejoicing and mourning, our great Sage, the Chida, reminds us that "Lag B'omer is the celebration of never becoming hopeless or despondent. It is a day of tenacity, resilience, and a commitment to carry on our magnificent heritage and sacred mission in the world. Just as the bonfires will burn out and Lag B'Omer will come to an end, there will be time to light the Shabbat candles, and we will keep the fire burning."

May we each be blessed with the commitment to lead the lives we are capable of living and spread our Light and courage, by lighting fires of kindness and love on the Shabbat after Lag B'omer, despite tragedy.

We count the Omer every day with the consciousness of who we are and how we must grow into the best of ourselves. We must learn to revere ourselves as creatures of God and love ourselves into intimate relationships with others. We must protect our sacred earth which sustains us. Let us reject our unworthiness, our separation, our loneliness, and find the cure in our faith and in our love, in our inherent connection with each other and with all of life. Then maybe we will witness the beginning of the transformation of our world. Let us say Amen!

Behar

Our parsha teaches us about the law of *Shmita* (the seventh year) and *Yoveil* (the 50th Jubilee year) which, when observed in Israel, would teach us to respect nature rather than take advantage of it. It would leave the earth alone for a well-deserved rest once every seven years. It would charge us to refrain from overproducing, not to engage in cutthroat competition, and to avoid the cultivation of greed. It would in essence allow us to see the world as God's creation, given for everyone's benefit. Our parsha begins with the verse, "When you come into the land that I the Lord have given to you" (Lev. 23:2-3). It does not say the land that you have acquired on your own. This is to remind us that it is given on condition to act ethically. It is a gift, thus contingent on our behavior and gratitude in carrying out the laws and values of *Shmita*. The Torah reiterates this in our parsha once more. "For the land is Mine, for you are sojourners and residents with Me" (Lev. 25:23). We read this idea as well in this week's study of Pirkei Avot, "One who says, 'What is mine is mine, and what's yours is yours' is the characteristic of a Sodomite [or a mediocre person]. One who says, 'What is mine is yours, and what is yours is yours is a pious person [a Hasid]' (Pirkei Avot 5:10; 5:13). Our Sages state that the destruction of the first Holy Temple and the desolation of our land were consequences of the failure of earlier generations to observe and respect the *Shmita* and *Yoveil* years. Rashi says that the Babylonian exile lasted for 70 years because the Jews failed to observe 70 Sabbatical (*Shmita*) years in Israel. Even when the sixth year was abundant, there were some Jews who were still anxious and greedy. They imagined, "Maybe next year we can make even more!"

Once the world and its resources are indiscriminately exploited, as if they were made only by and for humans, the godliness that should pertain to the care of nature is replaced by human destruction to satisfy greed. War and desolation, ecological disaster, and perpetual pollution are the result. God's plea to respect nature and observe the laws is today a universal imperative.

It is our faith in Hashem that gives us the peace of mind to know that innate sustenance is a reality if we do not abuse our gifts on this earth. The purpose of this commandment of *Shmita* is to root the Jewish people in faith and trust in God. For it is natural to assume that when the people came to the Holy Land, they would probably occupy themselves with working the land in a natural manner; and that when they prospered, they might forget that this is a gift from God. They instead might turn away from this realization when they prosper, thinking that it was only their own strength, the might of their hand, that produced their wealth; they might erroneously think that the world is conducted purely by their own natural talents, and there is no authority superior to them. Therefore, the Torah commands the people to leave the land uncultivated during the seventh (*Shmita*) year, and thus the farmer implicitly acknowledges the sole supremacy of God over the land and the Providence that is always present in our world. In this way, the fallacies and illusions of human power are stripped away, and the truth of our partnership with God and the mandate to carry out the laws of the Torah for the benefit of all humanity remains.

Moreover, as we observe *Shmita*, the quality of life is tangibly improved through the affording of a breathing space from the bustle of everyday life. The individual recovers from the influence of the mundane at frequent intervals every Shabbat; what Shabbat achieves for the individual, the *Shmita* year achieves for the nation as a whole.

The nation as a whole has a need to express from time to time the revelation of its own divine light, not suppressed by the cares and toils of everyday life. The temporary suspension of the normal social routine raises the nation spiritually. A year of solemn rest is essential for both the land and the nation, a year of peace, quiet, and time for spiritual contemplation. At this time there is the cessation of the exercise of private acquisitiveness of our produce; allowances are made for those who have to repay loans; "Those Israelites who were impoverished and sold to work for others must be released and returned to their families in the Jubilee year" (Lev. 25:39-43); and thus the covetousness of wealth stirred up by commerce is forgotten. Gratitude for the blessings of God over the earth is affirmed.

According to Rav Avraham Yitzchak Hacohen Kook, normal economic conditions—including equality and freedom from oppression—do not constitute the ultimate aim of society, but are merely an essential condition for preventing the suppression of divine spirit and a means of promoting its moral elevation. The institution of *Shmita* invested the whole nation with a spirit of forgiveness and repentance, remedied the injustice of the past, and allowed the Light of spirituality to become manifest once more. Thus, *Shmita* was ushered in on the Day of Atonement, Yom Kippur.

So *Shmita* moves us from greed and insecurity to faith, from ego to soul, and reconnects us to the Light. We fully realize that we never totally control anything, be they slaves, land, money, etc. Our fight over land as if we own it should give way to acknowledging our land and possessions as gifts to be appreciated, shared, and celebrated with all who live amongst us; this is a prime value of *Shmita*. It is our faith in Hashem that gives us peace of mind; sometimes when we succeed with the land, we think it is only a result of our hard work and we forget the Source; we forget to give gratitude to Hashem. *Shmita* and *Yoveil* are reminders of our soul commitments.

At times of chaos and world suffering as we experience today, there is a tendency to lose faith, and rely on ourselves to create our own security; we forget that we are all interconnected in God's creation. The rejuvenation of our faith relies on the power of our soul to imagine meaningful changes that will help renew the force of love on our earth. The resiliency of our soul can always be revivified by our study of Torah, our prayers, our communal energies, our walking in nature. It is our power of faith translated into good deeds that our world needs now more than ever. It is precisely at times of despair when our Godly natures, our inner souls arise to find the necessary level of depth and strength to turn things around in the human heart, renewing the world of the Jubilee where all of us can share God's bounties together. It is at times when we feel that "all hope is lost" that a deeper sense of hope and faith can arise.

May we all be renewed with the spirit and power of *Shmita/Yoveil* and bring a world of peace and jubilation in our time. Shabbat Shalom!

Bechukotai

My eyes flow with tears,
Far from me is any comforter,
We are all forlorn,
For violence has prevailed.
—*Lamentations 1:16*

The last parsha of Vayikra, filled with words of God's promises to the people of Israel and warnings to them, sums up what Hashem has offered the Israelites: how they can walk tall because they are no longer slaves and how the promises of Sinai will be fulfilled. The parsha begins with the words, "*Im Bechukotai Tailaichu*/If you will walk in my statutes."

"If" implies doubt; the word walk is used instead of keep; and the word statutes contains the meaning engravings. At the beginning of the parsha, God promises the Israelites will be looked upon with favor and be fertile and multiply; they will have rain for their crops and peace will prevail; their enemies will fail. The Covenant will be upheld, and the *Mishkan* will be placed among the people.

The parsha promises us that God will walk among us and be our God and we will be his people. For when God took us out of *Mitzrayim*, we learned to walk upright.

Let us examine what the words if, walk, and statutes teach us. The Ishbitzer suggests that the word *Im*/if implies doubt—for no one can be absolutely certain that one understands the whole truth, especially when chaotic events invade our world. Therefore, there is always some uncertainty even when we are following the path of the commandments.

It is precisely because of this state of doubt and surrounding darkness that humility is created, and it is humility that is required to allow understanding to enter into our hearts and minds beyond our natural state of ego-boundedness and rational understanding. Through this process, says the Ishbitzer, through humility and effort, revelations will occur—not through the intellect which usually culls through the advantages in all situations, but by proceeding with humility, which brings us something deeper and more profound. For in uncertainty, one feels distanced from God and therefore develops the need for greater energy to feel God's Presence once more.

God reveals God's Presence in this powerful yearning, from this place of crying out and from this reality of doubt, darkness, and distance. God reveals at that moment that one can fulfill commandments even in a state of confusion and lack of comprehension. And eventually one realizes in the trial of the moment that God is always Present and waits for us to proceed to greater depths and greater action from the depths of our doubt. If one proceeds even with doubt, new revelations and new healing will occur in our world. It is then that the power of Light emerges stronger than the power of darkness.

The Sfat Emet suggests that the word walk is used instead of keep to teach us that we each have a particular path to walk; a necessary, unique talent to contribute to the world. One who serves God, longing always to find the paths that are unique to them, will be led by God in a true way. The word walk implies movement, striving to find the way to righteousness every day. A person has the power to see the patterns God has inscribed in their soul—if they keep walking and discovering, and do not remain stagnant in keeping the laws. The suffering and chaotic moments in our world prompt us to move forward to new discoveries that were always hidden beneath the surface.

The laws mentioned here are called *chukim*/engravings, because they are carved within us. Even when we feel an urge to follow temptation, the soul contains pathways that distinctively lead to God. But to find that fulfillment requires Divine help, aroused by human desire and encounter with Torah. We discover this as we walk, discovering paths that are uniquely ours.

As we strive to grow in depth, and have the desire to concretize our insights and feelings into action, we are helped from Heaven. Our wisdom and awareness grow; our soul is redeemed through our longing and desire to serve our Creator. This witnessing of God's Presence, our sacred duty, becomes our blessing as we increasingly discover the manifestation of God in our lives. Each of us, and all of the people of Israel, are called witnesses—purifying and raising up all the good from the mixture in which we live. Nature itself is filled with God's greatness and goodness. Anywhere we go becomes a house of study, a place where we can learn and bear witness to the goodness of God. At every moment we have the potential of an encounter with the divine in each experience and in every place.

But if the people do not listen, if they do not walk with God—if our souls reject God's laws and we do not carry out the commandments and we break the Covenant—we will suffer greatly from the devastating curses in the *tochacha*. The *tochacha* is the admonition wherein we learn what happens if the people of Israel fail to follow Hashem's laws. These admonitions spell out the horrific consequences of disobeying the Torah, and the reader on the Bima recites these verses in a whisper loud enough to be heard by the *kehilla/* congregation. Among those consequences are terror, disease, warfare, famine, and desolation. Before and after the *Tochacha* is read, verses before and after it are also read to remind us that God would always remember his covenant with our patriarchs Avraham, Yitzhak, and Yaakov.

Before he died, an Orthodox Auschwitz survivor told his daughter that when he was on one of the interminable "inspections" by the Nazis, an officer in sparkling boots and spotless uniform came up to him and pulled a piece of parchment out of his pocket. Shoving it into his prisoner's face, he asked if the prisoner knew what it was. After a quick glance, her father told the officer, "It is the *tochacha*, the warning to the Jews who leave God's path."

The officer, satisfied that the prisoner knew what he was talking about, told him, "I will let you live to fill out the curse." In this case, the curse saved her father.

The parsha offers us a way to reconnect to God, a way of showing value for each soul. It is called tithing—giving a percentage of what we earn as a sacrifice in the Holy of Holies. The people may do it with shekels or land or animals and then consecrate it with priests in a holy manner.

We live in a war-torn world, in an era of mass murder. We are all feeling wounded and pained at the horrific, devastating loss of lives perpetrated by those who use dangerous guns to kill innocent victims in classrooms, dance halls, shopping malls, and workplaces. They tear the flesh of children and adults and create eternal wounds in their families and close friends. It makes us feel at times that there are people who are simply not capable of acting as members of a human species created in the image of God, people who are wounded and unstable, and people who act out of base motivations. The violence, greed, selfishness, and uncaring of these killers shake us to our core, and Amalek triumphs in our world.

It is so very human to express our painful feelings, but then we must consider ways to ameliorate our current chaos and not abandon hope. We must resolve to strengthen our commitment to build the good world we are charged to create. As always, we must begin with ourselves and remember that each of us are capable, responsible, compassionate human beings who can find guidance in our Torah on how to carve out the path to peace. "Thy ways are ways of pleasantness and all its paths lead to peace" (Proverbs 3:17).

We always have the opportunity to dig deeper—not to despair, but to discover our strong faith, and to use our strength to transform our world in the face of these crises. Even with doubt, if we walk the path with God, we will discover our souls are engraved in ways that are unique to our destiny, and necessary to heal our world.

May we each begin to forge a new path and join together in action as a wounded humanity to work together to create a world where violence is obviated and love, justice, and security prevail. Amen, and may it be so!

Shavuot

The ongoing wars between Israel and Hamas and Hezbollah, between Arabs and Jews, take their toll in riots, carnage, myriad deaths, wounds, and pain, shattering the illusion of peace. These actions reveal the latent and obvious feelings of hostility and anger in the hearts of enemies who refuse to learn how to live side-by-side in security and mutual respect. Until we address the underlying wounds and convictions dwelling in the hearts of our enemies and in the hearts of combatants, there will never be a true and lasting peace. How does the message of Shavuot impact our psyches to help us find a way toward rapprochement and healing, accountability, and forgiveness?

We mourn for the loss of lives on both sides. At the Sea of Reeds, when the Egyptians were drowned and the Israelites crossed to the other side, the angels wept for the loss of our enemies as well as for our own losses. Feeling anxiety about how much pain and loss is yet to come, I am reminded of the custom that when the Shabbat comes or when a Jewish holiday such as Shavuot arrives, we must end our mourning and absorb the energy of the holy day.

Of course, saving lives overrules this demand and we can replace the energy of Shabbat and holiday for this purpose. However, those of us who are not fighting in the war are obligated to observe Shabbat and the holiday of Shavuot. Legend tells us that Shavuot is a moment of transformation: the holy kinetic energy at Sinai was so powerful, that we were forced to yield to its demand even against our will. Legend says that God held the mountain over our heads at Sinai and said, "Observe these commandments or I will drop this mountain on your heads." Reading the experience at Mount Sinai and reading the Book of Ruth may give some indication of the values we must seek and implement to create a more peaceful world of love and harmony.

Why was the moment of accepting the Torah and the Ten Commandments so mystical? It was the moment when all of history changed in the psyche of the Jewish people. It was the moment that gave us meaning; we were charged with bringing a sublime message of ethics, morality, and the ingredients to make the world into a world of justice, peace, and love. Surely, it was one of the most significant events in human history. The world was never the same after our ancestors stood at the foot of the mountain and, amidst thunder and lightning, heard the words of the Ten Commandments.

It was the time that molded our character, regulated our behavior, and shaped our destiny. For on that day, something revolutionary and irreversible happened to our people. After Sinai, the Jewish people would never be the same. We became obsessed with and possessed by the Torah! Torah became our main calling. And through the generations, the Torah grew with added commentary after added commentary. We are known in history as the "People of the Book"—we carried the book and the Torah carried us. We resisted all the chastisement, prejudice, hatred, and pogroms. We persevered and became a special people. Yes, it was our Torah at Sinai that defined our uniqueness.

Let's examine some of the salient messages from the Book of Ruth that we read on this holiday.

We encounter the power of welcoming those who come from different cultures (Ruth was a foreigner, a Moabite), the power of one woman's faith and moral glow, the beauty of female friendship, the love between two human beings that brings forth the messianic seed, and descriptions of loyalty, devotion, and sacrifice.

And there are the Ten Commandments. The first of the Ten Commandments states "I am the Lord your God" in the singular construct (*Elokecha*) and not in the plural construct (*Elokeichem*), although it is a revelation to the entire Jewish people. It suggests that at Sinai everyone felt as if God was speaking directly to them alone, to the unique subjective reality of each individual. Each of us has a unique task in this world and extracts from the Torah that which is most resonant to our soul. Each of us contributes something unique to our world. Each of us must trust the voice inside us that hears the Voice or words in the Torah directed to us and follow that voice that calls, "I am the Lord your God."

There are times when one individual can make an extraordinary difference, when one individual takes a radical step to shake others out of their lethargy, one who cries out in the name of the Ten Commandments, in the name of God, to do what is necessary to create justice and peace. The prophets of Israel did this: Moshe at Sinai did it by creating a new set of laws and inspiring the people to wake up from their slave mentality to march forth in freedom to a new world.

These times call for each of us to find our inner Sinai on Shavuot and march forward toward peace. We are at a time of great crisis, and a time of great potential change. We must transform conditions on the ground and face the challenges ahead with a new vision prompted by Sinai. We must move from the slave mentality of following the herd blindly and awaken to the calling of the Torah!

However, we must always remember the call of our community, the call of our people, and the call of all people as well. The Torah was given as a unit to a whole community (the people dwelt in unity at the foot of the mountain, *vayichan ha'am!*). We are stronger as a community than as isolated individuals. We lend each other strength, and each person contributes something different, something necessary, that separate individuals are incapable of doing on their own. When we stood at Sinai, there were people next to us who were very different from us as well—strangers, elders, young ones, men, women, etc. But in the power of the great Light of the Voice, we heard the calling, and our souls "saw" it as well. We realized that we are all human beings, each of us with different stories that need to be heard with a compassionate ear and an open heart.

In the same way, God called out to our hearts at that moment, recognizing our uniqueness, our different temperaments and experiences. Our challenge today is to reach out to others, hear their pain, share our pain, and discover the humanity and dignity of each other, each of us created in the image of God—no matter the differences in race, religion, nationality, and culture. Let us share each other's stories and find our common humanity so we can work together to build a better world through knowledge of each other. This is the deepest message of the revelation, the ability to recognize that God created each of us in God's image, each of us carrying a different message to uplift humanity. Let us reach out to our own families, and to those who are from different backgrounds to expand our horizons and discover that all human beings are created with God's beauty and wisdom.

How can we share our gifts with others? How can we welcome the stranger the way Boaz welcomed Ruth—a foreigner, a Moabite? Through this liaison of difference, they created the messianic energy through their relationship. How do we do that? How do we return to Sinai on Shavuot to remember the responsibilities communicated to us in the Ten Commandments? How do we translate these edicts in our own days, in our own society, with gratitude to our healthcare workers, to heal the racial inequities in our society, to help those who need food and clothing? Will standing at Sinai reawaken us? Will studying the Torah until sunrise inspire us to carry out its mandates?

Will we now answer the call to be holy individuals; to be a holy nation as we all heard the mandate together as the Israelite people? We all have myriad opportunities before us. Let us commit ourselves on Shavuot to take on at least one task to uplift the world with our gifts.

Can we reach out with confidence in our strength, in our faith, in our dedication to God and the Ten Commandments to transform our enemies into friends? Can our attitudes and visions project a new future—a future where each nationality, each religion can have its own place, its own unique contribution to our world? Can we share land and build together as God has mandated us to do? Faith, love, and courage are necessary to achieve this cherished goal.

We as a Jewish people derive our strength from the Torah, from being inspired by its wisdom, and thereby elevate ourselves to become the best we can be. We must overcome our fears and join with others of good faith who also want peace and justice in this world. Is it merely a coincidence that the counting toward Shavuot and the fasting of Ramadan occur at similar times? This season of holiness for Jews and Muslims commemorates the revelation of our sacred texts. Shavuot marks receiving the Torah and *Laylatu Alqadr* marks receiving the Koran. We say *Chag Sameach*, and the Muslims say *Eid Mubarak*. Are we not all awakened to the call of the Lord, the call to our higher selves, to our responsibilities, to feel gratitude for our creation and to partner to create the beautiful world we are capable of creating?

Each one of us knows how it feels to love someone dearly. No matter our political beliefs, we are members of the human family. We are perfectly capable of understanding and relating to people who on the surface may seem very different from us. Let us begin to understand that we must treat all people for who they are—family. We, of course, also see how different we are from each other in ways ranging from gender and race to geographical location and religious beliefs. But the truth is, in our personal families as well as in the human family, we really are the same.

May peace emerge from the chaos, bloodshed, and madness. May war bring peace, may tears lead to joy, may we awaken to God's salvation by truly following the Torah, and seeing that we either embrace our brothers and sisters or destroy God's world. Let us move from selfishness, racism, and antisemitism to a society of love and justice. We are all human and we are all family. We all look at the same stars, we all laugh and cry. We all love and breathe the same air. We all have all been hurt; we all have cried.

As Rav Avraham Yitzchak Hacohen Kook says, "One day the song of the self, the song of the people, the song of humanity, the song of the world will all merge, lend vitality to each other and these sounds of joy and gladness, jubilation and celebration, ecstasy and holiness will be the voice of peace and wholeness and a new day will come" (*Lights of Holiness*, v. 2 p. 459). May that day be soon, Amen!

BAMIDBAR
Numbers

Bamidbar

In this week's parsha we read, "Count (Lift up) the heads of all of the congregation" (Num. 1:2). The expression *siu et rosh* literally means "raise the heads" of each person, intimating the importance of each and every individual. It was not simply a "counting," but distinguishing every individual as precious, so that the individual knows that they are precious. Hence, the charge to lift up through counting.

Probably the most efficient way to take a census is to ask the head of each household for data regarding one's family. Having Moses count each and every person, and to name them, was very inefficient, and extremely laborious and tiresome considering the great numbers involved. The census process was put in place to teach the value of the uniqueness of each individual. No one can be treated as a mere number. Moshe had to meet each Israelite and show each one the honor and respect they deserved, being the image of God (Sanhedrin 37a). It feels awful to be taken for granted, to not be known. As Martin Buber suggests, every person wishes to be confirmed in one's individuality and wishes to have presence in the being of another. To be seen and to be heard is soul-fulfilling; it means to be listened to carefully, not to be mistaken for someone else, and to feel another's heart is opened to us. We all want to be seen in our uniqueness and appreciated for the complex human beings we are.

The Torah affirms the reality of uniqueness, designing the flag of each tribe with a distinct logo signifying the unique nature of that tribe—*Ish al diglo b'otot l'veit avotam* (Num. 2:2). For example, the flag of Judah depicted a lion, the king of the animals, because the royal house of David was descended from him. Zevulun's flag showed a ship, symbolizing their occupation as seafaring businessmen, which enabled them to support the Torah study of Issachar. The Torah may be suggesting that in our desire for uniformity, for outward similarity, we have frequently brought division into the very center of our community. Therefore, the Israelites were distinctly commanded that so long as the tribes were stationed around the Ark, each was to march under its distinguishing banner.

This biblical picture of the ideal community is quite elegant. It consists of a common center, around which are grouped diverse bodies. Its foundation is unity but not uniformity. That is the pattern we should keep before our eyes as being worthy of embracing. Picture the scene in the wilderness. They are aggregated by a common attachment to the central sanctuary, the Ark. It is in the center of the people; around it on all sides and in all directions are the twelve tribes, not as one indivisible mass, but as distinct sections, each recognizable by outward symbols. Every Israelite was in their place under the tribal banner to which they were attached. There was to be a Oneness, a unity created by accepting the diverse elements around the Ark. Although each tribe was distinct, they were bound up in a common destiny. Each tribe was to maintain its separate identity, and yet be a unit in the whole. By such arrangement and in such formation, the Sanctuary was properly honored, and thus the people marched on to their goal.

This is the ideal flourishing and vital community. This is an arrangement that leads to progress and harmony. Yet we persistently neglect it. We want every member of the community to march under one banner. We fail to make provision for differences in temperament, upbringing, education, and taste. We refuse to admit the elementary fact that what suits one may not suit another. We demand that others should be like us or should be all alike. The result of this attitude is that others drift slowly away from Judaism, or they form themselves into a separate and distinct body for the satisfaction of their religious needs. In this way, we give rise to division in the community, and often mutual hostility. It seems apparent that such a policy is not the best strategy to create a harmonious community. Instead of one strong body, we have several attenuated groups that could benefit from greater connection to a dynamic center. Our energies and resources are currently dissipated instead of being strengthened by interconnections.

The word religion is thought by some to be derived from a Latin root meaning to "bind together." Accordingly, it should be a force that unites people. And sometimes it actually does. But at the same time, there are sometimes judgments that reside within its walls that create anguish and distress within its members. At times religious groups have been the cause of frightful atrocities and persecutions. Inhuman crimes have been committed in its name. Sects and factions have fought against each other; and why? Because of the differences of opinion on matters in which it is unreasonable to expect agreement.

If Moses had tried to obliterate the differences between the tribes and demand uniformity, it is quite probable that internal troubles would have constantly disturbed the national unity. But by wisely recognizing tribal distinctions, and even encouraging and affirming them, a harmonious community was born. It is the acceptance of diversity that creates harmony and peace; where each individual has the freedom to discover, give birth to, and contribute their unique God-given talents. Having to conform to one way of behaving creates an impossible tension that splits a community; it is not peace that is then achieved, but stress. Anger and flight are the consequent outcomes.

Unity is more important than similarity! And unity can only be secured by diversity! God has not made us all alike, either physically or mentally. We differ in appearance, thought, and inclination. Our Scripture recognizes these differences; so why don't we do the same? Why do our communities drive away people who are as eager as we are to uplift our world, but stand under a different banner from ours? Such an attitude is contrary to Jewish ideals and retards progress and eventual harmony. May we begin this Shavuot to embody this acceptance of diversity, each resonating with one's particular Torah message, or Torah verse, or Hebrew letter joining together under the banner of the Lord and the Torah. And may it be so!

Naso

This parsha asks us to focus on the theme of inter-community strife that is prevalent and dangerous to our mission as a holy community and to continuity as a wholesome, evolved people. Can there be hope for dialogue in our split communities that will lead to peace? Will it occur after these most tragic wars? What is the Jewish charge for successful dialogue and partnership? The Talmud discusses the disputes between Hillel and Shammai and provides us with some insight into proper dialogue between rivals. The Talmud states, "For three years Beit Shammai and Beit Hillel disagreed. The house of Shammai said the halakha is in accordance with our opinion, and the house of Hillel said the halakha is in accordance with our opinion. Ultimately, a Divine Voice emerged and proclaimed, "Both these and those are the words of the living God. However, the halakha is in accordance with the opinion of Beit Hillel" (Eruvin 13b).

The Talmud asks, "Since both these and those are the words of the living God," why was Beit Hillel privileged to have the halakha established in accordance with their opinions? It was because they were agreeable and forbearing, showing restraint when confronted; and when they taught halakha, they would teach their own statements *and* the statements of Beit Shammai. When they formulated their teachings and cited a dispute, they prioritized the statements of Beit Shammai to their own statements, in deference to Beit Shammai."

Though the houses of Hillel and Shammai had many disputes and disagreements throughout history, some even leading to violence and destruction, the Mishnah reports the constituents of the two schools intermarried despite their disagreements. How is it possible to remain respectful of the other side while retaining strong disagreements of opinion?

The Mishnah points out that the way we disagree is as important as one's argument. Beit Shammai's rulings are just as valid as those of Beit Hillel, but we follow the latter because of the civility and deference they demonstrated. In our climate of ever-increasing polarization, this passage is often cited as a plea for intellectual and political discourse that is respectful and intellectually humble. Like Hillel, we should seek to understand opposing arguments and relate to them with respectful disagreement, instead of trying to prove that we are right. Mere cordiality and lukewarm respect are not sufficient to create a deeper, honest relationship with others.

One of the main challenges we face today is that we live in separate communities, based on religious practices and differences. We live in bubbles corresponding to the narrative of our own side. Our opinions of the other are sometimes based upon authentic experiences and also on distorted perceptions based on ignorance. We also do not see how the other sees us and our actions. Our fear of the other dominates us, and our despair of ever finding understanding with the other lingers. We believe "they will never understand me," and don't make an effort to understand them. While it is true that we may have some truths, we do not own the complete truth. Only in true courageous dialogue can a larger and healing truth be revealed.

Superficial niceties and polite conversation are not sufficient for deeper, honest relationships. We may not even be aware of the prejudices, fears, and repressed anger of the other. True friendship and reconciliation mean confronting deep wounds and pain. It means listening deeply to the feelings of others that are difficult to hear. It means honoring perspectives that are different from ours and developing empathy through this deep listening without judgment. It also means taking responsibility and acknowledging mistakes that we may have made in our thinking, ignorance, and fear. We also must be able to forgive ourselves in the process as well as forgive the other. We must rid ourselves of inner negativity to truly face our own imperfections as human beings, as well as the imperfections of others. It takes great courage and strength to open our vulnerabilities and accept our fragile humanity. But we are also beings who can rise to great potential and transformation! This is the real work that must be done if we are to move beyond strife, contentiousness, and violence of spirit and body.

When everything seems to be on the edge of destruction, we can also be on the verge of great awakenings and life-changing revelations about our own inner nature. We can become open to ways of contributing to the ongoing pulse of life. We can create a tomorrow based upon an existence in which our common futures are integrally tied to the well-being and peace of the other.

I learned this on June 5, 1967, as I sat in a *malben*, a home for the elderly, on the border of Jerusalem, in Talpiot. How did I get there? After graduating from Yeshiva College, I went to Israel to study in a yeshiva before entering rabbinical school. We studied Talmud day and night for more than 10 hours each day and lost weight on a diet of eggs, tomatoes, potatoes, and Israeli salads with lots of oil. We shivered at night, crouching close to the gas heaters, and rarely had hot water for showers. But we were committed to mastering the ethical teachings of the Talmud. The theme of the particular text we studied was the Laws of Damages (Nezikin). Not only did we learn the intricacies and severities of damaging another person, but also that another person's property was precious in the eyes of the owner and thus needed to be honored and protected. Bottom line: It was sinful to harm another person, even if one had to sacrifice one's own comfort and suffer loss through honoring the rights of others.

After 10 months in Israel, in May 1967, Arab armies on all sides of Israel threatened to drive the state into the sea. The rabbis instructed us to ignore the shots intermittently heard in the streets and devote ourselves to our Talmud study. But on the morning of June 5th, the punctual, dedicated rabbis did not come to the Beis Medrash. Instead, they phoned us and instructed us to call two taxis and go to different rabbis' homes. War had broken out! As we climbed into the taxis, heavy gunfire broke out in the neighborhood, and the Haga (internal security) police ordered the taxis to halt. The roads were too dangerous, so my fellow students and I were forced to go instead to the home for the aged across the street from the yeshiva. We entered the Jerusalem stone building with no electricity and found elderly men and women who were frightened and worried. Many were Holocaust survivors, and the sounds of the planes overhead and large Howitzer guns hitting buildings along the street created panic. We helped the older individuals gather together their belongings and spent the six days of the war in the building's basement area, rationing food and praying for a miracle.

When radio communication was restored, we learned that a miracle had occurred: Israel had experienced a tremendous victory, even managing to enter the Old City of Jerusalem, which had been divided since 1948. We were elated, and when we opened the doors of the senior home, squinting into the sun for the first time in days, we hoped and dreamed that this might usher in a new era of peace between neighbors, one the Prophets had predicted.

The Jewish holiday of Shavuot arrived, and we marched together, singing and dancing toward our cherished destination, the Western Wall. On the narrow cobblestoned streets of the Old City, we saw Arab merchants huddled against their shops—nervous and worried—and little Arab children attempting to sell trinkets and memorabilia to the Jewish marchers. Two young children, shy with large brown eyes, approached me and said, "We don't hate you; we only hate the Americans who provide weapons to the Israelis." I kept my American identity to myself and nodded a reassuring smile at them as I continued excitedly to the Wall. When we reached the plaza that had been rapidly opened up, there were thousands of people celebrating in dance and song in a rapturous rhythm, and we felt blessed by this miraculous turn of events in our lifetime.

But my dream of two peoples living together side by side was soon shattered. The Arab nations, having experienced a heavy defeat, met in Khartoum and decided that no peace accord could be reached. The balance of power had been reversed, and the victorious Israelis could not reap the fruit of victory until clear conditions promoting empowerment and equal partnership could be created. Perhaps the hope of a reversal of this defeat was prominent in the minds and hearts of the Arabs, but it was clear that my fantasy of a quick rapprochement between enemies would not be realized.

Ironically, during that whole year, I was immersed in studying the Laws of Damages and how careful we had to be in the treatment of others, even enemies. And here before me was the possibility of actually interacting with my enemy in a loving manner. Could my simple, small act have a helpful impact on the wound in the other that was so deep and raw? The complexity of this task was overwhelming, especially when extremists on both sides, both suffering wounds and mirroring the way they saw each other through lenses of fear, anger, and hatred, acted out in cycles of violence. Was I still obligated to try to enact the sensitive Laws of Damages in the face of others who now hated me? A small voice within me answered, "Yes." For as Pirkei Avot 2:16 says, "It is not up to me to complete the work, to find the 'right' solution, but neither am I free to desist from beginning it." We are each called to do the godly act in the moment, not to worry about the result.

Two weeks after the war, when we had returned to the yeshiva, housed in an old, large Jerusalem stone two-story home, a large Arab family, two parents and their eight children, knocked on the door of the yeshiva with a large key in their hands. They claimed the yeshiva had been their home until 1948, when they left during the war. It was hard for me to comprehend that reality. I had never encountered that possibility before. But we welcomed them with some tea, and communicated human to human, without language but with an understanding heart. They left humbly, having been heard, and I never saw them again.

Two weeks previously, we marched to the Western Wall in joy and hope. Now, decades later, marches inside the walls of the Old City are not hopeful. These marches are still filled with joy, but also with anger, including hostile signs deprecating the Palestinians, and encouraging them to leave the city.

My hope is that we keep the Laws of Damages at the forefront of our human souls and that we will each do our part to heal wounds through human interaction—listening and hearing the distinct narrative of the other, and understanding that each of us must painfully sacrifice our optimal dreams for the sake of peace and justice.

As our ancestor Aaron taught us (Pirkei Avot 1:12) being a "lover of peace" means taking responsibility to try to change reality, and it can only be done with a loving attitude that sees each human being as created in the image of God. It demands courage to talk, to meet reality as it is, to strive to change that which is changeable with equanimity and patience, and to yield to things we cannot change. It may require sacrifice to achieve larger goals instead of meeting all our needs with a sense of righteousness. It means restoring trust and faith through communication and meeting with each other.

From the cherubim in this week's parsha (Num. 7:89) we learn that when we truly face each other with passion and compassion, then God dwells between us. Only when we see the humanity of the other looking at us will we achieve peace and wholeness. The forces of fear, division, and hatred can be overcome. This includes facing the underlying injustices and grievances that others endure because of our actions or lack of action, in order for a lasting peace—not just interim false peace followed by destructive war. Let us work for a better future we can create with the help of our faith and God's blessing. Amen!

3

Beha'alotcha I

Parshat Beha'atlotcha offers some guidance about the prime responsibilities of a Jewish leader in its description of the duties of the high priest (*Kohen Gadol*). The verse in our parsha states, "When you go up to kindle the lamps, toward the face of the Menorah shall the seven lamps cast light" (Num. 8:2). The *Kohen* must clean out the Menorah and light it with olive oil each day. He must go up though the Menorah is only 18 handbreadths tall and he could light it without going up. Since the Menorah symbolizes Torah, it must be uplifted.

The verse implies that Aaron is rising up and causing the flames, the sparks of holiness within the people, to rise up as well. One of the prime goals of a Jewish leader is to raise their people to a higher spiritual level, to spread the light of the Torah. The lamps must be kindled toward the central lamp, the inner core where the Torah's depth resides. The wick of the central lamp was pointed West, toward the Holy Ark. The Menorah represents wisdom, and all the wisdom in the world must be directed toward the Holy Ark, to reveal God's presence and the enlightened teachings of the Torah. It says, "And Aaron did so" (Num. 8:3), which implies Aaron epitomized this ideal by kindling the Light in his community.

The shape of the Menorah, with multiple branches made completely from one piece of beaten gold, symbolizes how each segment of Torah, as a whole unit, contributes to the elevation of society and all its inhabitants. The Jewish people are charged to take this light from God's shining Torah Light and kindle it so others can connect to its radiance, for "Its ways are the ways of pleasantness, and all its paths are Peace" (Proverbs 3:17). Aaron was imbued with this Light, and it is said, "He loved peace, and actively pursued peace by imbibing from its light and sharing its depth and wisdom with others, bringing people close to the Light of Torah, the Light of Peace" (Pirkei Avot 1:12). This is indeed the purpose of Torah: to allow its wisdom to transform us, to enter us, so that we become a vessel of peace.

All our future Jewish leaders have the capacity to create a world of peace and harmony.

The Midrash (Mechilta, Parshat Yitro) teaches that the Revelation at Sinai was given in the desert, not on the Temple Mount, to teach us that the Torah is not meant for the Jews alone, but for all humanity. Our particularistic disciplined path of observing the commandments in a distinct way must lead to a universal message to benefit all humanity.

Just prior to the Revelation, Israel is charged to be a "Kingdom of Priests"— teachers to all humanity, purveyors of a God of love, compassion, morality, and peace (Sforno, Ex. 19:6). This universal charge is given to the Israelites to make of themselves a sacred nation (otherwise we would hardly be an example to emulate), a nation of *Kohanim* to embody and convey the Light and beauty of our teaching to the world (Isaiah 2; Micah 4; Zechariah 7, 8, 9). This is the true significance of the *Kohen's* kindling of the Menorah: to spread the message of Torah beyond the Sanctuary to the rest of the world.

It is the duty of the new leaders of our generation to demonstrate to the world that we are taught paths to seeking justice, and to radiate humility and lovingkindness so that all humanity can celebrate the gift of life and God's blessings. We are taught through righteous decrees and ordinances that we are "our brothers' keepers" and we must hold hands and hearts with all humanity (Deut. 4:8). It is the *Kohen* Gadol in the days of the Messiah and the educators of today who must convey these laws of compassion and justice to encourage our whole world to live a life of lovingkindness, gratitude, and generosity. We must be ambassadors to the world, who will bring the light and warmth of Torah as a blessing to all the families on earth. (Gen. 12:1-3).

And finally, our parsha teaches us that a successful, noble, exalted, dignified leader must be sensitive to their community and adaptive to the needs of the current reality. We must pay attention to and listen to the complaints of our community members as Moshe did when the people complained about the "boring daily manna in the desert" (Num. 11:1-15).

Moshe was confronted with a new generation. The youngsters who left Egypt were maturing and had different needs and expectations from those of their parents. Each successive generation has new dreams and visions. It is our challenge to be sensitive to their voices to maintain Torah ideals, and always remain alert to the honest changes and needs that call for response. Boredom can be transformed into excitement when each member's vision, insight, and contribution are actualized.

A mature and prudent leader cannot be too far ahead of their community, nor can they fall behind because of an inability to truly listen to the unique needs of their community. This does not mean that we must fulfill all the needs and demands brought to us, but we must be able to listen and to help clarify what those needs are. The skill of active listening is very healing and will empower each member to reach their highest potential and live out their "soul dream." The community will be able to grow with a common vision under the guidance of a superb, sublime leader—one who honors change while maintaining the ideals of our tradition.

May we be peacemakers like our High Priest Aaron, and bestow love, justice, and pleasantness on our holy, blessed journeys. Let us pray for peace, joy, and healing. May pain and suffering be assuaged and let us say Amen.

Beha'alotcha II

A tale from Israel:

A new immigrant, just arrived from the Former Soviet Union,
was asked "How was life where you come from?"

"I can't complain," he answered.
"And how were your living quarters there?"

He said, "Well, I can't complain."
"And your standard of living?"

Again he replied, "I can't complain."

"If everything was so good, why did you come here?"

"Oh," replied the new oleh (immigrant),
"Here, thank God, I can complain!"

Our Torah tells us of various grievances of the people—voiced for good reason—in the desert, and how God responds positively to their complaints. For example, in Exodus 15:23, they complain about bitter water; at Refidim in Exodus 17:2, they complain of the lack of water. In both cases, Hashem provides them with water.

But in Beha'alotcha, there is a different response. The verse states "The people took to seek complaints and were like 'complainers' and it was evil in the ears of Hashem" (Num. 11:1). Here they are not complaining about a specific problem, but are complaining for the sake of complaining. The verses describe a small contingent, "the mixed multitude/rabble," which cultivated this "craving." Whining and fretting became a habit (Num. 11:10). Every social gathering led to lamenting and fault-finding.

What was the reason for these complaints? Two possibilities come to mind. Perhaps it was the boredom of the desert, and the repetitious daily Manna, or that the new commandments seemed to be a burden. The people fantasized about the past, claiming falsely that the conditions in Egypt were better. They said, "At least in Egypt we had meat instead of manna" (Num. 11:4-6).

The Ramban explains that the Hebrew word K'mitonenim, (complainers) can mean both complainers and also mourners. It was as if they felt that they had not lived! This aroused God's anger and Moses' despair, for it showed that they did not find meaning in the teachings Moses was bestowing upon them.

The marginal mixed multitude/rabble who were most dissatisfied succeeded in inciting the people to doubt and murmur against their lives in the wilderness. A small group of dissatisfied people can create major injury in a community when they are not singled out and dispersed. Sometimes, actively listening can address their complaints; sometimes, a harsher response is necessary.

It is probable that these people were bored with life in the desert, and sought new stimulation and recognition. The steady diet of manna may have been enervating. Rather than embrace discipline, they sought instant gratification. Perhaps the abundance of manna and the lack of challenge of working for their food led them to gripe.

Boredom can occur when we are not giving or open to life's challenges. The Jews did not work for their food in the desert; it was just provided for them. They did not have much experience in giving to one another, in joining together for a cause. Perhaps this led to a feeling of a lack of purpose. Sometimes being given everything (manna) may lead to a feeling of being spoiled, wanting more (a craving), and a feeling of never having enough. When we work for something, there is a feeling of satisfaction, security, and a willingness to be giving to others.

At times one can forget oneself in the serving of an all-absorbing ideal. But when there are no new opportunities to experience, an ennui can set in. To give is to live; to create something that will outlast time, that will contribute to the improvement of the world, makes life meaningful. Perhaps the discipline of the law, the repetition of the same food, and the restriction of rules also affected them. The gathering of the manna had certain rules attached to it (gather only enough for that day; do not gather on Shabbat, etc.) and it required discipline, so rebellion against this became a rebellion against the entire Israelite lifestyle.

The "'rabble" rejected control and instead demanded meat and instant gratification instead of manna. God reacted by making them see that instant gratification and abundance of meat is not the solution for what ails them (Num. 11:18-20). Even the most cherished material fantasies become ordinary, even repugnant, in excess. The initial pleasure satisfies a temporary need, but the deeper need for meaning and challenge remains. It was the lack of soul satisfaction that led the people to seek gratification in material things, and their effort was doomed to failure.

It is startling that these complaints in the desert occurred only one year after receiving the Torah at Mount Sinai. What made them complain and be ungrateful so soon after the Revelation? Was it the anxiety of being free after a life of slavery where everything was laid out for them? Was it the fear of death in the desert that led them to a feeling of despair? Was it the monotony of the desert that led them to complain and fantasize about the past (was there even real meat in Egypt)? Moses is overwhelmed by the people and his inadequacy in teaching them. He was not a great orator—it was Moshe's humility Hashem loved—and so God gives Moses assistance at this time of crisis.

Seventy spiritual teachers were needed to share the responsibility of opening the people up to the challenges of observing the mitzvot (Num. 11:16). These teachers were charged with inspiring the congregation's hungry souls to live a spiritual life which still was lacking. The people were still slaves and not open to introspection and empowerment. The leaders needed to challenge them, and not respond to the slave mentality. They needed to become partners with the Israelites. The people needed to learn the blessings of the unique lifestyle which had been given to them. This way of life included ethics, compassion, warmth, and love which they needed to share with all the families of the earth.

In our own lives, we must also recognize the source of our complaints. Often our boredom is a result of giving up on the yearnings of our hearts and souls. We must dig deeper into what makes us feel alive and use our talents to follow a path that allows us to express our unique life force in our world. Then our complaints will fade away and our soul satisfaction will create gratitude and appreciation of the challenges and gifts of our lives.

May we all be blessed to seek honesty, awaken our life-giving energies, and give the world what we are meant to express in this life. Then we will leave the desert with renewed energy, clarity, and the optimistic will to live every day as fully as possible. Shabbat Shalom!

Shelach

This parsha describes the power of evil speech, *lashon hara*. The spies sent to scope out the Promised Land committed that sin when they brought back negative reports about the possibility of conquering the land. Was it ultimate subjectivity that affected their perception? Was it their great fear of freedom or their lack of faith?

We read the words of the 10 scouts in the text, "Let us make a ruler and return to Egypt" (Num. 14:4). Also, "We are like grasshoppers compared to the inhabitants there" (Num. 13:33), and "They have walled, fortified cities there" (Num. 13:28).

Our Sages say that this was not their failing! For, after all, we all have fears which affect our perceptions. Their sin was that they used their fears to speak *lashon hara* about the land (Num. 14:36), emphasizing the strength of its inhabitants, thus discouraging the Israelites from wanting to conquer the land. They defamed the land and that was inexcusable.

These descriptions all point to a lack of self-confidence and a projection of fears that affected the meaning of what they saw. Or was it a fear of losing their power in a new political reality that would be created in the land of Israel? After all, they were now princes of their tribes; would that be lost in this new land? The Zohar says (of Num. 13:28), "It was the desire for honor that was the scouts' undoing. A person who desires honor and recognition cannot tolerate being on a lower status than their friends. This caused the scouts (the princes) to slander the land and brought death upon them and their entire generation. For they feared their honor might be diminished when they would enter the Land, and others would serve in their stead."

These tribal leaders manifested a lack of faith and self-confidence. But is this sinful? We all lack confidence at times; why should they be punished for this? The Rabbis concluded their sin was not their lack of faith; the sin was spreading a bad report about the land to the Israelites. Instead of providing an unbiased report, they added their opinions, creating fear in the people.

Interestingly, the Kli Yakar says they failed because there were no women among the scouts to offer a contrary, hopeful opinion.

Had they left out the word but, they would have stayed within the limits of a factual report—a land flowing with milk and honey, powerful people, fortified large cities, etc. When they added the word but/efes (Num. 13:28), it was no longer a factual account and became an attempt to sway public opinion. "Yes. . . . But." An insecure person who feels ill at ease with their mission in life will often slander and malign those they sense are opposed to them.

Realists always point out the naivete of idealists, but sometimes the realists have subjective motives of which they are unaware. The path of faith is always a courageous one and can be perceived to be blind to objective reality, to facts on the ground. But one must not chastise the realists—instead, we must recognize and honor their reservations and doubts and help them deal with them. All of us have qualms, worries, and dread—often based on our experiences and our perceptions of reality. Therefore, Rashi and other commentators say the spies were not punished for their fears, but for speaking *lashon hara* and embellishing the facts to reach negative conclusions instead of letting the people develop their own opinions.

The scouts' original charge was to view the land and report back to Moshe and give a neutral, objective report: *v'yaturu et ha'aretz* (Num. 13:2). Instead they evaluated the land in terms of victory and defeat. They were defensive; they gave their opinion because they did not really want to go into this new land and potentially give up their leadership in a newly organized framework. And when they reported their perception, it was given simultaneously to Moshe and the people, instead of giving it to Moshe in private, and they devalued the land with their words. They said *efes*/but... (Num. 13:28), planting seeds of doubt in the minds of the people—and that was the sin.

The 10 scouts were not punished for their subjectivity or reporting what they thought they saw but for their defamatory behavior. For this, they were responsible. In their reporting, the spies exceeded their authority. The verse says, "They spread an evil report against the land" (Num. 14:36). There is no greater harm in a time of crisis than frightening people into believing they lack the strength to stand up to their ordeal. The moment people no longer believe in their strength, they are defeated.

Indeed, the scouts did not tell any lies, and even brought back wonderful fruits from the land, to show how good they were. But they essentially said, "Do you really believe that people who possess such a wonderful land will let us take it away from them? After all, if it were a bad land, people would not mind very much giving it up, and moving somewhere else. But it is a good land, and thus they will fight to the death to keep us out. Even if, in the end, we would succeed in conquering one of the kingdoms, we could not hope to stay there. The Negev is settled by Amalekites. The Jebusites live in the hills. Along the seacoast are the Canaanites. Besides, all of them have already developed strong identities and allegiances. We, on the other hand, have just been liberated from slavery; we have hardly had an opportunity to develop the resolve necessary to triumph over this major challenge."

Perhaps the development of their faith would only be attained by daily work on their experiences for years in the wilderness—not just by witnessing the wondrous miracles that saved them. Our memories may fade, but the daily encounters with life are what strengthen our resolve and faith. During the 40 years in the desert, a new generation would grow up and be nurtured with intensive study. They would grow up strengthening their faith and would no longer entertain any doubts about God's omnipotence.

The incident of the spies also raises a larger question about perception. How does anyone see objectively, unaffected by one's prejudgments and fears? Doesn't our sense of who we are affect our perceptions? Will we realize that there can be 10 separate opinions on any event or object that we perceive?

This question has plagued philosophers for centuries. The esteemed German philosopher Immanuel Kant believed that one knows that they are duty-bound to follow a "universal system of law" that resides within each person—what a religious person might call a *neshama*—but Kant does not identify the outer source that created that system. His solution was that this inner good will is the authority. We impose these laws upon ourselves, and we are only under obligation to act in conformity with our own will—a will which then leads to universal laws. He called this the "autonomy of the will," the supreme principle of a universal set of laws. The existentialist Jean-Paul Sartre stated that human beings are the creators of their own values. But whereas Kant believed a human being's will was the primary source of a universal system of laws, Sartre denied the idea of a universal law. Rather, he suggested that the basis of morality stems from each individual's subjective experience.

The British empiricist George Berkeley concluded that we are all subjective in our perceptions and this influences the way we see things. In physics as well, Werner Heisenberg's uncertainty principle acknowledges that our perception changes the reality of what we are seeing. Under the guise of being objective, we are often subjective, affected by our unconscious biases. Although the great philosopher Arthur Schopenhauer claims genius is the completest objectivity of the mind, Heisenberg's uncertainty principle limits the precision to that which we observe, since the observables are not independent of the observer. We bring ourselves to what we see and thus our distinctness influences what we think we see. Therefore, what we see can take on a range of values depending on the observer, instead of having a single exact value. We can move toward greater clarity through an effort to become objective, but we can never fully reach absolute truth.

This is similar to what the Sfat Emet says when he points out that our sublime task in this world is to achieve faith, because the achievement of complete truth is impossible. And, indeed, the world was created this way so that we are driven, galvanized, and inspired to work to keep increasing truth until we reach the messianic stage of complete knowledge of Hashem (Sfat Emet, Vayichi, end of Bereishit).

How does Judaism resolve this problem? Judaism's answer has always been the mutuality between a theonomy and autonomy. The supreme principle of the law, its ultimate source of authority, is the will of God. The interpretation of the law (and its application to the innumerable and forever-changing life situations) is autonomous. Theonomy liberates human beings from destructive relativism, and autonomy protects us from the idea that the law is absolute and cannot change over time, and allows us to responsibly interpret the law in every generation. Judaism's answer has always been the dialectic between Divine law and autonomy. The supreme principle of the law, its ultimate source of authority, is the will of God; the interpretation of the law and its application to the innumerable, forever-changing life situations is autonomous. This is how halakhah becomes part of human history. It partners the law with new historical realities and, through dialogue, aspires to reach the highest level of truth in every situation. This must be based on studying tradition, precedent law, and principles that allow us to respond to evolving developments in society. We must attempt to discern God's will, but, at the same time, we are allowed to interpret the Torah on many levels.

Of course, there is often tension between individual subjectivity and the objectivity of the law, but the tension is necessary. There is creative energy in the continuous unfolding of the law in the passage of time through which each generation and individual discovers the layer of meaning in the law that God intended. We discover the intended meaning in the fullness of our individuality, which falls within the framework of the written Torah and our oral Torah—the wisdom of our Sages who toiled in Torah all day and night. It does not seem plausible for God to judge us if we are subjective and influenced by our fears. It is more likely that we are judged by our actions, such as speaking *lashon hara*.

The problem remains, as I suggested above, that there is no such thing as the one will of man. There are innumerable subjective human wills and values. There is no person in the abstract. There are only people, and therefore innumerable value systems. Today we see this has degenerated into international decadence.

The distinguished Jewish philosopher, Eliezer Berkovits, articulates this beautifully in *God, Man, and History*. He says, "There is, of course, tension between the subjectivity of faith and the objectivity of the law. But the tension is necessary. It is the creative irritant in the continuous unfolding of meaning and contents. By means of the tension, each generation, and every individual Jew, discovers the layer of meaning in the law of God intended for him and her. Not all is given. The meaning intended for us must be discovered by us and made our own in the fullness of our individuality within the frame of the reality of our situation, in which our very subjectivity, too, has its origin."

We attain our greater objectivity when we are aware of our subjectivity! This develops humility, deeper self-knowledge, awareness, and greater movement toward ever-emerging truth. We all contribute to the evolving greater truth that emerges in a sincere search for truth through dialogue and faith. We become closest to objectivity when we are deeply aware of our subjectivity.

May we each continue the struggle to discover the seen and unseen dimensions of our existence, coming closer to faith and Hashem in the process. May we all be blessed to journey toward greater clarity and increased faith. May we each contribute in our own small ways to increase truth in the world and be open to the growth of the moment. May we see facts as we perceive them and allow for the opinions of others and not slander those who differ from us. I wish you all a fulfilling Shabbat filled with honest, open dialogue that leads to harmony. When differences emerge let us not try to convince others through our opinions, but allow the facts each of us sees to have a merry dance with each other's facts and respect each other's right to disagree. Shabbat Shalom!

Korach

*Any dispute for the sake of Heaven will have enduring value,
but any dispute not for the sake of Heaven will not have enduring value.
What is an example of a dispute for the sake of Heaven?
The dispute between Hillel and Shammai.
What is an example of one not for the sake of Heaven?
The dispute of Korach and all his company.*
—Mishnah Avot 5:21

In Parshat Korach, we find some core ideas that weigh heavily on our national psyche. The parsha begins with the words, "And Korach took...." (Num. 16:1). It does not say what he took, and thus the rabbis point out that his nature was to take, he was a taker—egocentric, narcissistic, and thus always wanting more, stemming from a woundedness that could not be satisfied. He tried to find satisfaction for his ego when he really needed to address his soul to find satisfaction and wholeness.

When "Korach took," says the Targum, it means "he divided." This happens when each person looks out only for themself and creates a world of strife (Sfat Emet). The opposite view is the view of wholeness, created by adhering to Torah values, based on *shalom*/peace. The spiritual attitude must be that we are all interconnected, part of the whole, connected to the One. By realizing our gifts are from Hashem, we become aware of even more gifts present in our world. This brings us to a state of gratitude, a way of seeing and being that leads to shalom, joy, and willingness to give to others.

But because of his ego, Korach and his followers rebelled, and Moshe responded harshly to their arguments. Why was Moshe angry? After all, at the sin of the golden calf, and the complaints about the manna (they lost their appetite for manna), Hashem and Moshe forgave the people. Also, in the case of the spies, Moshe asked Hashem to forgive them; even though he was dissatisfied with them, he did not wish for their physical harm. But in the case of Korach, he was unwilling to forgive. Why?

Under the guise of asking for democratization, Korach attempted to usurp Moshe's leadership. When he said, "You take too much upon yourself Moshe," Korach attempted to acquire power for himself. Korach continued, "For the entire assembly is holy, all of them, and Hashem is amongst them; why do you exalt yourself over the congregation of Hashem?" (Num. 16:3) After all, Korach was part of the Levite tribe, a leader in his own right, and a family member. Yet, Moshe chose Aaron to be the high priest, and Miriam had a major influence; so where was Korach's honor?

The Midrash says that Korach was a very wealthy man, the treasurer of Pharaoh. But instead of gratitude for his wealth as a gift from God, Korach attributed it to himself. The spiritual attitude that we are all interconnected, realizing that our gifts are from Hashem, brings us to a state of gratitude, joy, and the desire to give to others. And when this loving energy is present in the whole community, we all benefit. But this was missing in Korach. He did not understand that we each have a unique contribution to make; thus he was jealous of the position of the high priest, Aaron. This feeling of interconnectedness and of gratitude was embodied by Aaron, a "lover of peace" (Pirkei Avot 1:12), as opposed to Korach, who took only for himself.

Aaron's approach was to bring greater honor to Hashem in the world and to express love to God's creatures. This attitude is spiritual and not egocentric. It brings peace to our world. It is different from the attitude of Korach, whose attitude was: "May *my* will be done and then I will recognize others." This leads to great strife in the community. Korach's orientation against Moses and Aaron was based on his own needs rather than what was best for the community.

Moshe fell to the ground (Num. 16:4), feeling shamed and disappointed. After serving the people selflessly for many years, he was shocked that they were able to be manipulated by an impostor, a fraudulent deceiver, in which 250 men were naively taken in by his rhetoric. It is tragic but true that people can follow a charismatic leader with practiced charm serving his needs and leading to disastrous ends (Milgram, *Obedience to Authority*).

Moshe may have understood the complaints, and so he invited Datan and Avirom to meet with him. He even went to them and was rebuffed. And so Moses counseled the community to distance itself from Korach (Num. 16:26).

Moshe's leadership was not based on personal honor but rather on the stewardship of the community, which required humility, openness, and respect for others. Yet Korach and his cohorts were not willing to listen. Therefore, there was no possibility of reconciliation or rehabilitation. It was insulting and arrogant, and a strategy they decided would lead them to victory. Their attitude was not one of discussion, but a delegitimization of Moshe. This is what made the discussion Moshe yearned for impossible and raised his ire. That's why Moshe had to uproot Datan and Aviram! When there is no willingness to talk, there is just a continuation of controversy which leads to eventual destruction. To prevent a greater evil, Moshe decided to end the resulting plague immediately.

Moshe carried out his duties with dignity and loving-kindness. He realized that differences of opinion and civil discussions were both inevitable and desirable in a community. They served to promote expanded truths in the collective; the path of free expression is one that leads to peace and progress. Our entire Talmud is an aggregate of diverse opinions expressed and heard by different Sages.

When human beings are not willing to speak to each other, to communicate the hope for peace, reconciliation becomes impossible. This similar plague is prevalent in our communities today and in the larger world. It is the source of great fear and pain in our daily reality. This occurs within our families, such as when those who were vaccinated against Covid were at odds with family members who chose not to be. We see Israelis and Palestinians unable to come together to communicate, and Democrats and Republicans who refuse to compromise and sacrifice their optimal goals for a lesser goal that may be achieved. All of these examples manifest the inability or unwillingness to have productive, relational interaction that may lead to greater peace.

Through giving rather than taking, the soul is opened up and satisfied. Feeding the ego inevitably leads to more desire and dissatisfaction. And yet all of us have ego needs, bodily needs, needs for love and affirmation from others. But this has to be balanced by self-love, self-acceptance, and feeling God's love in a circle of faith leading to meaning. This becomes a great challenge if, as children, we are either deprived of love or overindulged. We then are either hungry or always expecting an affirmation from others that is impossible to achieve.

Korach's trait of taking was his downfall. It expanded to an aggressiveness that destroyed the appropriate boundaries of the community and was a challenge to legitimate leadership.

Today, the campaign of White Nationalism, couched in religious terminology, under the guise of patriotism and wholesomeness, attempts to polarize the American people to the point where no compromise is possible. Each side wants victory over the other. It is an argument of rightness rather than an attempt to find greater understanding on both sides. Moshe astutely recognized Korach's evil intent and his evil character, and became angry. This was righteous anger, necessary anger, to assert and make clear that our leaders must uphold the highest moral and ethical standards and not use their office for their selfish benefit. Moshe did not do this to save his honor, but because Korach created controversy and a potential reversal of all the values and progress that were being developed in the desert. Moses had to uproot this controversy instigated by Korach.

This is one of the tragedies and dangers of the human condition that must be recognized; not ignored, but opposed. A dictator, a demagogue, immune to morality, can only produce tyranny and painful destruction. Tragically, their followers are generally gripped by inertia, and not inclined to oppose the group leader. They would rather seek the favor and the security of the group instead.

In Pirkei Avot, our Sages defined two types of arguments: the specious arguments of Korach—which lead to division and destruction; and the genuine arguments of Hillel and Shammai, which lead to harmony and growth (Pirkei Avot 5:17). If one party in an argument has selfish motives, it usually becomes acrimonious. Only when there is some common ground shared by the parties, and a willingness to listen and learn, can a dispute produce positive effects. When each person has the attitude of only looking out for themself, it creates a world of separation, a world of strife. The absolute certainty of one's point of view, and the delegitimization of the partner in the dialogue makes pluralistic endeavors and resulting peace impossible.

There is also a divergent opinion among our commentators criticizing the lack of empathy in Moshe's response to Korach. After all, Korach too, was from the family of Levi, and it is understandable that he might feel wounded that he did not get any official appointment from Moshe. Moshe did not understand Korach's pain (ego wound). Therefore, Moshe was punished and not allowed to enter the Holy Land. The same words used by Moshe in our parsha to Korach

(Num. 16:7) "*Rav lachem*/It is enough" are the same words God said to Moshe as he was about to enter the Promised Land (Deut. 3:26). This interpretation affirms the importance of empathy, unity, and connection in order to heal.

True peace can only be brought about when different voices are heard and respected. When one party asserts that it knows the "whole truth" and refuses to talk with the other, peace is impossible. When there is no real attempt to engage, no respect for the other, then separate, self-absorbed entropic groups are created. Each one owns its own truth. They deny that arguments are essential, or that they add to truth.

Insecurity and fear of change rule this outlook. Without communication, progress is impossible. Diversity of opinion, rather than homogeneity, is essential for progress. Fine-tuning our ideas, being willing to change our opinions, expanding our views, and yielding to new realities uplift our world. Without respectful dialogue, there is only continuing anger, war, and destruction. People who only speak to their own groups, stubbornly imagining assured victory, prevent potential peace, which can only be achieved by getting to know the other and thus developing some empathy. It is victory, rather than compromise, that becomes the goal of this attitude—an attitude that is prevalent in so many areas of our communities and our world today.

We must embrace the path of faith, reach out to others, and make sure the voice of Korach does not destroy the social fabric that we are mandated to create. We can reach out to others to create communities of love and interaction, ruled by the highest ideals we are capable of reaching with faith, struggle, and the blessings of Hashem.

Each person has a unique purpose and contribution, and there is no reason to be jealous of another's purpose and path. This value must be reflected in our entire community to make a positive impact on our world. This was the greatness of Aaron, the lover of peace, as opposed to Korach, who took for himself.

The Netivot Shalom cites the Zohar, which states, "The world only exists fruitfully when it is ruled by the principle of shalom, wholeness, interconnectedness. What Hashem detests the most is *pirud*, disconnectedness from each other. The Torah is filled with the value of peace, as nothing flourishes without the value of peace, as it says, 'It is a tree of life to all those who grasp it, its ways are ways of pleasantness and all its paths lead to peace'" (Proverbs 3).

The Zohar makes it clear that argument for the sake of achieving a selfish goal, even when pronounced in a way that suggests you are arguing for the greater good, creates a separation between above and below, and therefore the punishment is very harsh. It is only through the elevated perception of unity that the nation connects to above; when unity is absent, the nation loses this connection. Our Sages teach that our people were worthy of receiving the Torah at Sinai because at that moment they were like "One people with One heart" (k'ish echad b'lev echad).

Because of this holy moment of oneness, of true recognition of our interconnectedness, and our task of making this world a world of love and beauty, they were worthy to become a kingdom of priests and a holy nation. When they severed this connection, the Holy Temple was destroyed. And thus, the Zohar states, "Whoever creates disunity, attacks God because God's name is Shalom." Just as loving your neighbor as yourself is the most important principle in the Torah, the blemish of strife is the most egregious sin in the Torah.

Korach's arguments came from a lack of faith, not striving for peace, and by forgetting our interconnectedness to others. This is how hatred emerges— when we base our decisions on insecurity and selfish needs instead of what is beneficial for the larger community and the world. It is the perception of unity that leads to clarity of what is needed for peace and justice.

If we can live each moment not in a state of entitlement, but in one of limited privilege or a temporary opportunity to participate in life as part of the whole blessed creation, we absorb the energy of Moshe. Our charge is to live on earth as brothers and sisters, responsible to our whole family and as caretakers of the earth.

As Jews, we have the additional responsibility to study and share the values and practices of the precepts of the Torah to remind us of God and our gifts on this Earth, and to treat each other with love. It takes effort to become conscious through the study of Torah and to think differently; it is not easy to think from a spiritual perspective with the goal of creating peace, rather than seeing all of life from the point of view of "I am the center of the world." That's the way of Korach. We must think of ourselves not as a principal actor, but as a part of the whole, as part of unity, of shalom.

Looking at the birds, at the world beneath the sea, at the mystery of the cosmos, we must conclude there is more than the "I" that surrounds us! Let us wake up this day to reject the way of Korach, and choose the path of Moshe. And make it so! May we all join together to bring the Great Peace to our world. Amen.

Chukat

In Parshat Chukat, we read of the complex law of the red heifer/*parah ad-umah*. The introductory verse has a unique, emphatic way of introducing the law by saying, "This (*zot*) very law is the decree (*chok*/statute without a rational reason) of the Torah" (Num. 19:2). Why such emphasis on its importance? One Midrash suggests the red heifer comes to rectify the sin of the golden calf. The Jewish people had come to sin with the golden calf because they attempted to ascertain a knowledge of God that was beyond their grasp. They wanted to obtain a simple, secure connection to God obviating the mystery of the ways of God. They tried to find a fixed model of God in an idolized calf, a God they could control and rely upon, denying God's beyond rational mystery.

The Midrash says that when Moshe ascended to the Heavens, he heard the voice of Hashem teaching the angels the secrets of the *parah adumah*. This law is so puzzling it baffled the minds of the wisest people, including King Solomon! Yet, though it transcends human comprehension, and while every attempt to explain the law fails our rational capacities, the law remains. The mystery of the red heifer lies in this paradox: The ashes of the heifer placed in spring water cleanse the unclean, but defile the priest who performed the ritual (while it purifies the defiled, it defiles the pure). Perhaps the remarkable lesson is this: The paradox of the *parah adumah* exists in everything we do. We are all filled with paradoxes!

Simultaneously each one of us is both purified and contaminated, cleansed and defiled, essentially filled with opposites! Moreover, we can transform and elevate the most basic of impulses to an act of sanctification, or we can drag it down to the basest behavior. We can turn the skin of an animal into holy parchment for a Torah scroll. We can transform a table into an altar, food into sacrifice, or we can degrade the same food and throw it in the garbage while others starve.

The *parah adumah* is filled with innate contradictions. Quite often seemingly opposite feelings and ideas coexist within us as well. Sometimes when we feel sure of ourselves, we still feel uncertain about the outcome. We can feel righteous and highly motivated when we take on a new endeavor, yet we try to reinforce ourselves to ensure the success of our goal. Sometimes we stubbornly hold on to something in our minds without letting it go. Sometimes we hesitate and do not act, waiting to see whether something turns out well, and only then do we proceed.

The human spirit and intellect can and must concurrently acknowledge enduring the opposites. The tension of the opposites is part of the human condition. Enduring this tension, appreciating the positives of each side of the conundrum without obviating or repressing them, can often lead to creativity, growth, new insights, new balance, and new integration.

The complex laws of the red heifer become a constant reminder that there is a limit to how far our minds can reach. The laws of the red heifer relate to how we must behave in our encounter with the ultimate mystery, that which is beyond our rational grasp: the reality of death. Thus, it is no arbitrary choice that these laws, relating to purification from death, are labeled a "decree," a law beyond reason. As the text suggests, this decree, this incomprehensible law, relates to the incomprehensibility of death, and yet it must be followed. We must be able to live with death, and with all that we cannot comprehend fully, affirming our faith by following the *chok* (and all *chukim*—laws beyond our rational comprehension) that are commanded. It is the fact of death, of absence, loss, and non-being which makes our existence so difficult to comprehend. Life necessarily demands that the laws governing our contact with death are somewhat paradoxical, and cannot be fully understood.

The goal of the ritual of the red heifer is to nullify the way death touches the deceased's relatives and to help them accept death as a mystery beyond comprehension. Thus, the paradox of the ritual is, perhaps, to teach us that purification from death requires jumping to a non-rational place. The theme of death becomes reality in our parsha, since Aaron and Miriam die in its chapters.

Another possible reason for this law's importance is found in a midrash telling the story of Moshe ascending to heaven, where he heard the voice of Hashem teaching the angels about the *parah adumah*. Why does this mitzvah assume such an exalted place before Hashem? Many other mitzvot are called *chukim* as opposed to *mishpatim*—laws based on accessible reasoning. Yet this one *chok* is singled out as *Zot chukat hatorah*. (This is the law of the Torah). What is the importance of this particular *chok*?

And why, when every attempt to explain the law fails, does the law still remain? Perhaps the paradox itself is the secret! For the paradox of the *parah adumah* resides in everything we do. We are filled with paradoxes—with opposites! This revealed fact is most important to grasp and allows us to proceed even when confronted with mystery. It is a deep lesson for us!

At the same time, we are purified and contaminated; cleansed and defiled; filled with myriad opposites. We are also beings who can reach wholeness. This is the human condition, the world of "bet-duality." It is a *b'racha*/blessing leading to growth as we wrestle with discovering our opposites and our inner world. Through these discoveries, rather than fighting against these phenomena, we can transform and elevate our most basic impulses to acts of sanctification. If we ignore our complex proclivities, we may be led to act out and allow ourselves to degrade our holiness.

The *parah adumah*, filled with innate contradictions, teaches that we are all filled with innate contradictions (as Walt Whitman said, "I am all"). Quite often, seemingly opposite feelings and ideas coexist within us. Sometimes we may feel sure of ourselves; a moment later we feel uncertain of the outcome. We can feel righteous and highly motivated when we take on a new endeavor, yet we may also try to ensure the success of our goal. At other times, even when we feel hesitant and uncertain, we forge ahead with our plans with faith and resolution. We trust that opposites are part of the journey, and trust Hashem's wisdom in creating us with opposites in order to probe deeper and discover the clear path. The opposites may blend together harmoniously, complementing each other, to produce a more profound understanding and outcome. Both confidence and caution can dance together, creating something new—a new song; a whole heifer.

The verse assures us of this when it says, "Take yourself a red heifer, whole and unblemished." This suggests that when we become aware of our complex proclivities, we must be aware that beneath the polarities we are whole and unblemished. God made us just the way we need to be, capable of reaching wholeness, always loved by our loving Creator. The challenges along the way are for the benefit of our growth, and we must always remember, "God has created the world for the sake of kindness" (Psalm 89:3), and not for self-flagellation. The evil in the world that seems so contrary to God's nature, obscuring God's Presence, becomes a veiled messenger of healing to be attained by our spiritual power. True love and gratitude may be born in the hearts of each of us.

There is another puzzling incident in our parsha that occurs after Miriam dies in the wilderness of Zin. She was the source of the people's water; with her death, a severe water shortage occurred. Moshe, perhaps for the first time in his career, did not know how to deal with the crisis. Confronted by heated demonstrations, he retreated to his tent and fell on his face. Hashem ordered him to "take the rod" and go back to the days of his youth when, with the rod in his hands, he would rise to overcome many crises. He was to talk to the rock and bring forth water. But instead of showing the strength of dignified leadership, Moshe lost his temper.

God told Moshe to speak to the rock before the eyes of the people so it would give water to the assembly to drink. But Moshe angrily says to the people, "Listen now, O rebels, shall we bring forth water for you from this rock?" Moshe then raised his arm and struck the rock with his staff twice; abundant water came out and the assembly of people and their animals drank.

But the Lord chastised Moshe for striking the rock instead of speaking to it as he was told to do.

Moshe, who had known how to face stormy situations in the past, who had previously set an example of how to treat his flock firmly but respectfully, lost his equanimity. Thus, he could not be the leader anymore. He would not be able to steer the people to the Holy Land. From the trauma of losing Miriam, he lost his spiritual energy and zest.

The Rabbis debated about the egregiousness of Moshe's behavior that would warrant the severe punishment of him not being able to lead the people into the Promised Land. Some Sages say this relates to the expression of anger and impatience by a highly respected leader of the people. As the role model that everyone looked to—every word and action of his was scrutinized—his behavior might lead the people to think that anger is okay. Or they might think that God was angry with them. The Sages suggest dignified leadership requires great patience; a leader should not be emotionally reactive. Anger might be appropriate in some situations, but it can lead to distortion in a given situation. Anger does not lead to discussion or to the potential sanctification of God's name. Therefore, leaders in particular must avoid rage as a direct response or a reactive gesture. Anger is only appropriate when done with a conscious motive, as it was with the golden calf, where Moshe broke the Tablets of the Law and was not punished.

Rav Levi Yitzchak of Berditchev says there are two types of rebukes: one that uplifts people and one that downgrades them. The difference between the two is that one who rebukes with good words raises the soul of the person to a higher level, always indicating the great potential of the human being. Such a person is worthy of being a leader in Israel. But one who rebukes with harsh words is not worthy of their position. This is why God said to Moshe, "Because you did not believe in me to sanctify me, you will not bring the people into the land."

Another creative interpretation is that Moshe's inability to lead his people into the Promised Land was not a punishment at all, but a necessary change for the sake of the people. Miriam's and Aaron's deaths were very traumatic for him. The complaint of severe water shortage happened right after Miriam's death, a terrible blow for Moshe. It was only then that he realized how dependent he was on his big sister, the one who, when he was still an infant, stood with a heavy heart on the riverbank to make sure her little brother would not drown. He probably did not realize until she died how much he needed the support of his close family circle in his dealings with the people. They had been a natural trio—Miriam, Aaron, and Moshe. Now it had ceased to exist.

Our parsha also includes one of my favorite teachings in the Torah—the teaching of the secret of healing (Num. 21:4-10). We read that as the people continue their journey to the Promised Land, they again complain, "Why did you bring us up from Egypt to die in this wilderness, for there is no food and no water, and our souls are disgusted with the insubstantial food." As a response, God released fiery serpents against the people. They bit the people, and many died. Moshe prayed for the people, so God instructed Moshe to build a copper serpent and place it on a pole. Anyone who was bitten would look at it; they would be cured, and live (Num. 21:9).

This is a message of healing! To heal we must look past the symptom (the bite) and get to the root of what ails us. We must examine that which bit us; face it, acknowledge it, feel it. Only then can we grow and heal. That which bites us is also the source of our healing—if we can truly face it. The symptom awakens us to what needs to be addressed. It is a blessing if we have the strength and wisdom to see that all God brings to us is a blessing—if we have faith to know this and pursue the path of healing, even if it includes facing pain.

If we do not, the symptom will recur in many ways. For the Jews in the desert, the same complaints came up repeatedly, until they faced their fears. Only when they investigated their anxieties and complaints to reveal the source of their discontent and woke to the fact that God was with them did they learn that faith is possible and that life can become a blessing. As is the principle in, that which bites us is the source of healing when we use our power to reflect and extract its blessing. Israel learned that the source of life and death is God, and that which bites us also heals us.

As human beings with hearts and souls, we have the capacity to look at that which needs healing and use our tension points as that which must be faced, bringing our renewed energy to our world. We can use faith as a motivating force to move beyond insensitive behaviors such as perpetuating racism and xenophobia by standing idly by and not helping our brothers and sisters. We must look boldly and honestly at our past lack of action and do our share to heal our world, joining people of all faiths and creeds to work for justice and sustenance for all. Facing our behavior will be the first step in moving higher and higher toward a world of bright Light, song, and celebration for all who share our world.

May we all experience a healing from the obscuring darkness that raises its head and demands our conscious response to the hatred and intolerance that still darkens our world. Amen.

Balak

Balaam and Balak are the stars of this parsha, characters in a very complex story. It is one about the power of the human mind to rationalize fulfilling one's worst impulses. Perhaps the story will highlight an internal alternative trait that allows us to attain clarity and lead us to a deeper knowing that goes beyond the complex, impressionable mind that has not yet gained deep self-knowledge or training.

Our story unfolds as Balak, the king of Moab, summons his prophet Balaam and begs him to curse the Israelites, as they are too mighty for him to defeat in battle. The tribes had just defeated the Amorites, occupied the kingdom of Bashan, and were now camped along the Jordan River, close to Moabite territory. As a result, they were growing in number and power. Out of fear, Balak enlisted Balaam to curse them. He said to Balaam, "For I know that whomever you bless is blessed and whomever you curse is accursed" (Num. 22:6).

What were the deeper roots of Balak's hatred and what might it teach us about the roots of antisemitism? Perhaps Balak is fearful because of the Israelites' faith and their values of freedom and honor of the individual, and he thinks his people will desert him and join them. He may have discerned their faith in God. Their values of redemption for all people might lead his people to rebel against him. His commitment to power and domination led him to perceive the threat of the Hebrews and he decided to destroy them. Their spiritual presence was a threat to his earthly presence (power), and the logic of God's redemptive presence meant the downfall of the wicked and evil at the hands of the Israelites.

To be fully redemptive means conquering evil. That is where God's name is sanctified. Balak trembles and hates the Israelites and never mentions them by name. Hitler, too, writes in his diaries that the Jews introduced democracy and conscience into this world, and that made him feel unfree. He refused to accept Jewish-inspired morality and way of life in Western Civilization; he succeeded in killing 60 million people in World War II, 10% of them the Jewish people.

Jew-hatred is hatred of God's redeeming presence, and other people's hatred of people who are not like themselves, hatred of the different others who seem threatening to their way of life. Therefore, these different people must be wiped out. Some in our tradition state that only the Messiah can relieve the fear and loathing of the Jew-hater. *Eisav Soneh et Yaakov*—the enemies of the Jews will be eternal, until the Era of Peace.

Throughout history, there have been many different reasons for antisemitism. There has been religious antisemitism—hating us for not accepting the Assyrian religion; Caesar and the temple in Rome; the Christian savior Jesus as the Messiah. Ensuing religious hatred spread, for centuries, throughout Europe. This religious conflict was experienced in Muslim countries as well, and during the Inquisition, the blood libels, the pogroms in Russia and Poland, and, of course, during the Holocaust.

Another reason for antisemitism is jealousy—manifested by libeling the Jews as Shylock money-lenders who control the economy of the world as bankers and heads of governments, or media manipulators. Another phenomenon was seen in post-Enlightenment intellectuals who labeled the Jews who left the ghettos as dirty, uneducated vermin. The Jews were hated for being too powerful or too weak; for being non-believers or being too pious. They were also hated as the Chosen People, "dwelling apart" (Num. 23:9), separating themselves from others—wrongly believing the reason for this was that we think we are superior to them. Jews are often perceived as being restrained by the laws of their religion which control our daily life in all its phases, so Judaism itself is a barrier separating Israel from the other nations, causing them to live apart.

Throughout the parsha, Balak and his messengers never mention the Israelites by name. They are called "the community" (Num. 22:4), "the nation that has left Egypt" (Num. 22:5), "this nation" (Num. 22:6), etc. Not once does Balak mention the Israelites by name. This is his way of dehumanizing them. The victims of all racists remain nameless. Moreover, when Balak wants Balaam to curse Israel, he takes him to a place where he can only see part of the nameless people. Conversely, when Balaam sees that God wants him to bless the Jewish people, he shifts his viewpoint so he can see the entire nation.

God told Balaam, "You shall not go with them. You shall not curse the people, for they are blessed" (Num. 22:12). But Balak continued to send higher-ranking emissaries who told Balaam that Balak would honor him greatly if he fulfilled Balak's request. Balak was apparently aware of Balaam's greedy and arrogant nature and assumed that by sending higher emissaries and suggestions of ample reward, Balaam would eventually agree to his request.

Balaam refuses again, for he will not transgress the word of Hashem even with the promise of gold and silver. But, after a time, he weakens and is driven by his greed to try to fulfill Balak's request. He becomes desirous of this great wealth and says, Let me check with God again. God tells him that he may go to Balak but he may only do what God will instruct him. Balaam tells the emissaries that God has said that he may now go. But he leaves out the condition attached—that he may only do what God will tell him to do. He does not indicate that he may be bound to give a blessing. He lets the emissaries believe that he had been given permission by God to curse the Israelites. He deceived them because he was so driven by his greed. The warnings of Balaam's intuitive donkey, who sees a fiery sword in their path as impending danger, are ignored in the face of Balaam's lust for the promised wealth that Balak offers.

The Mishnah states that Balaam's nature was characterized by three traits: an evil eye, an arrogant spirit, and a greedy soul (Pirkei Avot 5:19) The Talmud, elaborated upon by Maimonides and Abarbanel in their commentaries on Mishnah Avot 5:19, suggests that a greedy soul refers to Balaam's obsession with sex to the extent that the Talmud states he had intimate relations with his donkey! (Sanhedrin 105a-106a).

As the story proceeds, Balak's ongoing promise of increasing riches prevails and leads Balaam to succumb to the temptation of cursing the Israelites and rationalizing it, although initially he was clear it was the wrong thing to do. As we are tempted by riches and other benefits and our minds weaken, clear perception succumbs to temptation. Our mind rationalizes, our will wavers, and we may give in to the baser impulses of our nature.

How do our Sages teach us to choose the right path? What can we rely upon? Torah study, discipline, and desire to do the right thing in the eyes of God are great antidotes to selfish needs. But our parsha gives us an additional constructive aid to bolster our clarity and foster our perspicuity, with the tale of Balaam's donkey.

When Balaam sets out toward Balak, God sends an angel with an unsheathed sword to block his path (Num. 22:21-34). The donkey, untarnished by ulterior moves and moved by pure bodily instinct, was able to see the angel; while Balaam, dominated and manipulated by his agitated mind, could not. The angel blocked the donkey's path three times.

The first time, the donkey veered off the path and Balaam hit him. The second time, the angel stood in a narrow walkway; when the frightened donkey moved to the side, Balaam's foot was squeezed against a fence. Again, Balaam hit the donkey. When the angel then presented himself, on an even narrower path in which there was no place to turn, the donkey settled down on the ground, only to be hit a third time by an angry Balaam. It was then that a great miracle occurred. The donkey spoke! He rebuked Balaam for embarking on his journey, a rebuke to which Baalam was unable to respond.

Finally, God permitted Balaam to see the angel, who asked him, "Why did you hit your donkey three times?" Balaam replied, "I have sinned for I did not know that you were standing opposite me on the road. In my confusion, I was not able to hear your voice."

While Balaam went on his way to curse the people, his donkey hesitated and sensed danger ahead. The donkey's instincts and his body contained deep wisdom, simple wisdom, something we humans can also rely upon. "Monkey mind"—the wavering of our minds in the face of complexities, blatant self-interest, and thinking that we can get away with bad behavior— overcomes our initial instinct to do the right thing. The donkey teaches us to trust our bodies and our hearts to reveal truths far more reliable than the rationalizing mind.

Balaam attempts to carry out Balak's charge to curse the people three times. He, like Balak, never mentions the Israelites by name when he curses them the first two times. He says, "This nation," not Israel. This is his way of dehumanizing them. It is only in his last attempt, when he blesses them, that he calls them Israel. (Num. 24:1-2). Earlier, he can only see a part of the people: "He saw the outer edge of the people from there" (Num. 22:41). When you only see a part of a person and not the reason they behave in the way they do, you judge that person and curse them. You will see their edge and not their entirety. One must see the whole context to find compassion, as we see it happen the third time Balaam sees them and God's spirit comes over him (Num. 24:1-2).

Often, we give up what our instincts and our hearts tell us—when money, prestige, honor, and recognition are served to us on platters to convince us to do something we do not want to do even though we know it is wrong. Our bodies, our intuition, reveal a more reliable truth if we are trained to listen to their voices. "Hear O Israel! The Lord Our God, the Lord is One."

The whispers of the infinite, of the deepest holy path, are always singing to us if we learn to listen to the soul within. This is a genuine, reliable guide to fulfillment, enlightenment, and the confident path that God always opens to us—if we are willing to listen to it. It will not lead us astray, just as the holy words of the Torah rise to guide us to holiness. Perhaps ESP, bodily wisdom, the wisdom of the belly instead of the rationalizing mind can be trusted when we are faced with a major decision. Perhaps trusting our bodies is imperative when our minds are bewildered by conflicting choices. Perhaps the body knows. Our animals may own wisdom from which we can learn. They can often sense danger and that which can be trusted when we cannot.

Balaam was so blinded by greed that he could not see the danger lurking ahead. The instinctual animal, the donkey, was able to perceive truth with his instinct, more so than a human being whose mind is easily distorted and thus often prone to err.

Can we learn to trust our instincts more? Can we learn something from the animals with which God blesses us? We must learn to balance instinct with our minds to use all our God-given qualities. We must pay attention to our bodies. They can inform us of truths our minds refuse to see. Rav Avraham Yitzchak Hacohen Kook once said that the return to Israel, to the land, enabled the yeshiva student to rebalance the overemphasis on full-day learning through working the land and imbibing its blessings. The integration of body and mind brings us to a wholeness that cannot be achieved by trusting the mind alone. The mind can be a fickle instrument when tempted by wealth, fame, or flattery.

As Balaam gained clarity and reconnection to the prophetic voice within, he recognized this with the blessing he gave in place of the curse. "How goodly are thy tents O Jacob, thy tabernacles O Israel" (Num. 24:5). Amen.

212

Pinchas

Parshat Pinchas causes us to confront many complex moral issues and allows us to grow through our study of Torah. It also opens a door to understanding the principle of change in Jewish law. May we be blessed to continue to do so and grow closer to God through our study.

This parsha is the story of Pinchas (the lover of peace) from the priestly family of Aaron. It took place when the Israelites made friends with the people of Moab and Midian and began celebrating their gods with sexual rituals and generally had intimate relations with them. To punish the Israelites, God sent a plague; 24,000 of them died.

During the plague, Pinchas sees two people—Zimri, an Israelite man, and Kosbi, a Midianite woman—having sex in public. In a radical, extreme act, he flings his spear at them and murders the fornicators who were publicly and brazenly acting out in the camp. The verse says that his act restored the *Brit Shalom*, the covenant of peace in the community. However, our Sages point out that the writing of the Hebrew letter *vav* in the word Shalom in our Torah scroll (Num. 25:12) is intentionally broken to indicate that violence never leads to complete peace.

You might think Pinchas would himself be punished for killing two people. But Hashem tells Moshe that Pinchas, through his zeal and courage, ended the plague when he ended the bacchanalia. God says, "I give him my Covenant of Peace, because through his zealotry he ended this orgy, restored the values of a Godly community and made atonement for the Children of Israel" (Num. 25:13).

When plagues are present, humans who stand up for righteousness can change conditions and create healing. Pinchas witnessed the power of immoral pleasure introduced to the Israelites by the Midianites, behaviors he felt would be hard to eradicate—behaviors that would be in constant danger of re-emerging. He had to convince God's people that what they thought was a tempting pleasure was really a threat to their very existence. He shocked them with his stunning murderous act to save their legacy and their purpose in this world.

In the Talmud, our Sages said when Pinchas the Zealot slew Zimri and Kozbi, he did break Torah law (Yerushalmi Sanhedrin 9:7), but what he did was permissible because his motives were pure. Their proof was that God sanctioned him and said Pinchas restored peace among the Israelites (Num. 25:11-15). This momentary impulsive act by Pinchas murdering the participants, this violent act, should not be interpreted as normative or a path to peace. It is an exception due to extreme circumstances, for violence usually leads to reactive violence, revenge, and deep darkness.

Pinchas would have been guilty under the normal adjudication of the law, but because God rewarded him, we learn that at times the law can be changed for the larger benefit of the community, especially when one's motives are pure (Sanhedrin 82b).

Michael Walzer, in his classic book *Exodus and Revolution*, notes that in every revolution or march toward progress, there comes a crucial moment when a resistant crisis must be addressed or the revolution will fail. Must it take radical extreme action to eventually move forward again? Can there be a more moderate educational intervention that would achieve the same end?

In this parsha, a hostile reaction blemishes the blessing of peace. The removal of the Hebrew letter *yud*, one of the letters of God's name, from the name Pinchas (Num. 25:11) suggests an ambivalence toward his violent response. Many sources in the Torah and oral tradition make it clear that peace comes from peaceful action; Pinchas' act was an aberration, an anomaly. Perhaps he thought it was necessary and appropriate to address acts of desecration, but his action was not to be defined as a normative intervention in the pursuit of peace, and it did set a dangerous precedent for zealots to break laws for their causes. The cycle of violence and retribution does not make any of us safer.

The Netziv, the esteemed biblical commentator (1817-1893), suggests that Pinchas' characteristic personality trait was his enormous commitment to making our world more just and peaceful. He may have acted impulsively at the sight of the orgy and felt obligated to respond with murder. If he hadn't done that, there may have been a complete breakdown of the Israelite community and their connection to God and Torah. More deaths would have occurred if the immoral behavior were allowed to continue. Ultimately, Pinchas was blessed by God with the *Brit Shalom*.

Sforno posits that Pinchas' action and his zealous devotion were motivated by compassion for his brethren. He wanted to stop the plague that raged among them because of the orgy (Sforno, Num. 25:11,13). The thought of his brothers perishing was his driving motivation. The term zealot is usually associated with an angry, rebellious individual acting violently toward others under the banner of religious conviction. Many zealots in our own day have taken the story of Pinchas as justification to commit violence in the name of God. But Pinchas was overwhelmed by his intense love for his fellows and concern for the well-being of the community. His act saved countless lives. When we feel motivated to act zealously to protect others, it is different from the common usage of the term zealot. It is taking a risk, making a self-sacrifice for the sake of saving the lives of others.

Although the egregious, extreme act of Pinchas may elicit an intense re-action from anyone who reads the story—some with outrage, and some with resigned understanding (a volitional affirmation of the obligatory)—there is a much less volatile intervention in our parsha that achieved an important change in the society and is the preferred model in our tradition. This is the story of the daughters of Tzelafchad (Num. 27:1-11), which illustrates a very powerful, benign, and effective protest model to achieve change.

Our parsha tells us the five daughters of Tzelafchad protested to Moshe that because the laws of inheritance are passed down only through sons; they argued that the laws were discriminatory and excluded the sisters from inheriting their father's property. After hearing that only men were counted in preparation for the distribution of land, the daughters complained that because they had no brothers, their family would be without land. Because they stood up for justice and their cause was right ("Justice, justice, shall you Pursue" — Deut. 16:20), Torah was changed to include the rights of women to inherit.

God affirmed that the women's holy assertion saw what Moshe did not see: that they were entitled to their father's portion. We see here that a just and insistent protest by a small group of women can be as powerful as the action of Pinchas, and indeed is more in the spirit of the Torah than violent intervention. The verse states that this new law the women demanded is a decree of justice (*chukat mishpat*—Num. 27:11) and that the power of justice can supersede an ancient law that needs revision.

These two incidents (Pinchas, and daughters of Tzelafchad) illustrate an important principle that resides in the system of Jewish Law (halakha) and its ability to adapt and continue the spirit of the law in new circumstances. Our tradition understood that as time passed, new realities and insights would arise to necessitate new decisions that would obviate previous precedents, and lead to the changing of the law. This principle is built into the legitimate process of adjudication, which includes an obviation of a biblical mandate when necessary to expand God's law. Of course, it is to be done very carefully, thoughtfully, and with the wisdom of the scholars of the law. This principle of acting outside of the boundary of law in the face of extreme circumstances is found in several sources in our tradition, based on the scriptural passage in Psalms 119:126. "There is a time to act for the Lord and void the laws of the Torah!"

The Talmud, in Berachot 54a, explains that Ezra, the prophet/priest, proclaimed the name of God in full to exalt God in the national assembly as the people returned from Babylon (1 Kings 19). This contradicts the law which forbids pronouncing God's full Holy name outside of the Sanctuary. Ezra felt he had to do it because the occasion was unprecedented; the people returning from Babylon were determined to start a new chapter in Jewish history. In fact, at that time, in 6 BCE, they became known as the Jewish people. Ezra had to create a new law for that hour, an hour of holy inspiration, and so he spoke the name of God in its fullness. The original law was meant to be observed at normal times in the life of the people. But this unique hour called for a unique expression, and so he violated the law.

This process of obviation does not relate only to laws of divine service. At times it is permitted to suspend a biblical law for an action that is altogether humanly social. For example, in the Mishnah in Brachot it says that one is supposed to greet one's fellow person in the name of God, just as Boaz did in his fields. This is in contradiction to the biblical law, "Thou shalt not take the name of God in vain" (Ex. 20:7). But as Rashi explains, "At times one abolishes the words of the Torah in order to do for God" (Psalm 119:126). Here, where one's concern is for one's fellow, one is doing the will of God. For it is written, "Seek peace and pursue it" (Psalm 34:14). It is permissible to bypass the Torah and do what appears to be forbidden (Berachot 54a).

Another example shows the economic pragmatism of the Rabbis. Regarding the law of *Shmita*, Rabbi Yannai says to the people, "Go out and sow in the seventh year because land tax has to be paid to the non-Jewish authorities." The Rabbis were fearful the people would be fined if they didn't pay their taxes. If the fines were not paid, the people could have been imprisoned and killed (Tosafot), or they may have been fined and part of their land taken from them, causing economic hardship. Therefore, they allowed people to work the fields during the seventh year, although the Torah says it is prohibited (Sanhedrin 26a). The rabbis also allowed interest to be taken on loans (even though the Bible prohibited interest) because people were refusing to give loans to others (*Prusbul*, Talmud Gittin: 34b-37b).

The law also says all debts are canceled during the *Shmita* year; but because this edict made it very difficult to obtain loans (for fear debts would not be returned to the lenders), Hillel created the edict that at *Shmita* all loans were to be turned over to the courts of law, and the courts could collect them. Thus, people who needed loans could continue to earn a living. The edict here gives priority to ethical sensitivity and allows a pragmatic and moral intervention that may overrule the original law. This principle is built into the legal system to ensure that the evolving system is humane. The Sages must adhere to this principle, even with the tension of opposite claims and precedents.

Another example of overruling a biblical law is related to Yom Kippur. One of the five prohibitions of the day is not to bathe. But the rabbis permitted brides, during their first month of marriage, to bathe on Yom Kippur so they should be beloved to their husbands—a case of moral sensitivity (Yoma 73a).

Yet another example is the famous incident of Elijah confronting the 450 Prophets of Baal on Mount Carmel (1 Kings 18). The prophets who worshiped the idols of Baal worshiped their god with sacrifices on the mountain. The people of Israel were restricted to offering their sacrifices in the Holy Temple. At that time, the people of Israel were ambivalent about the worship of Hashem and cast an eye toward Baal. Elijah proposed to the prophets of Baal that two sacrifices should be brought on Mount Carmel, and the god who would answer the call by sending a fire to consume one of the sacrifices would be deemed the true One God.

Elijah, because of the importance of the hour, overlooked the law that said that sacrifices must only be brought in the Holy Temple and agreed to bring the sacrifice on Mount Carmel. The Bull of Baal was slaughtered first and placed on the altar. The prophets of Baal called out all day for Baal to answer them. But nothing happened. Elijah built an altar and slaughtered a bull, at the time of *Mincha*, the afternoon offering. He stepped forward and prayed to be answered so the people would know that Hashem is the true God. A Godly fire came down and consumed the entire offering. The people fell on their faces, and cried out, "The Lord God He is the God!" This became another example where the principle "There is a time to act for the Lord and void the law of the Torah" was cited.

In the Torah itself, three biblical laws were never carried out: 1) the law of bastardy; 2) the law of the rebellious son; and 3) laws relating to the city of idol worship. The rabbis, through their creative logic, made them impossible to carry out and they were never meant to be applied. Why were these laws written down to begin with? The rabbis say, "To interpret them and to receive reward from God for studying them" (Sanhedrin 71a).

We can readily see from these examples that the Torah gives priority to ethical sensitivity and allows pragmatic and moral interventions that may overrule the law. This principle is part of the methodology built into the legal system to ensure that the evolving system remains humane.

So many more examples of the dynamism of Jewish Law can be given. In the meantime, we are given the opportunity to continue our lifelong study of Torah. We can infer from these few examples that a humane halakha dwells in the Torah's essential nature when used with integrity and for the betterment of the people. It is the most potent antidote to fundamental zealotry. The Sages of each generation are charged to deduce new particulars of laws appropriate for new situations. There are times when the law can be obviated (temporarily or for a longer period) because of a new reality. This is the power given to the Sages, and to all who make the effort to do serious study of the adjudication of the law. They are "turn it and turn it" so it remains the living energy gifted to us in order to create a society of justice and peace. With this responsibility comes great power and great responsibility to use this power to make the law live in each generation.

May we be blessed to benefit from a living, evolving, humane law that uplifts all humanity and contains the glory of God. We human beings, created in God's image, are mandated to concretize this gift throughout history, and especially in our day.

May we all be blessed to listen to the inner holy voice, to our instincts, to our hearts and souls, and recharge ourselves to heal the world, to reach out to our neighbors with love and care, and to bring joy to the world! Amen.

Matot/Masei

*"If you are on a journey, and the goal gets farther and
farther away, then the journey itself is the goal."*
—Joseph Campbell

In the double parsha of Matot/Masei, we read about the journey from *Mitz-rayim* to the Promised Land. This journey contains 42 stops, in physical locations not easily recognizable, before the Israelites reached the Jordan River. Our mystical masters discerned that this was not a physical journey at all. Rather, it was the outline of a spiritual journey from a place of restriction and brokenness toward a progression of greater wholeness, to a discovery of soul and connection to God. The number 42 is symbolic of the Holy name of God. *Eh'yeh asher Eh'yeh* ("I am that I am") as revealed to Moshe at the Burning Bush. *Eh'yeh* in gematria is 21; the double name is 21+21=42. Thus, this spiritual journey is one that leads to connection with the soul.

What are the secrets of this journey toward wholeness? What is the purpose of the separate mentioning of each stopping place? It shows a manifestation of God's kindness. The purpose of these wanderings was to rehabilitate the former slaves morally and spiritually, equipping them to enter the Holy Land with strength. Each stage of the journey is lovingly named. Just as the Israelites went through 42 stops along the journey, our commentators suggest that each of us go through these trials and growth steps in our lives.

Each of the 42 encampments was a stage in the growth of the nation. Each stage of sanctity the Israelites acquired in the desert was brought with them to the land of Israel. This journey reveals the universal truth that spiritual achievement is a lifelong excursion filled with challenges until we reach the "promised land." Each of us goes through our own 42 stops, just as our ancestors did in their growth toward maturity. Each of us starts with childhood experiences which we repeat until we take responsibility for our lives. The long and weary progress of the Israelites through the wilderness is a paradigm of this truth. And the separate mention of each camp illustrates the importance of each individual step in the journey. Each stopping place has value.

In each place, we learned something and grew. Our own lives, and the trials we face and from which we grow, confirm this. Accordingly, it is the journey, not the goal or destination, that is emphasized. In the history of the spirit, it is the painful, seemingly endless process toward sanctity that is the essential part of our growth. The journey of 42 stops in the desert allowed our people to experience struggle, and to see the part that was self-created as well as its origin, and why we cling to it.

The journey awakened them to self-knowledge and to greater meaning. Our attitudes and actions recreate realities. Faith is developed in the midbar (desert); it manifests a deep belief that life's experiences need not be over-whelming, because they will all move toward greater integration, held in the framework of helping others, of giving hope and meaning to the struggles against loss and pain. Suffering becomes a bridge to interaction with others. "Hashem Echad" becomes palpable as we realize we are all connected in this life, each one of us a unique part of the whole.

The journey begins in Mitzrayim and continues in isolation in the desert. As we move forward, we gain greater insight and understanding, but not completion. We stumble along the way and often regress. The wholeness must be brought back into society until we wind up in Arvot Moav—to the 42nd stop, Eh'yeh—the plains or "mixture" of Moav, connoting interdependency and connection. Everywhere, there is imperfection, incompleteness, and unrealized ambitions. But from the spiritual perspective, this was no deterrent at all. Each motion of the heart toward God is cherished and valued for its own sake. "We are not responsible for completing the task, nor are we free to desist from beginning it" (Pirkei Avot 2:16).

"Each of us is born into the midst of things and dies in the midst of things," says Rav Dessler (Michtav Me'Eliyahu). Just as the Israelites went through the process of growth, each of us encounters trials that bring us to growth and discovery of our unique purpose, and we feel blessings of gratitude for our creation.

Journeys are the nutrients of our roots. Abraham left the world of his father, "Leave your home and go to a land which I will show you" (Gen. 12:1). His destination was not specified. Moshe treks through the desert but never reaches the Promised Land. It was the journey, the willingness to sacrifice, to move ever onward in search of God, that was demanded and treasured as the archetypal spiritual adventure. This realization brings optimism and true wisdom. We all go through the Exodus from Egypt, the 42 stages, to reach Eh'yeh (wholeness).

As we proceed through our lives and meet their challenges (each one a stop on our journeys), we emerge with greater consciousness as we continue our passage through life. There is, of course, a natural comfort in the mind's capacity to forget the fearful past, the trials, the so-called failures. But this consolation would be questionable if loss of memory also leads to loss of the insight gained from the trial and the gratitude for successfully passing through it.

We have the freedom to create new meanings, especially to open ourselves in times of pain to the roots of our compassion. When we cross the bridge from self-protection to compassion and self-knowledge, we change the world. Without human suffering, it is not likely we would ever find that bridge. Our suffering and our actions bring us to conditions that provide just what we need to awaken greater compassion and consciousness. It enables us to overcome our wish to be in control—which sets us apart from others.

This life is assigned especially for our learning, for awakening, for consciousness, and for repairing our world. So, everything is just as it should be if we do not resist it, and pain has its purpose—to awaken us to questions of meaning and purpose in life. We also must learn to step back from creating our own suffering. Without this capacity, we are cast morally and spiritually adrift.

There is a difference between a spiritual and a material journey. The latter emphasizes results and efficiency; the former focuses on process and effort. A material journey mainly measures results and efficiency; the less effort needed to create a product, the better. The act must be completed to achieve its goal, to have an impact. Effort as a value has no meaning in the material quest. The more one can reduce effort or streamline the project, the more successful it is.

The spiritual journey differs from the material journey. It differs in its goals and in the very process and values attached to each movement toward the goal. The effect of intention alone is considerable. The process toward the achievement is valued, as well as the awareness that develops through the journey. It is not as interested in the goal as an end in itself. Sometimes the goal even gets in the way and inhibits alertness and awareness of our reactions.

The sincere purposeful movement of spirit affects our inner lives and the universe. The spiritual journey is about effort, awareness, potential, and a meaning that often develops through suffering. Effort has significance and value. It honors sincerity and the inner life even if the final achievement is not reached. In spirit, each moment has value. A smile brings forth another smile! The movement of the spirit, sincere and purposeful, affects the inner life, even if the final achievement in the outer world is lacking. It is the journey toward wholeness that is meaningful. As our Sages teach, it is the effort that God adores, not the result. The latter is in God's hands or in variables beyond one's control, and the disappointment of not reaching one's goal has more to do with our ego's desire than our soul's nascence.

The long weary progress of the Israelites through the desert is a paradigm of this truth. And the separate mention of each of the camping stages illustrates the importance of each individual stage in the journey. Achievement alone is not recorded here in the history of the spirit; rather, it is the painful, seemingly endless process toward sanctity that is recited. Each motion of the heart toward God is cherished and valued for its own sake. The biblical imperative to remember the triumphs of the past as well as our trials and violations teaches us that we learn from so-called failures. We recognize that they contribute to our insight and growth, and acknowledge with gratitude their necessity.

Another ingredient in the spiritual process is pain (l'fum tzaara agra). Why is pain necessary in this spiritual process? After all, it can depress and inhibit us. Yes, there is pain that leads to regression and suffering, but there is also pain that leads to growth.

Two forms of suffering lead to depression, separation, and alienation. One form is deflation, and the other is inflation. Deflation is when we feel "less than," and inflation is when we feel "better than." In our early history, we experienced both forms of suffering. First, we were slaves in Egypt, which led to powerlessness (deflation), a feeling of not believing in self-power, dependency on others, and giving power to them to solve our problems instead of taking responsibility for ourselves. God's intervention, leading us out of Egypt, led to a sense of specialness, of entitlement (inflation), with high expectations and the inevitable disappointment and resentment that often follows. Inflation may create despair, resentment, envy, and self-pity, interfering with our discovery of meaningful compassion as inflation enlarges our self-importance.

But there is also a positive dimension to pain. The pain may lead to alertness and a need to search for reasons for it, leading to finding potential meaning and reaching out to God, or to a secular spiritual path. Suffering is often the first opening we have into deep curiosity about what is going on around and within us. Suffering leads to questions of meaning and purpose in life. This propels us into opportunities for development. Although we may resent the pain and hate those whom we blame for it, we cannot learn about ourselves without it.

When we become conscious of why we suffer, and how we continue to be responsible for our suffering by acting from our childhood place, we find self-knowledge, compassion, creativity, independence, and meaning. A larger spiritual meaning always gives context to our suffering and growth. We move from the seclusion in the desert and arrive at Arvot Moav, the last stop, a place of mixture and interdependence. The journey begins in the desert in isolation, reaches wholeness, stumbles—because the wholeness has to be brought into society, and finally winds up in the plains of Moav.

Our Sages suggest we each go through these 42 challenges until we reach enlightenment. We must face our deflation, powerlessness (our *Mitzrayim* remnant), and the remnant of inflation where our great expectations throw us off balance. This inflated feeling becomes a barrier to development when we regard it as more important than what stands before us. When we insist on our inflated fantasies as the "chosen ones" redeemed by God, we are flooded by feelings of resentment and self-pity for not achieving inflated fantasies. We also may allow this inflation to deride, exploit, and harm others.

This clinging to the past psychic remnant creates the kind of suffering that is debilitating and inhibits growth. This type of suffering interferes with our potential to change. It may take 42 steps till we finally use the suffering in a positive way, to use the pain for transformation, to reach a place where we can find a larger context for meaning. This permits us to translate deficits and losses into potential for new development. We can no longer maintain the façade and hang on to false hopes. The suffering finally forces us to create a new attitude and a change in outlook, to translate losses into future potentialities, and to recognize that the past is behind us. Each of the 42 stops was necessary to move us in this direction. Each stop necessitated another experience of growth we had to master. Our psyches are so complex; they ferociously want to hang on to the old and not embrace the new until we make progress along our journey with all the mishaps along the way. These mishaps become our teachers. Thus, not only our joy, but also our suffering, becomes our teacher.

Sometimes it is a trauma or a crisis that moves us forward, but for many of us, it is the daily grind of facing life's challenges that promotes our growth. Often it is when we open up to others, acknowledging the beauty of the human beings that we meet that we begin to feel grateful and connect to a larger secure home base, something beyond our own ego needs. We begin to feel part of the whole, interconnected, under the blessing of God.

We truly live when we let go of our old selves. To engage in life, we must "die" many times. Our people went through 42 death and renewal experiences at each stop. We can then see with fresh eyes; discovery becomes available since we don't habitually look to reactively and obsessively impose old meanings on things.

Jews believe that there are reasons for our life circumstances and that our fate is an expression of a principled universe. We can accept and discover meaning even in loss and trauma, in encounters on all levels of existence. We must understand how and why adversity can sometimes lead to transformation and at other times lead to only more suffering. How can it lead to a sense of purpose? Through new self-awareness and insight. Indeed, we may learn from both good fortune and bad fortune. Yes, bad fortune can be a means to shape and strengthen our character. We must pay less attention to what is happening to us and more to our own reactions to it. This will make sense out of pain and teach us to see it as a new opportunity for development, a new learning experience. We must reduce our intense focus on goals and pay attention to the present; we must make a full effort to be open, to be in the flow—alert, calm, and focused. And remember, an attitude that allows us to learn from every experience brought to us by God is a requirement. Thus, faith makes life less stressful, and makes it a blessing.

However, it takes more than pain or trauma to bring about the death of an old self; it takes a change of attitude—action, effort, courage. We change the world with movement from self-protectiveness to compassion and self-knowledge. Without human suffering, it is unlikely we would reach the promised land of wholeness, compassion, and connection to others.

When we become conscious that we are all on a spiritual journey, we will move from a state of habitual wanting to a state of habitual having. We will discover that we are parts of the whole. We will then move from ego-consciousness, the sole pursuit of pleasure and material gain, to soul-consciousness. From *Mitzrayim*, ego-boundedness, and the whining "why me?"

to enlightenment and meaning. To become vulnerable and to use pain for transformation, we must expand and support our desire for growth and clarity within a larger context of meaning. This is usually in a spiritual context, whether religious or secular, and it permits us to translate deficits and losses into potential for new development. It is important to realize that when we let go of our expectations and wishes—our old selves—then we will discover something new. We truly live in the present!

If we do not do this ourselves, a crisis or pain can shake us out of our habitual attitudes and demand we change. At this point, a supportive community can help us in our growth journey. Resistance to this growth journey is created by our wish to be in control, just as the Jews tried to deal with their trials in the desert. Only when we stop ourselves from imposing old meanings on our actions can we encounter something new. We must not move compulsively from one thought to another, but allow ourselves to be free to look at the serendipitous events that always surround us if we are awake to spirit. Our Sages teach that this life we are living was designed especially for us, containing lessons that are not arbitrary, but quite personal. Our tradition informs us that all life is a journey from which to learn and it contains a benign core.

Until we take responsibility for our own subjective lives, we repeat the same mistakes we learned in our childhood, blaming others for our faults. When we face our greatest fears directly, we will discover that we have more courage than we ever imagined. Our difficulties, our trials, will become the sources of our development. We can then move from the *Midbar* to *Arvot Moav*, from uselessness to useful suffering. Along this spiritual path lie the gifts that lead us from pain and separation to transformation and connection, to self-determination. We will retain the ability to extract meaning from each of our experiences. We will see ourselves as the authors of our own stories. We will look in the mirror and see our capacities and potential as beings created in the image of God. When faith emerges, we will believe that life's experiences cannot be overwhelming, because we have discovered God in this extraordinary journey called life. We will discover that the determined soul is on a spiritual journey, the same path that our ancestors took. We can then, from our suffering, create a coherent story of unity, purpose, and compassion.

The three weeks before Tisha b'Av begin this week. It is a most appropriate time for growth and to embark on our journeys from ego-consciousness to soul-consciousness, from *Mitzrayim* and separateness in the Midbar, to integration with others in Arvot Moav. Tisha b'Av is the birthday of Moshiach—on that day God and God's name will be One.

Wishing you all great success on your spiritual journey! Shabbat Shalom!

DEVARIM
Deuteronomy

Devarim / Tisha B'Av

Tisha B'Av, the Ninth of Av, is considered the saddest day on the Jewish calendar. Many disasters throughout history befell the Jewish people on that day. These include the destruction of both the First and Second Temples; the First Crusade in 1096; the first expulsion from England in 1290 and from France in 1306; the expulsion of Jews from Spain in 1492; and on June 22, 1942, the Great Deportation from the Warsaw Ghetto to Treblinka also began on Erev Tisha B'Av. We read Parsha Devarim every year at this time, on the Shabbat before this somber anniversary.

Some also regard Tisha B'Av as a day of hope. Tradition teaches that on this day the Messiah is born. The purpose of observing this fast day is to direct ourselves to the causes attributed to these terrible disasters and transform ourselves to create a reality worthy of the messianic realm. This new reality is always potentially accessible.

On every fast day we are given the charge: *Va'aneetem et nafshoteichem*, typically translated as a need to afflict our souls on that day. But the word *Va'aneetem*, usually translated as afflict, can also mean answer. Therefore, Tisha B'Av can also be a call to answer the call of our souls. Our souls know how to bring out the best of our deepest spiritual potentials, and it is our duty on this day to make the time to listen to our souls!

At night, when we begin the observance, we read the book of Lamentations/Eicha attributed to our Prophet Jeremiah as he walked through the streets of Jerusalem, lamenting the pain and suffering in the wake of the Babylonian invasion of 586 BCE. The book begins with the words, "How lonely sits the city …that was full of people." The word how/*eicha* contains the same letters as the word *ayeka* which means "where are you?" That's the question God asks Adam in the Garden (Gen. 3:9).

Where are you in relation to yourself, to your as yet unfulfilled potential? This is a time to reflect and awaken to the Call of your Soul, to contribute to the world's transformation. It is important to also recognize that Jeremiah does not give up hope in our ability to fulfill our calling with the help of God. As he says in Lamentations 3:21-25, "Because of the Lord's great love we will not be consumed, for God's compassion will never fail…. The Lord is good to those who hope in the Lord, to those who seek the Lord in truth, God's tender mercies will be renewed every morning."

In Yoma 9b, the Talmud asks, "Why was the First Temple in Jerusalem destroyed [in 586 BCE]?" The answer? Because of three evils in the Jewish community: idolatry, promiscuous immorality, and bloodshed. … Why was the Second Temple in Jerusalem destroyed in 70 CE, when during the time it was extant, people occupied themselves with Torah, with observance of mitzvot, and with the practice of Tzedakah? Because during the time it stood, baseless hatred, *sinat chinam* prevailed! The Sages teach us that *sinat chinam* is deemed as grave as "the three sins of idolatry, forbidden sexual relationships, and bloodshed together." Such is our complexity! The same heart that can genuinely love some people can simultaneously harbor unwarranted hatred toward other people (the opposites). This hatred is so poisonous that it can lead to the destruction of a whole community.

This type of hatred is illustrated in the Talmud and related by Josephus in the story of Kamtza and Bar Kamtza—the word *Kamtza* is from the root *kemitza* which means separating, suggesting a culture of dividing rather than uniting (Maharal, Netzach Yisrael, Ch. 4-8).

This is the story:

"There was a certain wealthy man whose friend was named Kamtza and whose enemy was named Bar Kamtza. He made a large feast (by invitation only) and said to his servant: 'Go bring me my friend Kamtza.'

"The servant went and mistakenly brought him his enemy Bar Kamtza. The man who was hosting the feast came and found Bar Kamtza sitting at the feast. The host said to Bar Kamtza, 'You are my enemy. What do you want here? Arise and leave.'

"Bar Kamtza said to him, 'Since I have already come, let me stay and I will give you money for whatever I eat and drink. Just do not embarrass me by sending me out.'

"The host said to him: 'No, you must leave.'

"Bar Kamtza said to him: 'I will give you money for half the feast; just do not send me away.'

"The host said to him: 'No, you must leave.'

"Bar Kamtza then said to him: 'I will give you money for the entire feast; just let me stay.'

"The host said to him: 'No, you must leave.' Finally, the host took Bar

Kamtza by his hand, stood him up, and took him out.

"After having been cast out from the feast, Bar Kamtza said to himself: 'Since the Sages of Israel were sitting there and did not protest the actions of the host, although they saw how he humiliated me, they must have been content with what the host did! Perhaps the Sages wanted to remain in the good graces of the host or were afraid of opposing him. I will therefore go and inform the king against them.'"

"He went and said to the emperor: 'The Jews have rebelled against you.'"

"The emperor said to him; 'Who says that this is the case?'"

"Bar Kamtza said to him: 'Go and test them; send them an offering to be brought in honor of the government and see whether they will sacrifice it.'"

"The emperor went and sent with him a three-year-old choice calf. While Bar Kamtza was coming with the calf to the Temple, he made a blemish on its eyelids, a place where, according to Jewish law, a blemish is not acceptable as a sacrifice. But according to the gentile rules for their offerings, it is not a blemish. Therefore, when Bar Kamtza brought the animal to the Temple, the priests would not sacrifice it on the altar since it was blemished, but they also could not explain this satisfactorily to the gentile authorities, who did not consider it to be blemished.

"The blemish notwithstanding, the Sages thought to sacrifice the animal as an offering due to the imperative to maintain peace with the government. Rabbi Zecharya ben Avkolas said to them: 'If the priests do that, people will say that blemished animals may be sacrificed as offerings on the altar.' The Sages said: 'If we do not sacrifice it, then we must prevent Bar Kamtza from reporting this to the emperor.'

"The Sages thought to kill him so that he would not go and speak against them. Rabbi Zecharya said to them: 'If you kill him, people will say that one who makes a blemish on a sacrificial animal is to be killed. As a result, they did nothing, Bar Kamtza's slander was accepted by the authorities, and consequently, the war between the Jews and Romans began.

"Rabbi Yochanan says: 'The excessive scrupulous ruling of Rabbi Zecharya ben Avkolas destroyed our Temple, burned our sanctuary, and exiled us from our land.'"

The Gemara continues, "It is taught, Rabbi Elazar says: 'Come and see how powerful the damage of hurtful shaming is, for the Holy One observed this deep humiliation of Bar Kamtza and due to this deep spiritual insensitivity, this plague of indifference, this breakdown of ethics, this shattering of intimate communion, this pernicious, corrosive, attitude is far more egregious than the superficial sacrificing in the Temple. Behaving with baseless hatred toward others is contrary to the most essential values of Judaism. Thus, due to this deep humiliation and the ceaseless behavior of *sinat chinam* prevalent in the community, God destroyed and burnt the Temple" (Yoma 9b.)

Anyone who studies the story of Kamtza and Bar Kamtza is shocked by the extreme hatred that drove the host of the banquet to forcibly evict his enemy, Kamtza, in full view of the entire community, despite Bar Kamtza's pleas to be allowed to stay and pay the cost of the entire affair, the host had him forcibly removed from the room. This, according to our Sages, is symptomatic of the disease of *sinat chinam* that was widespread among the people during that time (Gittin 55b, 57a).

The destruction of the Second Temple also stands out for moral reasons—*sinat chinam/lashon hara* among them. A statement in Bava Metzia 30b quotes Rav Yochanan, "The Temple was destroyed only because the judges ruled in accordance with the strict letter of the law, as opposed to ruling beyond the letter of the law." The scholars had become so insensitive that the embarrassment of a human being was less important to them than the offering of a sacrifice according to all the technical details of the halakha. They witnessed this disgraceful public embarrassment without protesting. This bystander passiveness, this reticence to offend the rich, this callousness, created a wound in Bar Kamtza that led to Exile and the total destruction of Jerusalem and the Second Temple.

In Shabbat 119b, we find several more explanations: The Temple was destroyed because the people desecrated the Sabbath; they did not read the *S'hma* in the morning and evening; they neglected the education of schoolchildren; because the small and the great were made equal in their eyes, causing disrespect to the learned amongst them; because they did not know how to correct others with sensitivity (Lev. 19:17) and they did not know how to receive correction with grace and appreciation.

Jews were living in separate enclaves/*agudot*, speaking *lashon hara*, gossiping, judging, belittling, and disparaging those who were not in their communities. This habitual lack of respect and honoring of others was obviating their soul journey of uplifting the world through love. The Chofetz Chaim wrote that the *lashon hara* that evolved from *sinat chinam* was the most egregious of all sins.

What have we learned from the actions of our ancestors? Do we indeed behave differently today? Do we allow the influence of wealth, the protection of those in power, to blind us to the commandments to act justly and lovingly toward all human beings? Are we too frightened or insensitive to stand up and do what is right instead of currying power from the elite?

Are we any different? Do we sit as helpless bystanders while Haredim and outsiders continue to hate each other? Do we stand idly by as *agunot* (chained women whose husbands refuse their divorces) wait endlessly for their freedom, suffering while "Sages" refuse to find a way to free them? Do we work tirelessly against poverty, homelessness, racism, and climate disaster, as loving human beings are expected to do?

Obviously, we are still afflicted with this insidious proclivity. We see the symptoms throughout our communities and throughout the world. Rather than expressing our opinions as just our own opinions and making room for the opinions of others, we express our truths as the only truth—which leads to animosity and baseless hatred of the other. We must become more aware of our behavior and rectify it. Our Sages were so sensitive to this egregious behavior, that they stated that even not speaking to someone because of ill will is considered *sinat chinam* (Sanhedrin 27b). Avoiding someone because of resentment, even without displaying strong hatred is also *sinat chinam*. We must make the effort to express our feelings directly, honestly, and humbly so as not to harbor ill will, which will grow if not addressed.

Our inability to connect with others, the baseless hatred that often defines our communal culture must be faced and overcome; *sinat chinam* is entirely incompatible with a revealed presence of God. We need to commit to practices and rituals that bring us together. We need encounters and interactions to foster the sense of communal *chesed* and communal togetherness. How can we create a community that ensures that everyone is uplifted? How can we create a renewed commitment to our soul calling, to the godliness within ourselves? Doing the mitzvot is what allows us to live for something larger than our own personal needs, to feel God's presence.

Our Torah encourages us to expand our world of compassion and embrace and include others, manifesting our inner godliness in this world, and discovering the very same godliness and potential that exists within others. We must not just mouth these values but live in such a way that actualizes these values. When we proclaim how much we value caring social behavior, but then describe others who are different as *those people* or complain about having to spend time with a particular person or group, we are hypocritical and (apparently) unconscious of our own prejudices, fears, and judgments.

Only when we transmit and demonstrate lived examples of love for each other will we truly heal the world and truly allow God to dwell among us.

There are two major suggestions by contemporary Sages that lead us toward a path of redemption. First is the suggestion of Rav Soloveitchik who explains that the word Eicha/How did this happen? is intertwined with the word Ayeka/Where are you?) in Genesis 3:9. This implies that to repair the current devastation and insensitivity in our world, we must investigate where we are—where are we in our responsibilities, in our consciousness, in how we see ourselves. Where are we in relation to others who differ from us in their points of view and practices, and how they treat us? Where are we in the pursuit of peace, unity, and working for justice? Are we beginning to realize that it is the judgment and disrespect of others that caused the destruction of the Holy Temple?

Let us learn not to repeat the sins of the past. From the ashes can come redemption, if only we would learn love for one another rather than emit hatred. The suffering of Tisha B'Av can awaken us to a new way of being.

This is not easy. We all face the tension between our minds and hearts, between our discipline and our desires. We all have conflicts at work and in our homes, between our authentic feelings and the need to conform to the demands and opinions of the groups to which we belong. Yet, at times like Tisha B'Av, when we confront ourselves and our tradition, there can be an opening to change and a commitment to the honesty with which we must conduct our lives. We can embark on our spiritual journey to discover the Divine which is truly prevalent in our world and in ourselves—only if we are open to it. As mentioned above, our tradition tells us that on the day of Tisha B'Av, the day of destruction, the Messiah is born. The darkness and the ashes force us to awaken and create the world we are meant to create and actualize the talents and gifts Hashem has bestowed upon us.

The second major exhortation by our contemporary Sages that leads us toward a path of redemption is the path of Rav Avraham Yitzchak Hacohen Kook, of the Chafetz Chaim, of the Ibn Ezra, and of the Netziv. They all say that the antidote to sinat chinam is ahavat chinam; hatred for no good reason must be replaced by loving for the sake of love.

Rav Kook taught us that ahavat chinam/unconditional love is the hugely powerful, constructive counterforce that must be harnessed to transform the destruction of hate. What does this mean for our everyday lives? What does unconditional love imply in terms of our actual behavior? Rav Kook elaborates in his poetic way:

> The heart must be filled with love for all. The love of all creation comes first, then comes the love for all humankind. It is Israel's destiny to serve this holy task of abundant love for all. And it is to be expressed in practical actions, by pursuing the welfare of those we are bidden to love and to seek their advancement. It must embrace every single individual regardless of differences.
>
> This is, of course, a major challenge for us to achieve, due to the complexity of our nature, filled with opposites.... Much effort is needed to broaden the love for people to the proper level. It is essential to understand the characteristics and lifestyles of different groupings and nations to know how to base our love of humanity on foundations that will readily translate themselves into action.
>
> The narrow-mindedness that leads one to view whatever is outside a particular nation as defiling, is a phase of darkness that undermines the effort to reach that state of spiritual development whose dawn is awaited by every sensitive spirit. The Torah's moral teaching, its commandments, good deeds, and studies, have as their objective the achievement of universal love that can spread and be available to all realms of life. (Middot haRayah:1, 2)

Rav Kook suggested that we are each capable of loving our fellow human beings, recognizing them as created in God's image. We are all interconnected sharing this gifted planet with others in order to give to each other our gifts and build a messianic world of peace and justice. How? By getting to know one another, which creates empathy and intimacy. We can only discover the beauty of another by communicating and relating to one another. We must not be satisfied with the illusion of dwelling with stereotypes, as if we know another when we have never broken bread with our fellows. We must overcome our fear and discover the solution of *ahavat chinam* by having the faith that every human being is deserving of our love and gifts. In this way, we can build societies that can coexist in a dignified way, in a way that honors and protects life in all its splendor.

A Holy Temple cannot endure in a generation that professes *sinat chinam*, disunity, and division amongst ourselves and separates itself from those in need of our care and deep humanity. The Talmud states, "That any generation in which the Holy Temple is not rebuilt is considered as if it had destroyed it" (Yerushalmi Yoma 1:1). This suggests that if we have not rectified the causes that resulted in the destruction, we perpetuate the darkness that continues destruction in our world. In our generation, we have the potential to address the causes of *sinat chinam*, heal the pain in the rejected other, and identify the place within ourselves where we have not addressed our inner resentment and ill will. Let us discover the deep love that is contained in our hearts and bring it to others.

In my opinion, the plague of *sinat chinam* is the most egregious condition that we must address in our generation. The Sages in different generations read different moral lessons that can be learned from the destruction of the Temples. In the Talmud (Shabbat 119b) many of the suggested causes are highlighted as lessons for their day. They read into the tragedy lessons which they thought the people needed at the time. Over centuries, the rabbis read into the past the faults of the present. Thus, some of the causes given may not be true in fact, but nevertheless are valuable lessons to be learned.

Let us listen to our souls to discover the very lesson we are meant to learn on this day and use our insights to help heal our world. Listen/*va'aneetem* and discern/*ayeka* your unique discovery and bring your revelation to our world. We are all in this together, and it is imperative that we build a world worthy of the Third Holy Temple. May this be so!

May we be blessed to move toward a healing of our world. Our holy loving Creator has given us the talents and capabilities to transform our world into a blooming garden of love and caring for all its inhabitants. It is our ultimate responsibility. May we succeed in doing so quickly in our day. Amen!

Va'etchanan

According to the Sages in the Midrash, if the Jewish people would keep only two Shabbatot, they would be granted redemption. Why do the Sages not stress that we should observe every Shabbat? One of our Rabbis comments that this saying refers to two special Shabbatot: Shabbat *Chazon*, the Shabbat before Tisha B'Av; and Shabbat *Nachamu*, the Shabbat following Tisha B'Av when we read Parsha Va'etchanan. In other words, if we succeed in living our lives according to the lessons of these two Shabbatot, which are linked, we will be living lives that are redemptive and meaningful.

The second Shabbat, Shabbat *Nachamu*/comfort (named after the beginning words in the Haftarah taken from Isaiah 40:2, "*Nachamu, Nachamu Ami*") reminds us that all this misery has not been the end of our existence. It shows that we can find comfort to sustain us, and to help us overcome every conceivable misfortune and ensure our future survival. We remember from the beginning of Jewish history how our father Avraham was forced to leave his family, bereft of property and protection. Yet in the end, he became prosperous because of his faith in the future, and in the destiny that God had promised him. The same thing happened when the children of Israel were in Egypt. They started as an assembly of tribes and even became slaves. But they had faith in the Lord and in Moshe, God's servant. They followed Moshe through the wilderness and in the end became a prosperous nation.

The same story has repeated itself over and over again, even in our lifetime. A people persecuted and decimated in a world war, a people destined for annihilation and disintegration, has succeeded in creating the State of Israel in the face of enormous and continuing challenges. This theme continues—and yet it prompts a bitter question: Is it really necessary that we should always suffer destruction before we can rebuild? Why does there have to be a Shabbat Chazon before a Shabbat Nachamu? Why should there be destruction before consolation?

Perhaps one suggestion is that we as human beings tend to become blasé and forget to express gratitude. Unfortunately, we forget the source of our gifts when things go well. We operate under the illusion that we alone are the source of our success and forget the fact that the reason we have gained this success is due to more than our efforts. We forget to express gratitude to God, an attitude that leads to the love of God and inner happiness. Thus, sometimes it takes setbacks in order for us to develop this attitude of appreciation for what we have when we regain it (*nachamu*) and develop the proper attitude of faith that is expected of us and that ultimately benefits us.

We are responsible for our efforts, but the success of our efforts depends upon many interactive dimensions beyond our control with the blessing of our Creator. When we only experience success, we get angry when we lose something. We assume we have the right to it and forget it was given to us and is never absolutely our own. Indeed, we may never have learned to be grateful when we received this gift. Raised in abundance, we expect abundance. Often, we are much more grateful, appreciative, and empathetic to others when we have been raised with challenges. The rabbis suggest that if I am angry at God for losing something, I should not forget to praise God for all that I once had. All my possessions are really on loan to me, and this consciousness enables me to truly appreciate them and express gratitude when I regain them.

That is why Tisha B'Av—and perhaps any type of suffering—can be viewed as an element enabling us to elevate our consciousness to a new spiritual perception and awaken us to count our blessings. It is this faithful attitude that leads to happiness. This consciousness is manifest on Shabbat Nachamu when the day is celebrated as a time when single adults come together to seek relationships that can lead to intimacy and commitment. I remember fondly, years ago, when I worked as a waiter in a Catskill Mountain resort in New York, that Shabbat Nachamu was the most crowded, most passionately anticipated weekend of the summer as happy young people came to meet other singles on this particular weekend. Moreover, the Rabbis point out that we only recite three Haftarot of rebuke in the weeks before Tisha B'av. We read Haftarot (from our Prophets) warning us of impending doom. But after the debacle, for seven weeks we read the comforting words of consolation and faith. Consolation is more powerful and prevalent as a loving and supportive energy after destruction.

Our Rabbis teach that loss and suffering are not really punishments. They are meant for our enlightenment. It only becomes a notion of punishment if we do not learn the lesson and punish ourselves as a result and get angry at the loss which was never ours in the first place. Shabbat Nachamu reminds us that there is always renewal after loss, and this comfort sustains us and helps us understand that the whole experience was necessary for our growth and ultimate happiness. Hence, the link between these two Shabbatot is a crucial lesson for redemption.

Life is filled with mysterious opposites both within our own psyches and in the world around us. Perhaps these unfathomable energies become more comprehensible when they are viewed as interlinked catalysts leading to a yet-to-be-achieved wholeness. They challenge our faith along the way, but it is the strengthening of our faith in the face of the intermittent darkness that sustains and moves us to a higher consciousness.

From the tragic events of Tisha B'Av, we move to the happy events of Tu B'Av, a very special holiday that arrives during the week of Shabbat Nachamu. The Talmud lists seven joyous events that occurred on that day, and states that this special day is equal in stature to Yom Kippur! The day also marks the beginning of the grape harvest. With the reading of seven weeks of consoling Haftarot, there comes a joy that surpasses the hardships and indicates the spiritual path in Judaism and its optimistic faith.

The Talmud states, "Said Rabbi Shimon Ben Gamliel: 'There were no greater festivals for Israel than the 15th of Av and Yom Kippur. On these days, the daughters of Jerusalem would go out and dance in the vineyards for joy. They would borrow white garments in order not to shame anyone who had none, and all would be equal.' They proclaimed, 'Do not set your eyes on beauty alone, but set them on sublime character. Grace is deceitful and beauty is vain. But a woman that fears the Lord, she will be praised'" (Taanit 26b on Proverbs 31:30).

After Yom Kippur, a spirit of joy and love would enter the hearts of the Jewish people, since they had gone through a day of fasting, cleansing, and repenting and felt worthy of returning in love to their beloved God. They knew they would be accepted with love and joy. They were rejuvenated and filled with ecstasy. The Light reappeared from the darkness. Similarly, on Tu B'Av, after mourning for the destruction of the Holy Temples because of unbecoming behavior, they committed to a life of holiness and purpose. Their openness and faith led them to consummate their natural need for love, communication, and intimacy. Their feelings of isolation and guilt were attenuated, and they wanted to return to the blessing of socializing and finding the warmth of human contact and understanding. Their return to God led them to an honest return to what their hearts and souls craved. They longed for the deepest form of fulfillment, the soul's yearning for wholeness, for connection to the Beloved—a movement from isolation to connection.

Because relationships are the most fertile agents of growth and transformation, we yearn for their presence and our reconnection. Who we are and who we become depends in part on whom we love, and our hearts always yearn for connection and the energy of God. As Buber says, "When two people say to each other 'You are the one,' then God dwells in between."

On Tu B'Av we release our yearning for love and joy. To love is deeply human. The soul needs connection and to be known. And yet, perhaps the most difficult thing required of us is for one person to care for another. This is the work for which all other work is but a preparation. We bring our whole being to another, both our bright and dark sides; and we work to be honest and vulnerable in order to love fully. It is a committed and enduring process, filled with changes and trials, and yet our soul calls us to it. The impulse to love and be loved is not simply an escape from loneliness. It is an opening in response to one another; it moves us beyond our selfish boundaries. It is really a gift given to us, something that calls our souls—two solitudes that greet each other. As we read in *Shir Hashirim*, "My beloved is calling to my soul" (Song of Songs 5:1). It is a grand blessed experience bestowed upon us, a natural part of knowing our world in the fullness and brilliance that God has created for us.

We should, if we could, spend time with our families to take in the beauty of the waves at the coast, the flight and songs of the birds, the lush mountains, the trees swaying in the wind, and open our hearts to a form of love and longing found in nature—to watch dogs romping spontaneously, and plants in gardens growing in their natural way. Love is drawn out of us to appreciate the beauty of the world we have been blessed to experience. To experience this beautiful mysterious wisdom that fills the earth down to the smallest thing—to the sea urchins, to the birds who play overhead without a care, is to feel a part of the love that is within us and leads us in gratitude to God. We desire to express this joy and share this bliss with others. Our souls are aroused and ready to dance in the garden, this world God created for us. From this physical world, our souls are uplifted to the eternal energy that always lies dormant within us. Out of the darkness comes the light. Then the expressions of our souls are transformed into words, sharing the soul wisdom of the Torah and the truth expressed by all the great poets, philosophers, and artists who capture the resourceful energy of connection and discovery.

It is the awakening and the attention fastened upon another person danc-ing in the vineyard, and the other person nourishing and reciprocating that at-tention that opens us up to God. Bumping into someone who can spark your soul is rare and a gift from above. It is a time when one confesses their true character, their essential nature, springing from the most profound depths of our being. Suddenly everything is illuminated; suddenly everything sings!

But this unique blessed energy may also obviate many details in life that give life its actuality; there is darkness in life as well as light. Often one be-stows one's concentration on one single aspect, his beloved, and this gives a limited aspect to existence although it is one filled with profound intensity. The remainder of the world must be sought out laboriously, too. His beloved has dislodged the world and replaced it with her presence. Without a paralysis of our consciousness and a reduction of our habitual world, we could never fall in love in this romantic way.

When we emerge from a period of falling in love, we feel an impression like awakening from a narrow passage crammed with dreams. For a period, we experience a deep melancholy and then a return to reality. The dance in the vineyard is interrupted. This is the nature of life. Change is constant, and ecstasy reaches its limit and we come down to earth. But this is also a blessing, for without this limitation we would be bereft of desire and occa-sional merging. This is the great dilemma. For once we possess the object of our desire, often our desire ends unless we are threatened with its loss; in that case, the desire turns into a fear of losing the deep love. The quest for absolute romantic love fails because life always changes, and fear creeps in because we realize that we do not possess the beloved. If we did, our desire would wane, because it is the fear of loss that reignites the desire. Anyone who seeks safety in romantic love is constantly frustrated because everything is doomed to die, as Shakespeare captures it in Sonnet 64, "Ruin has taught me thus to ruminate, that Time will come and take my love away, this thought is as a death which cannot choose but weep to have that which it fears to lose." Fearlessness exists only in the complete calm that can no longer be shaken by events in the future. But since life always changes, many people just yearn to be free from fear.

The Tu B'Av world of faith opens us to a different reality. In *The Little Prince* (St. Exupery), we read, "What is essential is invisible to the eye." Faith polishes the lens of our entire world. Our perceptions expand beyond the things that are apparent. New visions enter our encounter with God's creation. Our expanded love filled with faith is imprinted on everything and everyone we meet, encounter, or create. Our faith now has an enormous influence on our lives and the way we see and experience the world. It is because we know happiness, and our notion of happiness guides us in determining the respective blessings in life that then become our intimate gifts and friends.

This is the secret in the vineyard on Tu B'Av. For a fleeting moment, it is as though time stands still, and it is this *now* that becomes our model of eternity. Happiness is achieved when the beloved becomes a permanently inherent element of one's own being, when we embrace with faith, the eternal now, living in the present moment. We are so filled with faith that we do not dwell on the future and its inevitable loss. We are taken up by the blessed energy of God.

If we live in the present fully and do not worry about the future and inevitable loss, we have a chance to live fully with faith. We know that change and loss are within the nature of life, and that is as it is meant to be. We are to enjoy the holy present even with its limits. Finitude gives life more intensity and more pleasure even with the fact of loss. The exploration of this phenomenon exposes us to the Greater Mystery we accept without ultimate resolution. The meaning sometimes haunts us and eludes us, but in its very pursuit, we approach the Ultimate Mystery of life itself. We must learn to live with life as it is, with all its changes.

The 15th day of Av brings a change filled with joy as we move out of the darkness and learn to live with life as it is, grasping the joy when it exists. Can we learn to make every day a 15th of Av when change is rampant? Only by living in the present and not worrying about the future can this be achieved, together with acknowledging the mystery and the blessing of change.

Among the reasons for the specialness of Tu B'Av, we glimpse the mystery and depth of eternity, the dancing in the vineyard, which leads to expanding senses, and the encounter with nature—which leads us to the marvel of the universe and its overwhelming beauty. Through our cleansing from our misbehavior and guilt, we reconnect with God and thus return to our Beloved who is always present.

As the great artist Vincent van Gogh proclaimed, "You know, what makes the prison disappear is a very deep, serious attachment. To be friends, to be brothers and sisters, to love; that opens the prison through sovereign power, through a most powerful spell. . . . life springs up again" (Vincent van Gogh, in a letter to his brother).

May we all be blessed with a joyous and comforting Shabbat Nachamu, and may this comfort continue for enjoying the blessings of renewal during this summer season. Shabbat Shalom!

Eikev

Parshat Eikev begins with the sentence, "If you listen to these ordinances…" but the unusual Hebrew word *eikev* is used to connote *if* rather than the Hebrew word *im*, the more common usage for the word if. The word *eikev* also means the heel of a foot. Our sages suggest that in contrast to the study of Torah that is done with the head, the mitzvot are performed with the body, and are related to physical action. In accepting the mitzvot of the Torah, a person must commit their body to a certain way of life. It is with our actions, rather than just our intellect, that *eikev* is concerned, as the actions of Israel would determine its fate.

Judaism teaches that by doing the mitzvot which create a God consciousness and a behavioral pattern, we create a vessel that can act in a holy way. It is with our feet, with our movement and actions that we create a reminder to the world that our planet is meant to be a place of beauty, splendor, and holiness rather than a place of injustice, suffering, and meaninglessness.

Our parsha elaborates many of these holy little deeds that create the consciousness of connection to the magnificent cosmos, such as beginning a meal with a *bracha* (blessing) and ending it with gratitude by reciting grace after the meal. We place a mezuzah on the doorpost as we enter our homes. These little acts, the little tasks performed regularly and faithfully by people, are what set the tone, content, and character of our tradition. We are not called upon to perform extraordinary things; we are asked to perform ordinary things, little things, with extraordinary consistency.

In the higher dimension, one is not merely concerned with carrying out these legalities. Rather, the ultimate test of religious authenticity is when, through adherence to these acts, one has developed an ennobled sense of spiritual expansion. Through these acts, a spiritual dimension is reached; there comes a caring for humanity, and an enhanced compassion for all creatures.

These deeds give us faith and a unique way of seeing the world. We each struggle with seeing the world with either faith or fear. We can look at life and always see reasons either for grumbling or reasons for feeling grateful. We can feel we have been shortchanged or humbly rewarded. We can constantly feel that our cup is half empty or that "our cup runneth over."

One of the commandments cited in our parsha to enhance our faith is the trial experienced in the gathering and eating of the manna (Num. 9:16). There are many explanations as to what the trial of the manna tested: The commentators view it as a test of and a potential strengthening of faith. For example, would the people adhere to the exhortation not to gather manna on the Sabbath as God required? The manna represented a burden for the people who entered the desert without food and were totally dependent on it. It was a strange food that could not be stored. Each day they were assailed by the doubt that it would not suffice. Each day they felt the anxiety of whether it would come that day. They felt a strong dependence on God's Grace. Waiting for manna was a test of their faith, which became stronger as they relied on its constant manifestation.

Every day they became more accustomed to trust in God, and their faith became part and parcel of their nature. This faith did not mean that sorrow would never invade their homes, or illness would never strike them or their loved ones. Their faith led them to feel that God would always give them the strength to endure and the power to hold on and see things through. Their faith gave them the capacity to translate even trials and tribulations into moral and spiritual growth and learning.

Our parsha states that when Moshe came down from Mount Sinai, he was unaware that his face shone (Deut. 10:2). He was the vessel through which the emanation of Light was crystalized to create good in this world. He learned Torah on the mountain and it became part of his soul, for God's essence can enter our souls when we enter the depths of Torah. This was the radiance that flowed out from Moshe. It was an amalgam of learning, prayer, and humility. He thought the radiance, however, came from the Tablets.

It is taught that the reason for the honor that is paid to the wise in Torah is not solely for their technical knowledge or their mastery of facts and legal expertise, but that the Light of Torah has entered and penetrates the person. When one's whole personality is imbued with wisdom and understanding, that is the essence of Torah. When a human being exposes their innermost soul to the rays of Torah through learning, prayer, and deep humility, then they are irradiated throughout with its holiness.

What is extraordinary is that this being of Light, Moshe, is also capable of character traits that are less than laudable. Through the parsha, as Moshe relates the journey of the Jewish people and God's protective care, Moshe also includes the flawed moments that appear along the way. He specifically points out their various complaints and failings along their journey.

Was this really necessary? Moshe states, "Remember, do not forget, how you infuriated God in the wilderness. …From the day you left Egypt until arriving at this place you were rebellious against God" (Deut. 9:7).

He continues to chastise them about the golden calf and the fiasco with the spies and says, "You have been rebellious against God from the day I knew you" (Deut. 9:24). He does not mention moments of glory: the song at the sea (Ex. 15); following God into the wilderness (Jeremiah 2:2); accepting God's covenant and hearing God's voice proclaim the Ten Commandments (Ex. 19-20); or building the Sanctuary, among other successes. How could the loving, humble Moshe present Israel's history and focus mainly on their failures and ignore all the successes?

Why does the Torah include Moshe's angry presentation of Jewish history? Perhaps it is to teach us that no one, not even Moshe, is perfect. No matter how virtuous we are, we also contain flaws that need to be addressed (consider Moshe's anger as he strikes the rock or slays an Egyptian). The search for perfection often leads to guilt and self-flagellation. Perhaps the Torah is teaching us that even Moshe Rabbeinu is not a perfect figure and that that is true for all of us. It is the journey toward wholeness the Torah requires of us and a consciousness to address our dark sides as well as the Incredible Light—such as that which permeated Moshe's being.

The Midrash tells us that Pharaoh heard a rumor that a great leader was to be sent to lead the Israelites out of Egypt. He had suspicions that it might be Moshe since he was so precocious, principled, virtuous, and courageous. He asked his phrenologists and astrologers (the psychologists of his day) to do a personality check on Moshe. They came back with their conclusion: *No way could it be Moshe, for Moshe is gluttonous, he has anger issues, he has a tendency toward depression, he is licentious, etc.* The rabbis agreed that this was true, but Moshe's *awareness* of these traits allowed him, for the most part, not to act out on these traits, to become the great leader he was to be with all his complexity (imperfections). This is an important insight for us to absorb.

Our Sages teach a similar lesson related to the shattering of the first set of Tablets (Deut. 10:1-6). This first set of broken Tablets were included in the Ark with the second, unbroken set (Berachot 8b). Both sets are revered. We are all broken in some way, yet when joined with our capacity to grow and get in touch with the amazing soul potential within us, we can each make a unique contribution to our world.

We must affirm our strengths but never forget our weaknesses. This is our journey toward wholeness, integrating our strengths and weaknesses. We store both sets of Tablets within our inner Holy Ark. Rather than denying and repressing our shortcomings, we recognize them and grow stronger through our courageous encounters. This encounter with our dark side does not have to lead to becoming guilt-ridden, self-critical, or to developing inferior feelings of unworthiness. Our inclusion of our shattered selves with our God-given gifts promotes the actualization of our destiny. We develop humility and confidence as embodied by our leader Moshe.

This concept is also present in our daily recitation of the *Sh'ma*. The first paragraph states: "And you shall love the Lord your God with all your heart" (Devarim 6:5; 11:13; 11:22). The Rabbis say the word *all* teaches that you must love the Lord with both inclinations of your heart; integrating the bad inclination/*yetzer hara* with the good inclination/*yetzer hatov*, using both to achieve growth and wholeness. It is crucial to face our shadows, to look clearly at what steers us away from virtuous behavior, and to apply that insight as a catalyst to increase good behavior. What appears as an obstacle and creates anger and frustration may become that which is necessary to face in order to employ all parts of ourselves to uplift the world. This takes strong, daily work on ourselves, and leads to our healing of the shattering in the outside world, as well. God entreats us to develop all parts of ourselves (*b'shnei yitzrecha*) to integrate the opposites to achieve wholeness (Mishnah Berachot 9:5). Walking in all of God's ways means facing that with which we are uncomfortable, that which creates fear, and depression, in addition to all the beauty that meets us in our daily lives.

To walk in God's ways (Deut. 10:12), means to love and serve the Lord your God with all your heart and life. The Talmud defines this as emulating God's traits: acting with compassion (*rachum*) and grace (*chanun*) and love (*rav chesed*) to actualize concrete behaviors such as honoring your parents (*kibbud av v'eim*), doing kind deeds (*gemilut chasidim*), bestowing hospitality to guests (*hachnasat orchim*), caring for the sick (*bikur cholim*), clothing the naked (*malbish arumim*), burying the dead (*levayat hamet*), etc. (Sotah 14a). We recite this every morning in our prayer services.

Our parsha wisely includes the commandment mentioned 36 times, more than any other commandment in the Torah. It states, "You shall love the stranger, for you were strangers in the land of Egypt. *Ani Adonai Elohei-chem*—I am the Lord your God, the Lord of all of you" The word *you* is expressed in the plural."*V'ahavtem et hager*—And you shall love the stranger"—once more *you* is expressed in the plural. We are all responsible. Our faith, and more so our actions, must rise up in these very oppressive times. We are to emulate God's ways. Just as God is loving and gracious, so must we be loving and gracious. Do justice to the orphan and the widow; love the stranger and give them food and clothing. Take all of your selves (both inclinations) and have compassion toward all who need your love, including loving that part that is estranged within yourself. Bring it all to God, for as Rabbi Abraham Joshua Heschel says, "God is either the God of all people or the God of no people."

The ultimate test of religious authenticity resides in whether one adheres to the commandments and whether, through the adherence to these, one develops a vessel that actualizes one's Godly soul to all of life—all our brothers and sisters, and all life that shares the planet with us. Such a soul will radiate the shining Light of glory that Moshe brought down to the world as he experienced the truth of the Great Love of God's Presence and felt called to share this Light with the world. Each of us has the capacity, and indeed the loving responsibility, to share our light and gifts with others.

Be aware there are times when we may retain our faith in God but lose our faith in humanity. We marvel at the ingenuity and capacity of our fellow humans, but we also tearfully and painfully see the immense suffering that is still with us. And this suffering is often a result of insensitivity, crass indifference, and blindness to the destruction we have caused. We see our streets filled with homelessness and hunger, and it tears us up inside. We see the continuation of war and violence around the world and in our streets, and we are filled with despair. We see our forests burning. We see crippled veterans with limbs severed returning from wars, and countries decimated by bombing and indiscriminate power. There are times when the pain is so deep that we can't even express it, and if there is no one to listen to us, to support us, we may get so depressed and angry, that it can lead to suicide.

One of my favorite poems that captures this despair is "The Second Coming" by William Butler Yeats:

> Turning and turning in the widening gyre
> The falcon cannot hear the falconer;

Things fall apart; the centre cannot hold;
Mere anarchy is loosed upon the world,
The blood-dimmed tide is loosed, and everywhere
The ceremony of innocence is drowned;
The best lack all conviction, while the worst
Are full of passionate intensity.

It is understandable to despair, but our tradition counsels us that even with our doubts and despair, we must not give up faith. As Psalm 30 states, "In the evening I go to bed with tears, and in the morning, I wake up with joy." Every day can be a day of new birthing, of new creation of ourselves. We must rise from the ashes with greater strength and conviction to elevate the world, and the mitzvot are our guide to actualize our higher sensitivities.

Our *actions* are needed now more than ever to ensure the survival of our planet. We must protect the environment from climate devastation, find solutions for homelessness and affordable housing, safeguard animals from inhumane farming practices, and save our oceans from pollution. Many urgent issues require our immediate attention and action.

Our Sages express the importance of consistent, committed action as the antidote to destruction in the following midrash (Sifra 4:12).

The Sages asked, "Which is the most important verse in the entire Torah? Rabbi Akiva says, 'Love your neighbor as Yourself' [Lev. 19:18]. Ben Azai said, 'This is the book of the generations of Adam, on the day that God created Adam, God made Adam in God's image. [Gen. 5:1]. This is the greatest verse.' Ben Zoma says, 'Hear O Israel, the Lord our God, the Lord is One' [Deut. 6:4] is the most important.' And Shimon Ben Pazi says it is 'The first lamb you shall sacrifice in the morning and the second lamb you shall sacrifice in the evening' [Ex. 29:39, Num. 28:4], referring to the daily (perpetual) offering brought every morning and evening. Rabbi Ploni stood up and said that the opinion of Ben Pazi is the correct one!"

How is this possible? After all, Ben Pazi speaks about daily lamb offerings and the others talk about universal, fundamental teachings. The Maharal answers that Ben Pazi's opinion emphasizes that a person should serve God with absolute consistency on a perpetual basis. The only way to transform our lives in a sustainable way is through continual daily commitment. Believing in the lofty declarations of each human being created in God's image and therefore acknowledging that they must be treated with love and respect is obviously very important and a beginning of elevating our actions. But it is only through a continuous and consistent commitment, day in and day out, that change in ourselves and the world can be truly evoked. This perpetual dedication is at the heart of a moral and spiritual life. The repeated daily actions become habits and character traits that transform the person.

Judaism is more about deeds than creeds; more about good actions than lofty thoughts which are often lost in abstractions. We lift up the ordinary routines of daily life, every day creating a new day, a new day of birthing holy deeds in our world. Every day we create ourselves anew through our deeds, our very creation of our own selves. Every day the Torah is given anew; every day God creates the world anew. Hope is never lost, and we are the ones who must act to create our new world.

May we be strengthened with our faith to do so and may God bless our journey. Amen.

Re'eh

In this week's parsha, Re'eh (Deut. 14:1), we read, "You are children to the Lord your God, you shall not 'cut' yourself (mutilate your body)." Nachmanides suggests that despite the natural grief that we feel at the loss of a loved one, we should not be so anguished or fearful of death that we should then mutilate our bodies. It is very human and proper to weep and mourn at the loss of a loved one, but one must set limits and not despoil one's body as a result.

Reb Moshe Feinstein *zt'l* expounds on this verse and gives a novel interpretation that is very relevant to our contemporary communal reality. He says that the phrase has two meanings. One is that we must not injure ("cut") ourselves as a sign of mourning. The other (based on the talmudic statement in Yevamot 13) is that we must not polarize the members of our communities by forming partisan groups, "cutting" them off into separate units. Reb Moshe says that these two meanings actually mirror each other. Polarized groups wound the ability of the community to function, and injure the spirituality of the community. Thus, they make the community repulsive, just as self-mutilation injures a person and may create discomfort within the person's group. He suggests that we must strive to not only remain physically wholesome but also guard our communal spiritual status and the way we interact interpersonally with each other.

This teaching is of paramount importance to our communal stature today. Many people perceive our Jewish community as less than spiritual, based on communal strife, and as a result, do not want to enter our portals. Indeed, our charge to be a Light unto the Nations is compromised when we demean others in our community who may believe or practice differently than we do. Rather than praising us as a special people dedicated to spiritual and ethical practice, "How goodly are thy tents, o Jacob, thy Tabernacles, o Israel" (Num. 24:5), we are instead looked upon as an embittered community—divisive and unable to create the unity that is a reflection of recognizing that we are all One, each of us a human being that is a reflection of God.

We must not continue to harm the body of our communities; we should reflect upon our reaction to others who disagree with us, and take a broader more respectful perception of our fellows. The Talmud teaches us to "Hate the sin and not the sinner" (Berachot 10a), encouraging us to act with active tolerance toward others. This is what will make us honored once more in the eyes of those who look up to us and make the Spirit of God palpable in our communities. It will open the doors to people who search for spirituality and meaning but today search elsewhere to find it. They will now find meaning and beauty in the beautiful home that embodies the holiness of God's Presence, the *Shechinah*—experienced in the way we act lovingly toward one another.

The great 19th-century ethicist, Rav Yisrael Salanter, taught, "Rather than worrying about another person's spiritual level, and your own physical needs, worry about another person's physical needs and your own spiritual level." This is a noble goal to work toward so that we do not "cut" the beauty and soul from the body.

God appears to us, not when we are passive, but when we seek, *Re'eh*, the Presence of God and actively pursue it. God is made present through our deeds, not merely through our words; through our active energy, not merely through our passive platitudes. This is how we become "seers" and communicate this developed "soul" energy to others.

This Shabbat also heralds the start of the month of Elul. The letters of the word, Elul, form an acronym from the verse in the Song of Songs, *Ani l'dodi v'dodi li* (I am to my beloved and my beloved is to me). It is the time set to return to our beloved Creator, and to our souls within, for the 40 days from the first of Elul through *Ne'ilah* on Yom Kippur. We blow the Shofar every morning and are called to our responsibilities, to our gratitude, and to the return to actualize our unique destiny in our world. Daily, we read Psalm 27, moving from despair to awe, from judgment to compassion.

Our Sages tell us that God waits with love for our return to the path of introspection, insight, and feeling, strengthening the depths of our commitment through emotional heightening, and finally committing to action to elevate our world through our traditions. So how do we achieve this *teshuvah*/return? What must we do? How do we return to this love, the love that Hashem has for us? How do we find self-love and gratitude? How do we move from despair and darkness to the great awe that constantly surrounds us when we are open to it? How do we move from self-judgment to self-compassion?

The rabbis set a course for us during these 40 days; 40 is the minimum number required for ripening, says the Kabbalah; just as the Jews spent 40 years in the deserts, and Moshe spent 40 days on Mount Sinai. The path of return created at this time has three ingredients: *teshuvah*/intense repentance; *tefillah*/prayer; and *tzedaka*/charity. Each of these dynamics helps us to move from judgment to compassion. *Teshuvah* moves us through introspection, commitment to action, self-forgiveness, and a natural movement from judgment to compassion. *Tefillah*, through a deep emotional dive into sincere prayer, softens us up to a movement from judgment to compassion. It gets us in touch with our hearts and informs us to trust our gut. *Tzedakah*, giving charity and interacting with others through a process of giving, moves us from judgment to compassion and knowledge of the other. The Talmud in Berachot 7a teaches us that the one prayer that God makes is, "May my anger/judgment be overcome by my compassion," and says if God dwelt in anger and judgment in these days, who would survive?

Thus, our pious Sages spent hours during Elul, sitting in group prayer settings to arouse their deepest yearnings to return, listening to rousing songs that opened their hearts, and experiencing the tears of sorrow and joy of their companions who joined them in these special prayer settings during Elul. They also made extra effort to give increased charity to the poor during this season and were extremely careful in acting with the highest sense of ethics and kindness to others.

Our Sages instruct as well that one of the most fundamental attributes necessary for the *return* is the trait of gratitude. This discipline of gratitude, of recognizing all our gifts, is the secret to self-love. If we allow our own self-criticism to be projected upon Hashem, we may not be capable of doing *teshuvah*. Our guilt and shame will trip us up, as we may not be able to imagine a mercy great enough to pardon our sins. As the Talmud says, "Sin dulls the heart of human beings" (Yoma 39a). Self-flagellation may blind us to the seeing of the beauty and grace that surrounds us.

Let us each take a moment to recognize one thing we are grateful for and make it a practice to say thank you to Hashem each day of Elul through Yom Kippur. It takes commitment, 40 days of *teshuvah* practice to transform ourselves from the state of habitual wanting to the state of habitual having; recognizing and accepting the gifts that have been given to us every day.

During the month of Elul, as we move toward the High Holy Days, we have special obligations and opportunities to become more conscious and sensitized to our spiritual growth. We should seek out those places, houses of study and synagogues; and times, like Shabbat, where holiness is revealed. We must be alert to our behaviors and face them so the Holy Spirit will come to dwell in our midst. It takes serious commitment to work on our spiritual growth and sensitivity.

Perhaps the greatest challenges are in our homes and in our workplaces, where we encounter differences of opinions, behaviors, and temperaments. We can pretend and make minimal efforts while, at the same time, avoiding honest communication and sharing of authentic feelings with others where we most often dwell. True growth begins at home and at work. How do we endeavor to make our homes and workplaces into mini-sanctuaries of holiness? How do we enrich our schools to create a *ruach*/spirit of community to enable us to become vessels of ethical and spiritual Light? It is not enough to study the sublime teachings of our Torah and Sages. Elul, and every day of the year, is when we must commit to growing into the very one we are meant to be, actualizing the highest manifestation of the image of God within us.

This spiritual path springs forth from the daily routine, affirming our personal connection to a purpose and way of life. Practicing compassion, gratitude, forgiveness, and generosity are all part of our spiritual lives. It is a process that takes patience and habitual commitment. Please take the time to carefully determine the action, thought, and ritual that most speaks to your soul. Is it a morning *tefillah* experience; a soulful Torah study with a *chavruta*/partner; lighting the candles on Shabbat; making *Kiddush* and singing beautiful *niggunim*/spiritual songs? What lifts you to a higher ground and connects you to the greater whole and helps you discover the interconnectedness of all things and the oneness and glory of God's universe? Act on that!

I hope Elul wakes us up, forces us to look around and see where we are falling short. Then we can work to elevate the world we live in into a place of holiness, where people support each other in growing toward the *kedushah*/holiness required of us. Let us commit ourselves to this path of beauty and growth, so people will say, "How blessed are these people, how worthy is their motivation," and our house will become a "House of Light" to all people. This is how we can honor God and fulfill the purpose of the Jewish people and all those blessed to inhabit our world. And may it be so! Our journey may encounter stumbling blocks and darkness along the way, but we know the goal of holiness is always achievable, and our reaching out to God and each other will make it a reality. Shabbat Shalom!

Shoftim

Parshat Shoftim reveals the core of Judaism, the uniqueness of our tradition that not only preaches love and justice as a general ideal but spells out in the greatest detail our responsibilities to achieve this goal. The study of Talmud and Torah opens us up to the depths of the precise details expected from us and through the enormous brilliance of the ideas encountered we are led to an experience of God and an intimate relationship with the Ribono Shel Olam. It is these intricate laws of justice that begin to form the imprint of holiness that is the core of the Jewish tradition and the Jewish people's quest.

Shoftim is filled with many ethical commandments and revelations of truth. The first sentence, "Judges and officers shall be appointed in all your cities. . . . and they shall judge the people with righteous judgment" (Deut. 16:18), is given with great foresight and is germane to the life of our contemporary society. The Torah says "Judges and officers" must combine their energies to create a just and humane society. Unfortunately, the different temperaments of human beings prefer one over the other and often do not recognize the essential importance of both categories.

When we emphasize the importance of the rule of law to the exclusion of discerning and humane judgment, our society becomes too harsh and errs on the side of punishment without compassion, denies proper understanding, and hinders a human being's capacity to attain *teshuvah* and rehabilitation. On the other hand, if we overemphasize "looking the other way" by rationalizing evil behavior and underestimating the importance of boundaries and discipline, we may soften the grounds for permissiveness without limits that trample the rights of others. By combining the two, and taking strength from each energy, a just society emerges.

The extremism in politics, religion, and disparate groups we face today results from an inability to recognize the positive dimensions of the other side, and so we see it as the enemy. And this divisiveness is often influenced by power differentials which turn people against each other for their own benefit. We must be aware of the wisdom of the Torah and allow integrated energy from judges and officers to flourish for healing to occur. We need insightful judges and humane officers to contribute their wisdom and create balance and healthy interaction. Law officers/*shotrim* and judges/*shoftim* who embody psychological and spiritual wisdom must work together to create a humane and just society. One without the other leads to extremes that harm the body politic.

Here are a few examples of the profound mitzvot in our parsha. The Sages expound on each of the lofty teachings about pursuing justice in the Torah, revealing deeper meanings.

In Deuteronomy 16:20 we read, "*Tzedek tzedek tirdof*/justice, justice shall ye pursue so that you may live." The justice we seek must be done morally and honorably, for the means are as important as the end.

Many interesting interpretations of this powerful charge have been passed down by commentators. First, the verse's repetition of the word *tzedek* teaches that the justice we seek must be carried out justly. The Sfat Emet suggests the repetition of the word *tzedek*/justice means justice must be pursued incessantly because we never fully attain it in this world until we are unified. The Mei Shiloach comments that in your pursuit of justice, you must pursue and not be judgmental of others who are not pursuing it. Don't wait for others and don't be critical of others who are not as scrupulous, "that you may live." Don't wait for them; just do the justice that is demanded of you.

Each person's path may be different in their uplifting of the world—some may seek justice, and some may have a mystical proclivity or do quiet deeds of kindness all for the sake of uplifting the world with their own unique way. As the Kotzker Rebbe said, "Any way can be a way, as long as you make it a way"

In Deuteronomy 16:19 we read about the prohibition of bribery ("You shall not take a bribe"). The Talmud expands the various nuances of "bribery" to include even minor acts; so that if a litigant holds the door open for a judge, the judge is disqualified because he may unconsciously favor him. The detailed extension of the law, the profound understanding of the human condition, is what has always opened the portals for us to experience the profound depth of our tradition. We too, must make sure that we extend the implications of our laws to include new conditions that appear before us. As an example, we see how bribery affects politicians who receive large donations to influence their voting choices, leading them astray from safeguarding the welfare of our society. We see how bribes can influence our self-interest and detract from the greater needs of our communities.

Another example of our tradition's profound insight is found in Deuteronomy 20:4-10, which cites those who are exempted from military service in an optional war. The exemptions are one who is in the first year of marriage, one who has planted a vineyard, and one who has built a new house. In each case, one is "giving" of oneself, attached and in love with their partner or property, and therefore would be distracted from being an effective soldier. This shows a deep understanding and acceptance of human nature.

In addition, in verse 8, we find the Torah also exempts someone who is fearful and anxious, perhaps because he has sinned and did not think he was worthy of God's protection in battle. To protect this person's dignity, the Torah exempts him the same as those who recently built homes or got married, so when he leaves the field of battle, people would assume he was going for the same reason as the others, and he would not be shamed. This is a deep acknowledgment by our Sages of the importance of dignity and the egregious pain shaming can bring (Sotah 44a).

Another interesting law in our parsha is that when you find an unidentified murder victim between two cities, the elder of the city closest to the body must bring a sacrifice of atonement. This is because the elder may have been lax in his duty and did not know or care for all those in his care, or did not take proper precaution to prevent such crimes. If no one knows the victim, it indicates a deficit in the community and a lack of caring. Thus, the leader must bring a sacrifice for his negligence and the negligence of the entire community. Perhaps, as we peer out at the neglected and nameless homeless people on our streets, we each need to sacrifice something and take positive action on their behalf. The Torah realizes how challenging it is in every generation to create a just society.

Finally, our parsha speaks about how we are to interact with nature and the animal kingdom. For they, too, are part of God's blessed world, and we must protect them and treat plants and animals with compassion and respect.

Thus, we are taught in Deuteronomy 20:19 that fruit trees are not to be destroyed during war, teaching compassion and sensitivity to all of God's creations. The Talmud extends the law not only to fruit trees but to barren trees as well, as demolition is an effrontery to God. Trees are essential to life! They are symbolic of the Great Mother—Nature.

In the Talmud, Bava Kama 91b, we are told that Rabbi Chanina attributed the early death of his son to the fact that he chopped down a fig tree! After all, a tree is symbolic of life; it protects us with shade and nourishes us with its fruits. It is a source of life, exchanging oxygen with carbon dioxide. Rooted in the earth, it conveys permanence: it gives life and dies. It is a symbol of transformation—leaves and bark, living and dying. New scientific discoveries reveal trees also heal one another when a neighboring tree is suffering from weakness! How sad to witness the destruction of the majestic redwoods in California as fires rage among them because of our neglect of climate change!

Throughout Scripture we find many commandments about the treatment of animals, to increase our compassion for all creation. Some rules are, "Do not kill a cow and its offspring on the same day" (Lev. 22:28); "Do not kill an animal before eight days" (Lev. 22:27); "You must cover up the blood of a beast" (Lev. 17:13); "You must return a lost animal" (Ex. 23:4); "An animal must rest on Shabbat" (Deut. 5:14); "You must unload the burden on an animal" (Ex. 23:5); "Do not plow an ox with a donkey together—for they eat at different speeds" (Deut. 22:10); "Do not muzzle animals when they plow—so they may eat (Deut. 25:4), "You must feed your animal before you eat" (Deut. 11:15, Gittin, 62a), and "Do not eat an animal killed by a hunter" (Lev. 17:15, Ex. 22:31).

Here's another example: if a friend needs help loading his ox, and another friend needs help unloading a beast's burden, unloading comes first because the animal is in pain from carrying a heavy load (Ex. 23:5, Deut. 22:4). Perhaps the most noble charge we find in Scripture is how to engage with our enemies—i.e., if the ox of a friend needs unloading and an ox of an enemy needs to be loaded, the Talmud (Bava Metzia 31a) says to help load the enemy's ox first, even though his friend's ox may be suffering discomfort. For it offers an opportunity to turn an enemy into a friend by doing a kind act to him. This transformation is held to be so laudatory (the ability to create peace between enemies) that it takes precedence over the animal's temporary discomfort!

Judaism posits that at times the natural order needs to be interrupted to protect the weak, unlike Darwin and Nietzsche, who preach that nature wants the weak to perish because death is part of the larger ecosystem. Thus, survival of the fittest is nature's way. Judaism's path is different. All living creatures should be protected; the weak may need aid to protect themselves from the strong. If we must take life in order to survive, we need to do it with humility and a sense of gratitude for the animal or plant that essentially sacrifices itself for us in the circle of life. Furthermore, Judaism makes it clear: if there is a conflict between the natural and the moral, morality must prevail. We do not hold by the principle of survival of the fittest—we intervene to protect the powerless.

How blessed is our tradition, and how blessed are all those who study it! Our parsha reveals the core of Judaism, the uniqueness of a tradition that preaches love and justice as a general ideal, and spells out, in the greatest detail, our responsibilities to achieve this goal. The study of Talmud and Torah opens us to the precise details expected from us; and through the enormous brilliance of the ideas encountered, we are led to an experience of God and an intimate relationship with the *Ribono Shel Olam*/Creator of the Universe. Our studies highlight the intricate laws of justice forming the imprint of holiness at the core of the Jewish tradition and the Jewish people's quest!

As we enter the second week of the echo of Elul, we are reminded that love and *teshuvah*/return are what we need to create healing and consolation in our sometimes shocking world of confounding mystery and sublime grandeur. We are reminded that if we do not love ourselves, we will not be able to see the love surrounding us and become whole again. Many of us are cynical because we have never met anyone who is truly holy. We don't believe that it is possible to be that way because it is not part of our inner experience.

If we work on ourselves and find joy in the elevated teachings of Scripture, of the blooming of nature, and of the grace of the human smile, we will begin to see the majestic beauty of the world as well as the joy that is open to us. We will imbibe the love of God surrounding us in the magnificence of nature and experience the love bestowed upon us by our fellow human beings, partners, family, and community. How deep and sensitive is our quest to create a just society. How blessed is our tradition and how blessed are all those who study it. May we all be blessed to be graced by this abundant love, and to carry out our commitment to uplift our sacred gift of life. Amen.

Ki Tetzei

Parshat Ki Tetzei continues Shoftim's elaboration of laws and lists 74 commandments—many of them uplifting, ethical mitzvot. Some examples are: giving asylum and not returning a fugitive slave to its master; building a fence on your roof so no one can fall off; not oppressing a poor worker by not paying wages immediately since he needs the money for food and shelter; returning a cloak being held as collateral back to the borrower every night lest they be cold and unable to sleep; not to judge unfairly in the case of strangers or orphans (the weak and the vulnerable); leaving your extra crops for the poor to collect; and using honest weights and measures.

There are also laws that may have been appropriate for the level of practice with the constricted consciousness manifest at the time (and more progressive options thus may have been ignored or unattainable), but these latter examples were upgraded and changed over time by the Sages who had the responsibility and legislative power to do so. There are times when the Talmud clearly states, "Originally the ruling was this, but subsequently it was changed to this," because new conditions demanded a new adjudication. In addition, the Rabbis upgraded several laws by making them impossible to carry out (for example, the case of the rebellious son, the identification of bastardy) and used their ingenuity to fulfill their mandate of changing laws in a proscribed fashion.

Let us look into a humane law that has relevance for us today. The Torah states, "You shall not turn over to his master a slave who took refuge with you. He shall dwell with you in your midst, in whatever place he will choose in one of your cities, which is beneficial to him; you shall not taunt him with words or actions" (Deut. 23:16-17). At first sight, this may not seem fair to the original owner who paid for this slave. And some systems of legislation at that time ruled that the penalty for a runaway slave was death.

Our Torah's view has a very different response toward the treatment of those who are enslaved. It does not actually tolerate what is defined as "slavery." The term *eved*/slave might be better translated as servant. There were two ways to become a Hebrew servant. The first is when someone commits a crime and does not have the money to repay it, they must work off this debt through accrued wages (Lev. 25:39-40). The second way is if someone cannot repay a loan, they can work for the master to pay off the debt (Ex. 22:2) so that they do not become homeless. The servant gets shelter and food. He is protected by getting a better bed and better food, to the extent that the Talmud says that if one hires a servant, one hires a master (Kedushin, 22a). Also, if the master harms a servant physically, the servant goes free, as the Talmud says, "A brutal man cannot own a servant."

From these series of laws and practices related to servitude, it seems clear that the Torah's attitude is far more progressive and rehabilitative than the system of punitive incarceration in place today. The servant gets to live with the family he has harmed and through their relationship learns to acknowledge his wrongdoing, repent, and develop socially.

Moreover, the Talmud states clearly that brutality toward both Hebrew and non-Hebrew slaves is not acceptable. In fact, the Talmud points out that the case in our parsha (Deut. 23:16) is referring to a heathen slave who flees to the Holy Land for asylum (Gittin 45a)

Why should a slave run away from his master in the first place? Without a home and land of his own, he would have nothing to gain. He would be compelled to find another master very soon. Only one factor could be behind the ordinance and reasoning in the text that tells us not to return him to his master. That factor is cruelty by the master, who did not go so far as to inflict injury, which would legally ensure the *eved*'s freedom according to Jewish law. So, the verse says, "He shall dwell with thee... he is to be helped and encouraged to find a home."

Let us imagine how this commandment may shine light on our contemporary world. There are many immigrants from Central America who escape and seek asylum because of cruel and dangerous conditions in their countries. According to our Torah, if escapees are indeed endangered and facing cruelty, we are commanded to welcome them and help them find sustenance in our homelands. We have the obligation not to split up families, thereby inflicting more cruelty upon those who seek our aid. The verse commands us, "Thou shalt not deliver unto his master a slave that has escaped."

In our own painful Jewish history, our families who attempted to flee the Holocaust (and the Soviet Union) were turned away by many countries. Immigrants from Darfur, Eritrea, Ethiopia, and Arab lands who sought asylum in Israel, were hardly welcomed and faced challenges and limitations to entry: prejudice, hatred, imprisonment, deportation. According to the Torah, if escapees are in danger and facing cruelty, we are commanded to welcome them and help them find sustenance in our homelands! Those who escape Ukraine, Afghanistan, or drug cartels in Latin America should be provided with safe refuge. The verse explicitly says, "Thou shalt not deliver unto his master a slave that has escaped."

In our parsha, we read of many humane ethical commandments, and of some laws that are appropriately relative to the level of practice within the surrounding ancient cultures. In the latter case, more progressive options were not available for implementation at that time since they would have run counter to the widespread practices and restricted consciousness of that era. Thus, our Sages were given Sinaitic legislative power and responsibility to upgrade and change laws when appropriate, carrying out their mandate through interpretation and proscribed rules of adjudication.

In our parsha, there are many humane ethical commandments and some that are offensive to our modern consciousness. Here is where the wisdom of our Sages, given the mandate to change the law when appropriate, step in and carry out their mandate through interpretation. They are given the opportunity to create *takanot*, literally "repairs" and extensions of Jewish law, to promote the common good and improve Jewish life: revising ordinances that no longer satisfy the requirements of the times; to create *gezerot*, extensions of Jewish law to protect religious observance under changed conditions; and to create *hora'at sha'ah*—temporary, ad hoc emergency legislation which suspends a Jewish law that, if implemented, would undermine the Jewish polity. Within the Talmud itself we find examples of changes in law in debates between the Sages. More than 100 times in the Talmud, the rabbis declare, 'The law was once thus, but is now thus' when new conditions arise or more powerful insights emerge that demand a new ruling.

Two commandments in our parsha pose moral challenges to our contemporary consciousness and the rabbis overruled their literal rendition. The first is *Mamzerut*/Bastardy (Deut. 23:3) and the second is the Rebellious Son. (Deut. 21:18-21) In the former case, a *Mamzer* (defined as one born of an incestuous union whose marriage can never be valid according to Jewish law, such as a union between a brother and sister) is not permitted to enter the congregation of the Lord. Why should this offspring suffer when they had no part in creating his or her birth? When the law proves inconsistent with community norms, the law may be abandoned for the sake of preventing an individual's shame. When laws are contrary to the ethical norms of contemporary society, the Sages often suggest an ever-changing negotiation between the verse and its application in contemporary society.

There are times when the text in the Torah does not offer the law in practice. Some of the most interesting cases of real-world interference in theoretical discussions involve laws that, while technically acceptable according to the rules of legal interpretations, cause difficulties when implemented, and this difficulty obviates the textual law. In some cases when a particular textual law threatens to undermine the ethical norms of the day, the Sages declare a change in the law, *mipnei darkei shalom*/for the sake of peace or *mipnei tikkun haolam*/to heal the world. This is certainly the case with *mamzerut*, children born of incestuous or adulterous behavior. The literal text of the law may have acted to prevent incestuous behavior, but the rabbis made the actual carrying out of the law impossible by creating such strict evidentiary standards to *mamzer* status that proof of this status is impossible to establish.

An example of such reasoning is that at the time of the child's birth, perhaps the parents of the child were married, and it is impossible to prove the child was born under different circumstances. The Talmud gives the example of an inability to prove *mamzerut* when the mother gave birth while her husband was away in the army, by asking "How do we know the husband did not sneak away one night and impregnate his wife?" They used ingenious or extreme reasoning to obviate the possibilities of this law, making sure it would never be carried out.

The second case is that of the Rebellious Son who is to be brought to the elders of the city and be publicly stoned to death because of his gluttonous behavior and drunkenness (Deut. 21:18-21). The rabbis also made this ruling impossible to carry out. The law certainly contradicts our notions of justice. Does this death fit the crime of rebelliousness? Does this law contradict the image of the nurturing Jewish family? We must look at the law in the context of the time. It was an advance over the prevailing authority of the father in other legal systems. Even in later Roman law, the father had the power to commit capital punishment over every member of his household.

The Torah seeks to limit the power of the father. Now, he could not denounce the son by himself. The verse states, "His father and mother shall take hold of him." The mother must now agree with her husband. Furthermore, the son must be brought "in front of the elders of the town." This suggests the community must investigate the case and agree with the father before stoning can take place (Sanhedrin 71a). Finally, we see that the townspeople, and not the father, do the stoning, taking the punishment out of the father's domain.

Still, we are offended by the father's power to inflict capital punishment upon his son for being disloyal or defiant. The Sages were equally disturbed by this biblical law and made it impossible to carry out by imposing impossible conditions on it. They limited it to a son who must be between the age of 13 years and 13 years and three months (Sanhedrin 68b). The son must steal the money from his parents to buy wine and meat or drugs and consume them in a gluttonous manner in front of his friends. He has to be warned by two witnesses and must repeat his crime. Only then is he punished, since the Torah predicts he will eventually steal and murder to fulfill his lusts, and so the Sages declare, "Better he leaves the world while still innocent rather than after he is guilty of serious crimes" (Sanhedrin 72a). The biblical law was changed by the rabbis of the Talmud. As the Talmud often says, "The law was thus and now is thus."

A novel ethical lesson can also be learned from the verse itself. According to the Mishnah (Sanhedrin 8:4), since the verse says, "That his father and mother shall lay hands upon him," the rabbis teach that if either the father or mother was maimed in the hand, or lame, or blind, or deaf, the son cannot be condemned. What does this teach us? According to the commentator Pinchas Peli, it teaches us an ethical lesson about the responsibility of good parenting. "A son is not to be blamed if his parents are maimed, i.e., if they do not lift their fingers and change the environment in which he is raised; or if they are lame—if they do not go out of their way to give up their comforts in order to raise him properly; and he is not to be blamed if the parents are 'blind' and overlook or disregard the problems he faces. Finally, he is not to be blamed if the parents are deaf and will not listen to his voice, which may be an outcry for more love and understanding, for more sensitivity and consideration." Since there are no perfect parents, there is no possibility of carrying out the punishment of breaking the law of the 'Rebellious Son.'" As the Talmud states in Sanhedrin 71a, "The case of the execution of the Rebellious Son never occurred nor will it ever."

May we continue to study our beloved Written Torah and our sublime Oral Torah, mandated to ensure that our Torah continues to grow throughout history when new circumstances arise and new consciousness emerges. Our Sages were given the task to study the Torah in its entirety, extracting the holy sparks contained within in every generation. We, the heirs of that tradition, must continue to study and apply its holy principles in our own day. The Holy Sparks of the Torah are ever-evolving and wait for us to reveal it anew every day. It calls on us to use its Light to create a renewed world of beauty and justice for all. May we be blessed to do so, partnering with the Light of our Creator, and uplifting our world with the inner Light that resides deep within us. And may it be so! Shabbat Shalom!

Ki Tavo

Our parsha this week begins with the mitzvah of *bikurim*, the bringing of the fruits of harvest to Jerusalem. It instructs us through the *bikurim* to bless God in gratitude for all that the Creator has bestowed upon us: our first fruits; the freshness of life; the truth of newness. The Rambam describes the approach of the large procession to Jerusalem. The pilgrims bearing their first fruits would be joined by official representatives of the communities they passed through, and together they entered Jerusalem.

The pilgrims would sleep in the streets of the city. In the morning, they would wake up and march; the ox for the peace offering would walk in front of them, its horns overlaid with gold and a wreath of olive branches on its head. The flute would be played until they arrived close to Jerusalem, and the whole way the people would chant, "I rejoiced when I was told to the House of the Lord let us go" (Psalm 122:1).

When they arrived close to Jerusalem, they would send messengers to inform the inhabitants of their arrival and would wreathe their first fruits and decorate them with the ripe fruits on top. Then the leaders of Jerusalem would come out to greet them. And when they entered the gates of Jerusalem, they would all begin to dance and sing, "Our feet are standing within your gates, O Jerusalem."

The pomp and ceremony served a positive purpose. It gave the mitzvah the beauty and deep significance it deserved: the truth of newness; the God-given freshness of life; the renewal of the wonder of creation and its radiance produced every day by our Creator and the work of our hands ("*Hamechadesh b'tuvo b'chol yom tamid ma'seh bereishit*"). This is the consciousness that should always be blooming, flourishing, arising, and flowing within our souls every day.

The first fruits are concrete proof that achievement through effort and the awareness of God's blessing bring us infinite joy. It gives us a natural reason for rejoicing. When we can live on this level of gratitude for God's eternal providence, we become joyous. Joy is what comes spontaneously when one lives to see the first fruit of one's labor. Why is it then ordained as a law? "And you shall rejoice with all the good that God has given you" (Deut. 26:11).

The new harvest of God ripens within us every year and, indeed, every day. The nature of life, its constant change, opens us up to the faith that growth and serendipitous energies are always present! As the Psalmist says, "In the evening I go to bed in tears, and in the morning, I wake up with joy" (Psalm 30). The discipline of gratitude, of recognizing all our gifts, is the secret to self-love. Alternatively, if we project our own self-criticism on Hashem and allow it to dominate us, we feel that we are so bad that Hashem cannot possibly forgive us, so we don't even bother doing *teshuvah*, or returning. Our guilt and shame trips us up and we cannot conceive of a mercy great enough to pardon our sins. As the Gemara in Yoma 39a states, "Sin dulls the heart of human beings." Self-flagellation, the attitude of "An eye for an eye," says Gandhi, makes the whole world blind!"

All too often, we are not ready to rejoice when good comes to us as much as we are ready to complain and lament when the reverse happens. When we can live from the level of gratitude and feel God's ever-present kindness, we live with inner joy and thus it becomes an important mitzvah for our well-being. The discipline of gratitude, of recognizing all our gifts, is the secret to self-love as well.

Looking out at the Channel Islands, watching the majestic whales, the brilliant dolphins, and the colorful, musical singing birds in Ventura, we see the ocean with its white dancing waves and the sublime interaction of the ecosphere. We experience interdependence of all life and it leaves us with such joy. This is the time of the year, pre-Rosh Hashanah, when we should recognize with gladness and wonder the lessons that this season offers us— above all to allow the harvest of God-awareness to ripen within us.

Let us each take a moment to recognize at least one matter (rare or usual) that we are grateful for every day during the month of Elul until Yom Kippur. That will be 40 days of committed practice to increase our joy and recreate the joy that our tradition expects from us. Our parsha insists that our commitment to joy and practicing loving kindness as a result of our inner abundance is what will create a world of blessing.

Our parsha remarkably states that the reason for the curses mentioned in it and all the suffering attributed to our reality is solely because *Tachat asher lo avadita et hashem elokecha b'simcha u'vtov leivav mairov kol*/You did not serve the lord your god with *joy* and *gratitude* with all the abundance that you have received." Amazing! Not only are we required to do the mitzvot, but we must do them with joy! "The world is created for the sake of kindness" (Psalm 89:3) and we are commanded to love ourselves, to experience joy so we can share the blessings of our world.

Our Sages state that if, for some reason, we stray and lose our mission of experiencing and creating joy in our world, and hence bring pain, suffering, and curses into existence, this is not the end of our story. The Kabbalists indicate that there are a total of 676 words in the verses of the curses in our parsha. The Sages teach that the number 676 is the total found when 26 (the letters in God's name—yud, hey, vav, hey—add up to 26) is multiplied by 26. This suggests that even in curses there is a path to lead us to growth and joy. For within the curses, within the darkness, is found God's compassion waiting to be discovered, as God's eternal Light will guide us to return to the joy of creation and its blessings. As suggested above, let us each take a moment to recognize one thing we are grateful for and make it a practice each day of Elul through Yom Kippur to say thank you. It takes practice, commitment, and those 40 days of *teshuvah* to transform ourselves from the state of "habitual wanting to the state of habitual having"—recognizing and accepting the first fruits that are given to us every day.

Let us remember the Mystics declaration that God's compassion is found within the curses, awakening us to do *teshuvah*, to return to God and the joy of creation. If we accept the curses as a learning experience, they become a source of joy. All of life, whatever we face, is a learning experience. This is the recipe of God's blessing for achieving joy and gratitude in our lives; faith that all that is before us is a blessing. This necessitates acceptance—the "volitional affirmation of the obligatory" (Otto Rank, *Art and Artist* ([1932] 1989) p. 64).

Let us, then, practice the trait of gratitude, of returning to the One who loves us, and return to the God within ourselves. If we do not love ourselves, we cannot see the love in others. We cannot imagine that love exists in the world because it is not part of our own experience. So let us work on self-love, on God's love, so we can see the love around us and become whole again.

If we accept the curse/darkness as a potential instructive experience necessary for our awakening, these dark experiences will also become a source of growth and joy. God will never fully abandon us and just "waits for us"

(Psalm 27:14) to reawaken our gratitude for the blessings of first fruits in our world. We will then fulfill our obligation to share our abundance with others out of our joy.

Ki Tavo (coming home) also talks about returning from the vicissitudes of the world. Going out in the world can mean growth and individuation, but it can also mean danger, tragedy, and evil destruction. The tragedy, anguish, and pain of the families whose men, women, and children are mercilessly blown up all over our world leaves people inconsolable. My words fail me, and my heart breaks when I confront the horrific continuous wars on our beloved planet; the destruction, suffering, and tragic loss of lives are heart-wrenching. The anguish and grief, heartbreak, and misery of human beings who cannot sleep at night nor rest during the day, fearing for the lives of their children and families, is heartbreaking. We cry as a nation and as individuals who bear witness to this barbarity, these cursed wars, which send hundreds of innocent human beings to their deaths. Danger and darkness remain part of our reality as we grapple with this insanity even during Elul, a month known for love and a return to our highest selves. As we weep with tears for the lives of every individual lost in war, and every individual suffering, we pray that a lasting peace and political settlements with understanding and dignity for all will emerge in our lifetime. And war will be no more! We pray for a day when "Nation will not lift up sword against nation, and never again will they learn war any more" (Isaiah 2:4).

How do we deal with this tension of opposites, those parts of our reality in the outside world and within our own hearts? We cannot solve this dilemma by simple rational deliberations, as our minds are often filled with rationalizations that are not fully accurate. We must recognize that the mysteries of the universe and the behavior of human beings are beyond simple analysis and deliberation. Our bodies, our hearts, our guts, are sometimes more reliable in discovering when something is terribly wrong, and those may be the places where the deepest heart truths can be discovered and acknowledged.

The month of Elul, when spelled in Hebrew—*aleph, lamed, vav, lamed*—is the acronym from the verse in Song of Songs, *Ani L'dodi, v'dodi li*/I am for my beloved and my beloved is for me (Song of Songs 2:16). The 40 days from the first day of Elul until Yom Kippur is the time set to return to our beloved Creator and the soul. We blow the Shofar every morning and are called to our responsibilities, our gratitude, and *teshuvah*/return to actualize our unique destiny in our world. We read Psalm 27; we move from despair to awe, from judgment to compassion, and our Sages tell us God waits with love for our return to the paths of introspection, insight, feeling, and action. We strengthen the depths of our commitment through emotional heightening and seriously commit ourselves to action to elevate our world through our traditions.

How do we return to achieve this *teshuvah*? What must we do? How do we return to the love Hashem has for us? How do we find self-love and gratitude? How do we move from despair and the darkness within to the great awe constantly surrounding us when we are open to it? How do we move from self-judgment to self-compassion? The rabbis set a course for us during these 40 days (40 is the minimum number required for ripening, says the Kabbalah; just as the Jews spent 40 years in the desert and Moshe spent 40 days on Mount Sinai). The path of return created at this time has three ingredients, *teshuvah* (intense repentance), *tefillah*, (prayer), and *tzedakah* (charity). Each of these dynamics helps us move from judgment to compassion.

Teshuvah moves us through introspection, commitment to action, self-forgiveness, and a natural movement from judgment to compassion. *Tefillah*, through the expression of our emotions and a deep emotional dive into sincere prayer, softens us up to move from judgment to compassion. It gets us in touch with our hearts and informs us to trust our gut. Finally, *Tzedakah*, charity, and interaction with others through a process of giving, moves us from judgment to compassion and knowledge of the other. The Talmud teaches that the one prayer God recites is, "May my anger be overcome by my compassion" (Berachot 7a), for if God dwelt in anger and judgment in these days, who would survive?

Our pious Sages spent hours during Elul sitting in group prayer to arouse their deepest yearnings to return. They listened to rousing songs that opened their hearts and heard the tears of sorrow and joy of their brothers and sisters who joined them in these special prayers during Elul. The Shofar was blown, and committed communities did the work of Elul—returning to their souls and the God who loves them. They also made extra effort to give increased charity to the poor during this season and were extremely careful to act with the highest sense of ethics and kindness to others.

Many of us are cynical because we have struggled before to do *teshuvah* and then slowly return to previous behaviors. We don't believe that it is possible to change, and achieve *teshuvah* because it is not part of our inner experience. But if we work on ourselves, find joy in the elevated teachings of Scripture, of nature in bloom, and the grace of the human smile, we will start seeing the majestic beauty of the world and find the joy expected of us.

When tragedy abounds, as it does all around us, it is challenging to find joy. We must dig deep into our faith and allow this darkness to deepen our compassion; to move away from judgment and return to the love that is our salvation. It is in the echo of Elul that we are reminded that love and *teshuvah* are the restoratives for healing and consolation in our sometimes-shocking world of confounding mystery and sublime grandeur.

Let us dedicate ourselves during this season to find joy in God's Torah, and in the beauty of creation, so that we will rediscover the joy demanded of us!

May our Selichot be meaningful and accepted. Shabbat Shalom!

Nitzavim / Rosh Hashanah

What is *teshuvah*? Our Sages say it is one of the seven necessary energies created before the creation of our world. (Pesachim 54a, Nedarim 39b) Why is it such a blessing and a requirement for our world? A significant reason is that in God's wisdom for free will to exist in our world, one has the option to choose good or evil (Luzzatto, Derech Hashem). If choices were made to lead human beings to a path heading away from wholeness, there had to be some antidote to rehabilitate the stragglers. That is the gift of *teshuvah*. It is the gift that leads one to a higher plane than one could reach in a world without choice, a world with a single path leading to comfort but not growth. For example, remaining in the Garden of Eden, never leaving it, would be living in a world of naive consciousness, but not living in a world of growth that would allow us to overcome evil by our choices. Freud points out that all movement to completely de-stress (rest without stress) is a death wish (Thanatos) instead of facing reality in our post-Eden world with all its choices (Eros) and growing, even with stress.

What is the definition of the word *teshuvah*? It is the *Tashuv Heh*—Return to the Lord, a return to wholeness, to the soul within, to the song of the Lord (Rav Kook, Sfat Emet). Rav Avraham Yitzchak Hacohen Kook says our natural state is one of wholeness and Light. But we need to enter the darkness to discover this. The Kabbalists suggest that this is why the Torah begins with a *bet*: B'reishit (duality), not *aleph* (a naive unity). The encounter with this duality (opposites that are ingrained in nature and within the self) leads to growth and blessing, and a conscious unity rather than a naive unity experienced in the Garden. Thus, it was planned for Adam to sin, to move from a state of naive unity in the Garden to consciousness that came via an encounter with otherness. Life is a journey from the Garden (the Great Womb) to a reality leading to conscious growth when we encounter diversity and discover the unity within that diversity—namely, that we are all made in God's image and contain the Divine Spark. When that happens, one can return to the beauty of the Garden awakened, enlightened from one's journey through life and return to home, to the Garden, in wholeness.

Yes, this journey is fraught with challenges—it is a process one must enter in order to individuate. Many people remain at the edge of the Garden and do not enter because it necessitates sacrifice of the ego, which is painful. They remain unenlightened, clinging to their ephemeral power, security, fears, and control. *Teshuvah* demands a sacrifice of ego-boundedness to discover the Soul that enriches and enlightens. *Teshuvah* remains a gift to all who can take hold of it.

According to Rav Soloveichik, *teshuvah* means to "answer" and face the question of our lives and give our unique answer based on deliberation and heart-searching. It is a gift given to us to come home to the Soul bestowed upon us from the Heavenly world and promotes a growth that elevates us above our previous level.

Our Sages teach, *B'makom sheh ba'al teshuvah omed, ein tzaddik gamur yochol la'amod ba*—In a place where the *ba'al teshuvah*/returnee stands, even a perfectly righteous person cannot stand! (Berachot 34b). Why is that? The Rabbis explain that it is because of the dissatisfaction experienced by the returnee in a place of darkness and distance from Hashem, that a great awakening and deep revelation occurs. An opening in the heart is revealed that promotes growth, a state of being that surpasses the everyday comfort and habits of even the righteous ones. The penitent has suffered and knows about the narrow line between good and evil, and develops a greater sense of humility and empathy toward fellow human beings. They know how easy it is to slip and are therefore less judgmental. This path we traverse for *teshuvah* in the days before Rosh Hashanah contains four stages, according to Maimonides and others.

The first is *charata l'avar*—suffering, regret, awareness of betrayal, etc. Yes, though betrayal of another, betrayal of God, betrayal of oneself (one's unique destiny) is not good behavior, it contains the seeds of Return. For without a betrayal, there is no experience of forgiveness, no motivation to heal the breach, so even betrayal/sin contains an element of potential redemption— the Light that can be discovered in the darkness. As the Kabbalists put it: *cheit*/sin=18 and *chai*/life)=18! Betrayal can become a catalyst to transform one to a higher level of being, to return to Soul.

The second stage is *azivat hachet*, abandoning your misstep and discerning how you got there; developing the insight and awareness of the roots of this behavior and the defenses erected to maintain it. You must examine the many triggers active in your life and how to unravel their hold, allowing you to face your fears and imagine following a more righteous path.

The third stage is *vidui*, the confessional—making your past deeds real by naming them; by developing the emotional intensity necessary for change that stems from deeply feeling the passion to return to a state of wholeness; to connect to the soul within and the loving Creator without; to develop the emotions leading to transformation. The importance of moving beyond our intellectual "knowing" to reach our emotional depths is essential for effective *teshuvah*. As our Rabbis teach, it is the Gate of Tears, the most effective form of communication, that leads to successful action.

Two heroines of our tradition, Rachel and Hannah, model this for us. Rachel, our Matriarch, weeps for the Jewish people in exile and prays for their return. Hannah (1 Samuel 1:1-20) travels to the Tabernacle in Shiloh and prays for a child, saying, "Lord, if you will only look on your servant's misery and remember your servant and give her a son, then I will give him to the Lord for all the days of his life." She prayed intensely and silently, and her prayers were answered; she bore a son and named him Samuel, which means "I have asked for him from the Lord." Rachel and Hannah's deep emotions were the catalyst transforming their realities, opening the gates to redemption.

Fourth is *kabbalah l'atid*, the resolve and commitment not to repeat bad behavior. It requires a change of action and reinforcement through deed. It is crucial to reinforce one's insight and emotional intensity with concrete action, reinforcing one's transformation and strengthening one's new path. Without this final action, to support the insight and emotional awakening, *teshuvah* is not complete and the powerful drive to repeat earlier patterns will return. Our Sages state emphatically that once one has the will to do *teshuvah*, and starts walking down that path, the Holy One will reach out and ensure their success.

To be sure, this exalted state of *teshuvah* does not always remain constant, for life is constant change. Approach and falling away occur in our daily lives, in our behavior, and in our search for God. We must remember God, though immanent in our world, the *Ein Sof*, is transcendent, beyond our world, making it impossible to totally and tangibly grasp God's Presence. One's spirit often retreats to a stage of melancholy when yearning is not satisfied.

When the Soul aspires to the most luminous Light, it cannot be content with trivialities that are part of our world of vanity. We are often angered, doubtful, or blame ourselves for our inability to directly apprehend the ineffable. Our tradition says that it was only Moshe who was able to experience God, face(s) to face(s) (Deut. 34:10), including all the various manifestations of God's relationship to us. The Midrash says Moshe experienced God through a bright mirror, whereas all the other prophets experienced God through a less lustrous mirror. But even Moshe was only able to see God's back from the crevice of a rock as God passed by, for no person can see God and live (Ex. 33:20-23).

Although we may never be able to directly experience God's transcendence, we can enter God's palace in all God's manifestations immanent in our world. In addition to the Gate of Tears, there are divine dimensions in the beauty and grandeur of our world, manifest in every living thing. We witness this in every insect; in every blooming plant and flower; in the ocean with its turbulent waves and undersea life; in magnificent architecture created by the ingenuity of human beings; in the blue skies and white clouds; in the imagination of poets and thoughts of philosophers; in the feelings of every human being; in the homeless person on our street corner; and in the heroic deeds of every person coping and surviving with resiliency on this planet. Thank God that God has bestowed these gifts upon us, and we are always uplifted by the whispers of God's beneficence and the gifts that surround us when we are open to them.

As we prepare for Rosh Hashanah, two emergent themes appear as we journey through Elul.

The first theme is inner honesty and authenticity. Our Sages suggest that this is a time to review our year and to assess "where we are in our particular way" (Buber). Are we on the unique path God created for us, or have we strayed from this path? Have we discovered our unique talents and used them to uplift our world, or have we ignored them? Are we still in the process of discovering them, or have we discovered that they have changed from earlier perceptions?

This takes courage and an honest discerning of our thoughts, feelings, and behavior. And if we indeed feel we are on the right path, have we put in the full, responsible effort necessary to succeed? One of the indications that we are on our correct path is a feeling of inner passion and joy in that with which we are involved. If we are not happy with what we are doing, can we change this in this coming year?

There is a striking story about one of the great Hasidic leaders of our generation. The great rebbe once walked into a Purim play where one of the

Hasidim was doing a perfect imitation of the rebbe. Everyone in the room was laughing except the rebbe himself. Instead, bitter tears began to roll down his face. Mortified, the impressionist ran over to the rebbe to apologize. "No need," responded the rebbe. "I was crying because you reminded me of all the times that I, too, was impersonating the rebbe." This was quite a deep and honest look at his inner self, mixed with the desire to become more authentic.

Though we may know that what others think of us may be their projection and expectation, but not necessarily the reality, we may still struggle with this and question our authenticity and motivation on our current path. Through this awareness, we may work harder to be more authentic (*tocho k'baro*), either by changing our occupation, or accepting that our lack of perfection is accepted by God, and that self-flagellation removes us from God.

Clearly, depression removes us from the joy that is a requisite for influencing others to an elevated state of being. And it is equally true that many of us endure depression, either sporadically or as a constant underlying melancholy. Hopefully, we can find proper relational support or mindful awakening when we become aware of this deflating energy and restore a robust, abundant faith. Moreover, healing tales, like the story of the rebbe, may help us realize that if a great rebbe feels that he is not inwardly at one with his vocation, we should not judge ourselves harshly if we, too, sometimes fail to live up to a perfect image of what is required of us.

It is only growth, *teshuvah*, that our tradition requires, not perfection. Actually, perfection is the enemy of the good: trying to be perfect creates feelings of inadequacy. We should strive toward the more humane goal of journeying toward wholeness—*teshuvah*—in the presence of a Loving God, who patiently waits for us to discover our destiny and actualize the inner gifts we have been given. Gabriel García Márquez, one of the great literary figures of our generation, insightfully revealed, "Everyone has a public life, a private life, and a secret life." And even if we impersonate ourselves or others, we can influence and elevate an entire community.

The second theme is the power of kindness, and the responsibility and benefit of following its path. If we take risks and engage in interesting conversations with new people; if we engage in a passionate conversation at our workplace; the experience itself—making real connections with people—reinforces the intuitive belief that we are all created with infinite capacity for good. It strengthens our belief and conviction that it is through connection, through expressing kindness and receiving kindness, that we create the capacity for a better world. When we listen with empathy to the hardships and pain of others, we transform ourselves from owning harmful, destructive stereotypes born out of ignorance and become human beings of spiritual elevation. We expand the boundaries of our narrow individual needs and connect to the complex lives of other human beings. We move from the realm of extreme individuality to the interconnectedness of all living creatures on our planet. To walk in the image of God means to act with empathy, responsibility, and faith. So, let us all dedicate ourselves to the path of kindness and believe in its transformative power. Let us dedicate ourselves to the development of compassion through interaction. Let us be blessed with serendipitous discovery through active listening to others, through sensitivity, through practicing kindness and forgiveness.

With patience, persistence, and prayer, we will put one foot in front of the other this year, transform our world, and place Light into the darkness through our faith and action. We will experience the love that is always there waiting for our acts of kindness. We will welcome the sweet, radiant, soothing embrace of peace and justice created by God's children as we pass the holy bread of kindness to one another. May it be so, may we make it so, and may it be God's will! May Rosh Hashanah and Yom Kippur bring us to a full Return to the Presence of the Lord, and a revelation of the Soul dwelling within us so the world may be fully blessed with *teshuvah*, higher consciousness, love, and blessing.

Vayeilech / Shabbat Shuva / Yom Kippur

For on this day (Yom Kippur) God will forgive you, and cleanse you,
so that you may be clean from all your sins before the Lord.
—Lev. 16:30

During this Shabbat Shuva season, the primary spiritual task in which we are asked to engage is a self-examination that will lead to growth and reconciliation. Any process that eventually leads to growth demands a seriousness of labor if it is to be successful. Now is the time for us to energetically dedicate ourselves to this process (through prayer, journaling, dialoguing, studying, group sharing) so that our High Holidays will lead to a successful culmination of this process rather than a laborious beginning.

As we pass through Shabbat Shuva, we anticipate and encounter the energy of Yom Kippur. Many associate this auspicious day as a day of *yirah*/fear; a day of *din*/judgment. Our Sages suggest it is more a day of *re'eh*—seeing clearly, a day to measure where we are rather than *din*. Most importantly it is a day of Grace, for God's love and forgiveness.

Our Sages say our confidence in God's love and our yielding to God's Grace on this day simply by observing its laws and energy makes this day a *mechaper*—a bestower of grace as the final step in our return home. We are to give up our enervating efforts (suffering, insight, emotional processing, and action) at this point—for though they have been necessary and laudatory till this point in the *teshuvah* process—it is still insufficient for a full, complete *teshuvah*. We realize it is only, finally, God's Grace, God's love for us, that ultimately makes our *teshuvah* possible and complete. We finally yield to God's Presence and say, "Thy Will be Done." We bow down in gratitude and recognition of the power of God's love and, in complete faith, our inner love is drawn out of us, loving God with all our might, with all our heart, and with all our soul.

If we feel rejected by God, or feel God's absence, it is hard for us to express genuine, honest love for God. We may feel doubt or anger at our incapacity to make this connection, and often blame ourselves. Each of us may have different concepts of God. Some may see God as the Creator of the cosmos and feel awe and gratitude at being given the gift of life in this majestic creation.

Others may see God as an oppressive power, judging us according to our behavior and adherence to the commandments, and therefore One who condemns us because of our failings. In this case, our resulting feeling of inadequacy and self-hatred is projected upon God and therefore we feel unloved by God. But if we have received and accepted the message that God is reconciled to us in this season due to the gift of *teshuvah*, a time of forgiveness and being drawn back to God's love, we will feel whole again.

On Shabbat Shuva there is a heightened feeling that God has created us with the power to succeed and express our gifts. God forgives our missteps and only wants us to return, to do *teshuvah*, and feel the incredible opportunities and blessings of life in this world. When we experience this within, everything changes. God's healing power—*kel na refa na la*—enters us, and we can affirm God and our own being. The others from whom we were estranged become connected to us again. At this moment we realize that God's love becomes and is part of our own being. To love this love is to experience God, and to accept life and love it. Being forgiven and being able to accept oneself are the same.

We realize our ultimate dependence on God, the All-Powerful, but are overjoyed that God's Essence is complete love for us, and our Holy Day thus brings forth great joy. Our love and effort have made possible the success of our *teshuvah*, and God completes it. Says the Lord, "Return to Me and I will return to you" (Zechariah 1:3).

Moreover, Yom Kippur is a day of joy; even if we failed during the past year, we are still given a second chance to return and become whole again, overjoyed to proceed with a clean slate. As the ancient prayer recited in the closing service of Yom Kippur says, "You stretch out your hand to sinners, and your right hand is open to receive those who want to return." We have come home, welcomed by our God. We have removed the impediments, the defenses, and cleared a way for the Light that is always there. Our desire to change brought us closer to Hashem, but we finally also recognized that it is only God's great love for us that makes our return possible. This is the understanding that it is the day itself, God within this day, which forgives us.

Not our "willing," which inevitably falls short, but the Grace God bestows on us because of our efforts during the Ten Days of Repentance. God's majesty, God's sovereignty must be recognized and accepted for the new rebirth to occur.

One of the goals in the process of *teshuvah* is a reconciliation within ourselves, with others, and with God, and some sense of achieved forgiveness. What do we mean by "to forgive and be forgiven?" And how do we achieve it? Forgiveness means reconciliation despite hostility. This genuine forgiveness, this reunion and participation once more with another, makes love for the other possible. We cannot love where we feel rejected, even if this rejection is done out of righteousness. We are hostile to that by which we feel judged, even if the judgment is not expressed in words. Moreover, this hostility and anxiety about being rejected by those who are nearest to us can hide itself under the various forms of love and friendship, sensual love, as well as conjugal and family love.

We removed the outer layers preventing us from coming close. God has compassion for us even if our physical needs and ego distractions overwhelm us. Trying and showing up are enough for Hashem to forgive us. We have been blessed to return to our community, God's ever-present love, and to our soul within, to the inner kernel of goodness we all possess. We celebrate in joy the opportunity to rediscover our true selves, to come home, to remember that we are souls within a body.

Once we take the steps to *teshuvah* and yield to the Grace of the Lord on Yom Kippur, we are transformed. That is why on Yom Kippur we wear a white *kittel* (a robe-like garment, also used on Seder night and as a shroud) symbolizing purity, love, joy, and affirming death to the old way of being, as we embrace our renewed state of being. We have been transformed by our efforts and by God's love. God's Grace has forgiven us and it is the season of joy, a time of transformation. We are free to begin again, having grown, having cleansed ourselves of much of our dross that distances our selves from Hashem.

Elijah the Prophet experienced "*Kol d'mommah dakah*/God is not found in the wind, nor in the earthquake, or in the fire, but in a still small voice" (1 Kings 19:12). We heard the still small voice and the clarion call of the shofar. When our consciousness is centered, not agitated, we become *seers*, opened to the Presence of God. In our silent state (removing our mind's distractions), we can hear the soft whispers of God surrounding us. Birds chirping, the wind rustling in the trees, the dog wanting to play—these are many gifts, many soul messages waking us to our duties and unique potential contributions. This day is a day of joy!

"Your children approach You with prayer, seeking You each day, speaking words of prayer" (Az Terem Nimtechu, a prayer written by Rashi).

"Seek Hashem when God is to be found, call God when God is near" (Isaiah 55:6).

"Return to Me and I will return to you, says the God of Hosts" (Malachi 3:7).

We break the fast with joy and come together with our friends and family, like celebrating a mini-wedding. At Mount Sinai, we were as bride and groom under the chuppah. Just as the bride in love reaches out to the groom, the groom in love reaches out to the bride, and God dwells in between. We remember who we truly are and return to *Shechinah*, to *Neshama*, to community, to God's love, to what we can become, to our unique destiny, to the truth to stand for what we believe in. We discover our identities and rediscover our loyalty to our commitments. We have gone through a process of assessing where we are relative to who we can become, and we are ready to face our challenges ahead. At the sound of the shofar, at the end of the *Ne'ilah/Ma'ariv* service, we wake up and recommit to redeeming the world, holding the energy of "Thy Will be Done."

In our joy, we must continue to find the good in ourselves. As Reb Nachman counsels, Hashem loves us, so we must never despair. Joy, laughter, and song are requisites along our journey. So let us celebrate Yom Kippur as the beginning of a year of Joy!

Finally, let us ask ourselves what our priorities are and who do we want to be in the coming year? What have we learned on this introspective journey, and how shall we grow from it? Here are 10 questions we may ask ourselves from Shabbat Shuva to Yom Kippur as we proceed forward on our journey:

1. When do I feel that my life is most meaningful?
2. Those who mean the most to me—have I ever told them how I feel?
3. If I could live my life over, would I change anything?
4. What would bring me more happiness than anything in the world?

5. What are my three most significant accomplishments since last Yom Kippur?
6. What are my three biggest mistakes since last Yom Kippur?
7. What project or goal, if left undone, will I regret most next Yom Kippur?
8. If I knew I couldn't fail, what project would I undertake to accomplish?
9. If I could only give my friends, or my family, or my children three pieces of advice, what would they be?
10. What are my three major goals in life? What am I doing to achieve them? What practical steps can I take in the next 12 months toward these goals?

May each of us find the strength to seek and find forgiveness, and hence to give out the love by which those around us are sustained. May we all experience a harmonious Shabbat Shuva and let the spirit of Shabbat continue to heal you, and lift you up to all that you were meant to be—Beloved and Loving. Shabbat Shalom!

Ha'azinu/Sukkot

As we come toward the end of the cycle of Torah reading, we learn that even Moshe did not reach the Promised Land. For that was not the goal upon which he continually focused. It was the journey. We were not to ignore our surroundings and inner soul-whispers along the way, oblivious to the ever-changing Holy Presence that met us and that brought a new serendipitous delight. The journey through life itself is the goal, not some hoped-for endpoint that defines us. If we focus only on the endpoint, we become so obsessed with it that we lose sight of the everyday blessings surrounding us. We also tend to judge ourselves harshly for our failure of not reaching the goal—and our inner turmoil leads to our perception that there is only darkness in the world.

Then we lose our joy and joie de vivre. Although Moshe did not cross into the Promised Land, he did not complain or define himself as a failure. He remained faithful, accepting the inevitability of his reality, and could look back at his life as one who truly lived fully through every present moment. This last bit of wisdom filled him at the end of his life.

Our journey takes us from the ethereal heights of Yom Kippur to the earthy reality of Sukkot/The Festival of Tabernacles. Sukkot is the holiday that symbolizes faith, peace, and joy in our tradition. In the desert, we developed our faith. The miraculous Clouds of Glory protected the Jewish people during their 40 years in the desert. The booths we dwelled in, the manna, the miracles we witnessed there at the crossing of the Sea of Reeds and Sinai and were manifest at that time built our faith. In this season, we also experience great joy, due to our successful cleansing and reconciliation, having done *teshuvah*.

Sukkot is the holiday where the fragrance of the *etrog*/citron and branches of willow and myrtle fill the sukkah, the dwelling under the sky where we are to dwell for seven days. On Sukkot we leave our stable homes and stay in the Sukkah, the tabernacle, the temporary abode we build to observe the holiday—bringing us closer to the Creator of nature.

Rav Dessler, in *Michtav M'Eliyahu*, says discord is created by an emphasis on materialistic values, inevitably creating competitiveness and hostility because of limited resources on our planet. Instead, the unstable nature of the sukkah demonstrates that the material world does not provide us with our greatest security. We have faith in God as our protector wherever we reside; affirming our spiritual values leads us to peace. We declare, by inhabiting this sacred space, that it is truly God who protects and provides security in our homes and in our temporary abodes, and that thinking material security is our protector is just an illusion. We don't need to turn luxuries into needs. Our faith in God alone leads us to true inner peace.

Just as our ancestors dwelt in booths in the desert, protected by the Clouds of Glory, increasing their faith, we too can accept God's ever-present partnership in our lives. We have this sudden flash of insight that we may not need the beautiful solid structures that shut us out from nature and are often created through major time-consuming, competitive, and stressful efforts. As a result, we no longer have time to remember who we truly are as members of a unique nation charged to uplift our world through our gifted capacities. We may begin to realize that our true security lies not in physical structures, but in faith. We can be protected by God in a sukkah just as well as in our beautiful homes. With faith, we can move through difficult challenges that appear beyond our control rather than fall into cynicism and despair that blunts our action. With faith, we can turn our anguish into concrete plans to heal our planet.

We literally invite our ancestors and antecedents from the time of Abraham and ancient Jerusalem into our sukkah to continue the dialogue, the conversation of generations, just as we invite our friends, extended family, and guests into the sukkah, to commune with them, to huddle together against the cool night air. We eat delicious delicacies—whether from the Ashkenazic or Sephardic traditions, prepared with love and grace for all to enjoy. We are blessed to have meals prepared with loving hands and continue the dialogue and conversations of the generations.

On Sukkot, four different types of fruits, the four species, are used together in the synagogue service and in the sukkah to symbolize acceptance of difference and diversity in our community—creating true harmony, instead of society's expectation of uniformity. We are instructed to wave the four species in six directions during the Hallel prayer service, affirming the omnipresence of God. It is also a way of teaching us about the beauty of nature and suggests that every human being must have the opportunity to experience and partake of gifts of nature. The heady, citrusy fragrance of the etrog (the Talmud says if we dream about an etrog, it means God considers us precious); the branches of the sukkah; the dwelling under the bright stars on moist evenings; it all brings us closer to nature and to the Creator. We hear the birds and crickets singing to us, the grass and trees treating us to their fragrant aromas, and we enter a new space in memory to join our ancestors who dreamed of a better world—where the whole earth would dwell under the sukkah of the Lord of Peace.

These ideas led our Sages to identify Sukkot with peace. We are also taught that to create true peace we must constantly work hard to achieve it. As our Aaron, the high priest said, "Be a lover of peace and a pursuer of peace; love people and bring them closer to the sublime values of Torah" (Pirkei Avot 1:12).

On our holiday of Peace and Joy, we are informed that a four-walled sukkah is not kosher; it must be three-sided, and the fourth side must be open to guests, strangers, and those who are needy so they can enter and join in our joy. We even invite the aforementioned spiritual, mystical guests from our ancient history, who may not be with us in body, yet live in our spirit as guides to moral and ethical behavior. They are called the *ushpizin*, and each night, one of our ancestors is invited into the sukkah. Avraham and Sarah, Yitzchak and Rebekkah, Yaakov, Rachel and Leah, Yosef, Moshe, Aaron, and David impart their wisdom and energy to lift us up to our responsibilities.

A three-walled sukkah also allows us to look outward to our neighbors and to those who may not have a place to eat. We welcome them with song and food and learn their stories and about their unique journeys in life. Last year we invited neighborhood Syrian refugees who escaped the destruction of their homes, friends, and family. They survived and reminded the world of the devastation of their countrymen and families, all victims created in the image of God, whose divine sparks were ignored. They awakened us to the horrors they experienced, and all the work we must do to attain a world of peace for all. In an interconnected world, it is not sufficient to enjoy peace in insulated communities. Those who suffer remind us we must reach out and work for peace for all who endure terrifying conditions in their homelands.

As a result of encountering their unique reality, they were invited to speak about the plight of Syrian refugees in several synagogues and educational settings, and inspired the community to continue working for peace and justice in our world.

The three-walled sukkah reminds us that our lives are not complete and that we must work to complete the fourth side, partnering with others to create a world of justice and respect for all human beings. As Aaron taught us, we must all be active peacemakers! In our prayer services on Friday evenings, we ask God to spread the Sukkah of Peace over us all, for it is only through God's protection and joining with others living in the Sukkah of Peace that we can create an interconnected world of joy.

Above all, Sukkot allows us to imagine what it would be like if we ourselves created a world of peace and opportunity for all. We must take time amidst our joy to plan strategies to bring more peace to our world in our short lifetimes, and know that God expects us to be peacemakers.

Let us make sure that we encounter diversity, equality, and inclusion in our sukkot, and that we invite people with opinions different than ours so that we can get to know them. Let it be a time of dialogue and learning and planning to work to ensure that next year we will all dwell under the Sukkah of Peace that we all deserve, and that the prophets of our past have proclaimed as a future reality. It is now our time to fulfill that prophecy!

Dwelling in a sukkah—living in a flimsy, temporary structure—exposes us to a small taste of the terrible conditions the homeless live with every day. Our three-walled sukkah is not complete if we do not look outward to our streets and embrace the vulnerable homeless. The three-walled sukkah gives us perspective; it reveals our insensitivity to the plight of our neighbors, who suffer daily in precarious huts of danger, illness, and hunger.

Every year Sukkot charges us with a mission to make sure everyone has access to a secure place to rest and sleep, to feel safe under the same stars we all see from our planet, and to discover the beauty of a star meant just for them! Let us commit ourselves to a path that will diminish poverty and increase justice. We need to remember who we really are—members of the Jewish nation with a special mandate to create a world of peace. We are brought into calendrical time, into a new space of memory, joining our souls to our ancestors. Thus, we take each of the four different species and bind them together, symbolizing the possibility of accepting differences all under one central motif. We realize that indeed, these very differences are essential necessary ingredients to create the wholeness and peace that our world deserves.

Let us be blessed in future years to invite to our sukkah both our friends and those who have not yet become our friends; to remain elated to discover their humanity along with the wonder of their "difference." Gazing at the stars from our sukkah makes us all feel humbled by the beauty and majesty of our universe, and awakens us to the fact that each of us is equal under the heavens. But will we also invite in people with whom we have strong disagreements politically and religiously, or will we only talk to those who are like us? The practice of only speaking with those who agree with us can hardly be the mechanism that leads to true peace and harmony.

And unfortunately, this is a norm that is prevalent in our communities. We must challenge ourselves to invite into our Sukkah people with whom we have strong differences as well. Conflict can create an opportunity for us to gain insight into our neighbor's point of view, create growth, and optimally develop new harmonious relationships with those whom we do not truly know and understand. Does anyone come to mind?

How can we transform hostile conversations into ones that lead to a greater understanding of the other? Perhaps the heads of the household can act as examples of bestowing respect on those who have different positions, and make an effort to listen and understand the underlying feelings that influence the other's position. This will improve the relationship with our guests even if the different positions are not fully resolved. When one feels respected rather than disrespected, the humanity of the other emerges, and this is healing to each party. The defensiveness is attenuated and a spark of shalom is ignited.

This is also the time of year when Jews celebrate the abundance of the joy from the fall harvest. According to some historians, our American holiday of Thanksgiving, celebrated since 1620, owes its origins to Sukkot. It is this faith and joy that leads us to inner peace. And now is our time to be surrounded by the energy of peace. Our holiday is called *zman simchateinu*/ our season of Joy, and is also referred to as *sukkat shalom*/ our sukkah of peace. Have a Shabbat and Sukkot filled with joy and the sparks of Peace, Blessings, and Love.

V'zot Habracha / Simchat Torah

We continue our journey to attain wholeness and closeness to God. We began in Elul, and continued through the majesty of Yom Kippur, in a never-ending journey, a continuous process, encountering the 'new' every day. Our Rabbis continued the process of *teshuvah* through Hoshana Rabbah and we dance with collective exuberance on Simchat Torah. There are never absolute endpoints that define us as good or bad if we achieve or fail to reach that goal. As we complete the Torah readings and begin them anew, we learn that even Moshe Rabbenu did not reach the Promised Land.

Our Hebrew calendar offers us experiences to express many emotions and spiritual longings during the year. As the Book of Ecclesiastes states, "There is a time to every purpose under heaven, a time to be born and a time to die…a time to break down, and a time to build up, a time to weep…and a time to dance…" (Ecc. 3:1-8). Thus Rosh Hashanahh and Yom Kippur were times of reflection and serious confrontation to the challenges we face. We then move from this space to a time of joy and celebration during Sukkot. This captures the cycle of life through which each of us must pass. How do we experience this moment of joy in this season? How do we move from the realm of sadness to the realm of joy?

We now enter a new opportunity to derive joy and express it on Simchat Torah! It is customary to dance the night away, releasing holy sparks with holy song, reaching out from the depths of our hearts and souls to God. We thank God for the everyday blessings and completion of the yearly reading of the Torah. Though we yearn for the "New Jerusalem," we remain in the present and work ourselves into a sweat through song and frenzied dancing, getting high on the completion and learning of the Torah.

Why such joy over the completion of the Torah, the heart book and the long continuous name of God? Because we have finished our yearly cycle of reading and studying the wisdom of our Torah, and are beginning it once more. There is no absolute end; the yearly journey itself is sacrosanct. Every year we discover something new. The circle of life is endless—as we change, as the world changes and interacts in complementary ways with each other, each part playing its holy role.

New insights are revealed; new ways of being and new opportunities are available in our encounter with Torah study. We will ask new questions from a place of greater radiant faith, for we have witnessed God's Grace, peering out to the mountains from the Sukkah of Peace. We have seen the circle of life from the moment of a child's birth through the many stages it passes in its lifetime. We have witnessed the infinite complexity of nature feeding the earth and of us caring for each other.

We have lived through despair and hope, through faith and love, staying on the journey until finding our place in the perpetual circle of life. Hopefully, along the way we hear the echo of the sounds emanating from the divine realm: "A voice that constantly reverberates in our inner heart and makes us aware of the waves from the higher realm that acts upon our souls ceaselessly" (Rav Kook/Orot).

Every time we absorb a high form of energy, our Hebrew calendar reminds us that there's an even higher form of energy waiting for us. Although Yom Kippur was an amazing day of Awe, Majesty, and Grace, we ascend to an even higher level through dance and song on Simchat Torah.

On Simchat Torah we take all the Torah scrolls out of the Ark after Kaddish Shalem, and hand the Torah scrolls to different individuals who dance with them around the bimah. We do this seven times; each time we recite verses from Scripture and break into dancing and singing. After each of the seven *hakafot* (circle dances), the Torah scrolls are returned to the Ark and given to different people for each of the next six *hakafot*. For each *hakafah*, we prolong the dancing and singing for as long as possible, and everyone is caught up in a collective euphoria. Everyone gets a chance to carry the Torah. It is an incredible custom in which we participate, and our bodies join our souls to reach the heights that only song and dance can create. In many synagogues, those who hold the Torahs go out into the streets to continue their dancing and singing there.

When I was a rabbinical student in Manhattan's Washington Heights neighborhood, the home of Yeshiva University, we danced in the streets for hours, until we reached a state of ecstatic exhaustion. The streets were roped off by the police for this holiday custom, and the entire neighborhood joined as observers or fellow dancers. Dancing with the Torah is one of the most spiritual experiences of the year, indelibly entwined in our memories and souls. After the seventh *hakafah*, all the Torahs are returned to the Ark, except for one Torah that is read to finish the final parsha of Devarim and to begin from Bereishit once more.

Incredibly, everyone in the synagogue is called up for an aliyah to bless the scrolls on Simchat Torah, asserting the democratization of our community; each one of us deserves the honor, even little children who are not of age for bar/bat mitzvah; everyone gets the opportunity to honor the Torah. How can we retain this joy for the rest of the year? By studying Torah; by connecting to community through our rituals; by doing good deeds and acts of kindness, and recognizing we are all interconnected on our planet.

Our joy on Simchat Torah and Sukkot is filled with the psychic/cosmic energy and realization that it is this joyful/peaceful Sukkot energy that affects the destiny of the world; for the holiday of Sukkot/Simchat Torah is not just about the recognition of the continual transformation of ourselves—our prayers and wishes on this holiday include the hope that sparks of peace will finally spread to create peace for all of humankind.

May each of us pray and dream on this holiday that someday all humanity will become restored to peace. This powerful vision of the future helps support our inner joy, as we pray for a world of harmony, free from the threats of hatred, and dream of a messianic era where this beautiful reality will be fulfilled.

Our rabbis suggest many reasons for defining this particular time as a time of joy. One classical reason is that Sukkot comes right after Yom Kippur, when we have reached an inner sense of commitment and purpose for the year ahead. We have come in touch with our special destiny and feel empowered to actualize our destiny, even with all the labor required to do so.

Another reason given for its joyous energy is that Sukkot promotes a sense of harmonizing the opposing forces within ourselves as symbolized by the four species. We take the *lulav* (spine), the *aravot* (lips), the *hadassim* (eyes), and the *etrog* (heart) and bring them together in a symphonic union. We find the courage (spine) to say (lips) what the heart (etrog) sees (hadassim). When we find unity within, we can see harmony without and not project our discord onto others.

The mitzvah of *hakhel*/gathering together as a congregation during this season (Deut. 31:10-13) is unique to Sukkot. In this mitzvah, all groups in Israel (men, women, children, and others) are commanded to come to Jerusalem to serve God in joy. In this social connection, joy is abundant. We are spiritually charged when we feel a sense of peoplehood with a common goal to celebrate the gift of life and love while absorbing the sparks of humanity. Our innate loneliness and periodic alienation are assuaged. We recognize that we subliminally yearn for the touch of the other, be it God directly, or the image of God residing in the love and acceptance of the other who accepts us. Our Sages teach that where there is unity there is abundant happiness, and the will to give and share.

Furthermore, the Hebrew word associated with the last day of the holiday, *atzeret*, connotes gathering and unity. It is the day when all the special light of the joy of the holiday comes together. We will celebrate Simchat Torah in ecstasy, singing and dancing with the Torah scroll as our souls reach a state of unity with each other, God, and the Torah.

In ancient days, the last day of Sukkot was spent celebrating the water libation ceremony, the pouring of water on the sacrificial altar, accompanied by music and song. The ceremony celebrated the recognition of water/nature, and the attempt to unify the heavenly and earthly worlds. Though we currently suffer terrible droughts and hurricanes, our ancient Sages saw this pouring of water as a fulfillment of the promise to the waters on earth, appeasing them. The waters originally belonged to the heavenly world, but they were brought down here by God in order for the earth to flourish. The waters were promised that they would be raised to the heavenly state again, and this occurred on the last day of Sukkot. We pray that the blessing of water again becomes a true blessing as we work to heal the damage to our planet caused by climate change. May Sukkot remind us once more of our promised blessings!

In ancient days, the unification of the upper and lower worlds with the water libation on the last day of Sukkot was accompanied by immense joy. The Sages designated it as the happiest day of the calendar. The Talmud says, "That on this day, the most serene and modest scholars danced in ecstasy and did cartwheels as expressions of their soulful elations. These festivities were called *Simchat Beit Hashoevah*/the joy of the water drawing, where the spirit of holiness was drawn down to earth on hearts filled with joy! The ceremony was held outside in the Holy Temple courtyard. The people danced with lit torches in their hands, singing with joy as the Levites played their harps and musical instruments. This was the joy of Sukkot, a moment of great connection to Hashem and God's manifestation in nature.

The Prophets Zechariah and Ezekiel add another dimension to the joy and sparks of peace that we experience on Sukkot and Simchat Torah. They declare that the transformation of the world and all the nations inhabiting it will take place at the end of the days on the holiday of Sukkot. At that time, all nations will recognize the majesty of the Almighty and will come to Jerusalem to recognize this new reality. They will all observe the holiday of Sukkot together (Zechariah 14:16). The 70 offerings brought in the Holy Temple on Sukkot correspond to the 70 nations descended from sons of Noah (whose descendants are the nations of the modern day) and who prayed on this holiday for the well-being of all and for universal peace among all nations.

We should feel God's love at the end of this holiday, connect to our loved ones, and derive joy from our honest communication and intimacy. Let us be grateful for all the gifts the Lord has bestowed upon us and be ever open to the whisper of angels that surround us. Let us help others, embracing their uniqueness, recognizing their beauty and soul. This will surely energize us, and raise our enthusiasm for life—even with all its challenges—as we dedicate ourselves to healing our water-challenged earth and creating joy for all.

It has been a privilege and honor to share Torah with you, my loving community, and I hope you will continue to study and absorb the Torah's wisdom, create your own commentaries as you soak in the words of our wise Sages, and bring your own creative brilliance to your study.

With Many Blessings and abundant love,

Rabbi Mel

About the Author

Rabbi Mel Gottlieb, Ph.D., is President Emeritus of the Academy for Jewish Religion, Ca. and served as well as the Dean of its Rabbinical School. Rabbi Gottlieb was ordained at Yeshiva University and holds a doctorate in Mythology/Depth Psychology from Pacifica Graduate Institute where he has served as an Adjunct Faculty member. Rabbi Gottlieb has also taught at Columbia University., Yeshiva University, and the University of Southern California Graduate School of Social Work. His essays have appeared in publications such as the *Huffington Post, Shma Magazine, Conversations: The Journal of the Institute for Jewish Ideals and Ideas,* and *Psychological Perspectives* and in the books *Illuminating Letters; Torah, Service, Deeds: Jewish Ethics in Transdenominational Perspectives;* and *Kashrut and Jewish Food Ethics.* He is a frequent guest lecturer at the C.G. Jung Institute of Los Angeles as well as synagogues of all denominations throughout southern California. Rabbi Gottlieb is the former Hillel Director at the Massachusetts Institute of Technology and Princeton University.

Recent books from *Ben Yehuda Press*

Judaism Disrupted: A Spiritual Manifesto for the 21st Century by Rabbi Michael Strassfeld. "I can't remember the last time I felt pulled to underline a book constantly as I was reading it, but *Judaism Disrupted* is exactly that intellectual, spiritual and personal adventure. You will find yourself nodding, wrestling, and hoping to hold on to so many of its ideas and challenges. Rabbi Strassfeld reframes a Torah that demands breakage, reimagination, and ownership." —Abigail Pogrebin, author, *My Jewish Year: 18 Holidays, One Wondering Jew*

The Way of Torah and the Path of Dharma: Intersections between Judaism and the Religions of India by Rabbi Daniel Polish. "A whirlwind religious tourist visit to the diversity of Indian religions: Sikh, Jain, Buddhist, and Hindu, led by an experienced congregational rabbi with much experience in interfaith and in teaching world religions." —Rabbi Alan Brill, author of *Rabbi on the Ganges: A Jewish Hindu-Encounter.*

Liberating Your Passover Seder: An Anthology Beyond The Freedom Seder. Edited by Rabbi Arthur O. Waskow and Rabbi Phyllis O. Berman. This volume tells the history of the Freedom Seder and retells the origin of subsequent new haggadahs, including those focusing on Jewish-Palestinian reconciliation, environmental concerns, feminist and LGBT struggles, and the Covid-19 pandemic of 2020.

Duets on Psalms: Drawing New Meaning from Ancient Words by Rabbis Elie Spitz & Jack Riemer. "Two of Judaism's most inspirational teachers, offer a lifetime of insights on the Bible's most inspired book." — Rabbi Joseph Telushkin, author of *Jewish Literacy*. "This illuminating work is a literary journey filled with faith, wisdom, hope, healing, meaning and inspiration." —Rabbi Naomi Levy, author of *Einstein and the Rabbi.*

Weaving Prayer: An Analytical and Spiritual Commentary on the Jewish Prayer Book by Rabbi Jeffrey Hoffman."This engaging and erudite volume transforms the prayer experience. Not only is it of considerable intellectual interest to learn the history of prayers—how, when, and why they were composed—but this new knowledge will significantly help a person pray with intention (*kavanah*). I plan to keep this volume right next to my siddur." —Rabbi Judith Hauptman, author of *Rereading the Rabbis: A Woman's Voice.*

Renew Our Hearts: A Siddur for Shabbat Day edited by Rabbi Rachel Barenblat. From the creator of *The Velveteen Rabbi's Haggadah*, a new siddur for the day of Shabbat. *Renew Our Hearts* balances tradition with innovation, featuring liturgy for morning (*Shacharit* and a renewing approach to *Musaf*), the afternoon (*Mincha*), and evening (*Ma'ariv* and *Havdalah*), along with curated works of poetry, art and new liturgies from across the breadth of Jewish spiritual life. Every word of Hebrew is paired with transliteration and with clear, pray-able English translation.

Forty Arguments for the Sake of Heaven: Why the Most Vital Controversies in Jewish Intellectual History Still Matter by Rabbi Shmuly Yanklowitz. Hillel vs. Shammai, Ayn Rand vs. Karl Marx, Tamar Ross vs. Judith Plaskow... but also Abraham vs. God, and God vs. the angels! Movements debate each other: Reform versus Orthodoxy, one- two- and zero-state solutions to the Israeli-Palestinian conflict, gun rights versus gun control in the United States. Rabbi Yanklowitz presents difficult and often heated disagreements with fairness and empathy, helping us consider our own truths in a pluralistic Jewish landscape.

Recent books from *Ben Yehuda Press*

Reaching for Comfort: What I Saw, What I Learned, and How I Blew it Training as a Pastoral Counselor by Sherri Mandell. In 2004, Sherri Mandell won the National Jewish Book award for *The Blessing of the Broken Heart*, which told of her grief and initial mourning after her 13-year-old son Koby was brutally murdered. Years later, with her pain still undiminished, Sherri trains to help others as a pioneering pastoral counselor in Israeli hospitals. "What a blessing to witness Mandell's and her patients' resilience!" —Rabbi Dayle Friedman, editor, *Jewish Pastoral Care: A Practical Guide from Traditional and Contemporary Sources.*

Heroes with Chutzpah: 101 True Tales of Jewish Trailblazers, Changemakers & Rebels by Rabbi Deborah Bodin Cohen and Rabbi Kerry Olitzky. Readers ages 8 to 14 will meet Jewish changemakers from the recent past and present, who challenged the status quo in the arts, sciences, social justice, sports and politics, from David Ben-Gurion and Jonas Salk to Sarah Silverman and Douglas Emhoff. "Simply stunning. You would want this book on your coffee table, though the stories will take the express lane to your soul." —Rabbi Jeff Salkin.

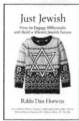

Just Jewish: How to Engage Millennials and Build a Vibrant Jewish Future by Rabbi Dan Horwitz. Drawing on his experience launching The Well, an inclusive Jewish community for young adults in Metro Detroit, Rabbi Horwitz shares proven techniques ready to be adopted by the Jewish world's myriad organizations, touching on everything from branding to fundraising to programmatic approaches to relationship development, and more. "This book will shape the conversation as to how we think about the Jewish future." —Rabbi Elliot Cosgrove, editor, *Jewish Theology in Our Time.*

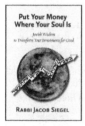

Put Your Money Where Your Soul Is: Jewish Wisdom to Transform Your Investments for Good by Rabbi Jacob Siegel. "An intellectual delight. It offers a cornucopia of good ideas, institutions, and advisers. These can ease the transition for institutions and individuals from pure profit nature investing to deploying one's capital to repair the world, lift up the poor, and aid the needy and vulnerable. The sources alone—ranging from the Bible, Talmud, and codes to contemporary economics and sophisticated financial reporting—are worth the price of admission." —Rabbi Irving "Yitz" Greenberg.

Why Israel (and its Future) Matters: Letters of a Liberal Rabbi to the Next Generation by Rabbi John Rosove. Presented in the form of a series of letters to his children, Rabbi Rosove makes the case for Israel — and for liberal American Jewish engagement with the Jewish state. "A must-read!" —Isaac Herzog, President of Israel. "This thoughtful and passionate book reminds us that commitment to Israel and to social justice are essential components of a healthy Jewish identity." —Yossi Klein Halevi, author, *Letters to My Palestinian Neighbor.*

Other Covenants: Alternate Histories of the Jewish People by Rabbi Andrea D. Lobel & Mark Shainblum. In *Other Covenants*, you'll meet Israeli astronauts trying to save a doomed space shuttle, a Jewish community's faith challenged by the unstoppable return of their own undead, a Jewish science fiction writer in a world of Zeppelins and magic, an adult Anne Frank, an entire genre of Jewish martial arts movies, a Nazi dystopia where Judaism refuses to die, and many more. Nominated for two Sidewise Awards for Alternate History.

Reflections on the weekly Torah portion from *Ben Yehuda Press*

An Angel Called Truth and Other Tales from the Torah by Rabbi Jeremy Gordon and Emma Parlons. Funny, engaging micro-tales for each of the portions of the Torah and one for each of the Jewish festivals as well. These tales are told from the perspective of young people who feature in the Biblical narrative, young people who feature in classic Rabbinic commentary on our Biblical narratives and young people just made up for this book.

Torah & Company: The weekly portion of Torah, accompanied by generous helpings of Mishnah and Gemara, served with discussion questions to spice up your Sabbath Table by Rabbi Judith Z. Abrams. Serve up a rich feast of spiritual discussion from an age-old recipe: One part Torah. Two parts classic Jewish texts. Add conversation. Stir... and enjoy! "A valuable guide for the Shabbat table of every Jew." —Rabbi Burton L. Visotzky, author *Reading the Book*.

Torah Journeys: The Inner Path to the Promised Land by Rabbi Shefa Gold. Rabbi Gold shows us how to find blessing, challenge and the opportunity for spiritual transformation in each portion of Torah. An inspiring guide to exploring the landscape of Scripture... and recognizing that landscape as the story of your life. "Deep study and contemplation went into the writing of this work. Reading her Torah teachings one becomes attuned to the voice of the Shekhinah, the feminine aspect of God which brings needed healing to our wounded world." —Rabbi Zalman Schachter-Shalomi.

American Torah Toons 2: Fifty-Four Illustrated Commentaries by Lawrence Bush. Deeply personal and provocative artworks responding to each weekly Torah portion. Each two-page spread includes a Torah passage, a paragraph of commentary from both traditional and modern Jewish sources, and a photo-collage that responds to the text with humor, ethical conscience, and both social and self awareness. "What a vexing, funny, offensive, insightful, infuriating, thought-provoking book." —Rabbi David Saperstein.

The Comic Torah: Reimagining the Very Good Book. Stand-up comic Aaron Freeman and artist Sharon Rosenzweig reimagine the Torah with provocative humor and irreverent reverence in this hilarious, gorgeous, off-beat graphic version of the Bible's first five books! Each weekly portion gets a two-page spread. Like the original, the Comic Torah is not always suitable for children.

we who desire: Poems and Torah riffs by Sue Swartz. From Genesis to Deuteronomy, from Bereshit to Zot Haberacha, from Eden to Gaza, from Eve to Emma Goldman, *we who desire* interweaves the mythic and the mundane as it follows the arc of the Torah with carefully chosen words, astute observations, and deep emotion. "Sue Swartz has used a brilliant, fortified, playful, serious, humanely furious moral imagination, and a poet's love of the music of language, to re-tell the saga of the Bible you thought you knew." —Alicia Ostriker, author, *For the Love of God: The Bible as an Open Book*.

Eternal Questions by Rabbi Josh Feigelson. These essays on the weekly Torah portion guide readers on a journey that weaves together Torah, Talmud, Hasidic masters, and a diverse array of writers, poets, musicians, and thinkers. Each essay includes questions for reflection and suggestions for practices to help turn study into more mindful, intentional living. "This is the wisdom that we always need—but maybe particularly now, more than ever, during these turbulent times." —Rabbi Danya Ruttenberg, author, *On Repentance and Repair*.

Jewish spirituality and thought from *Ben Yehuda Press*

The Essential Writings of Abraham Isaac Kook. Translated and edited by Rabbi Ben Zion Bokser. This volume of letters, aphorisms and excerpts from essays and other writings provide a wide-ranging perspective on the thought and writing of Rav Kook. With most selections running two or three pages, readers gain a gentle introduction to one of the great Jewish thinkers of the modern era.

Ahron's Heart: Essential Prayers, Teachings and Letters of Ahrele Roth, a Hasidic Reformer. Translated and edited by Rabbi Zalman Schachter-Shalomi and Rabbi Yair Hillel Goelman. For the first time, the writings of one of the 20th century's most important Hasidic thinkers are made available to a non-Hasidic English audience. Rabbi Ahron "Ahrele" Roth (1894-1944) has a great deal to say to sincere spiritual seekers far beyond his own community.

A Passionate Pacifist: Essential Writings of Aaron Samuel Tamares. Translated and edited by Rabbi Everett Gendler. Rabbi Aaron Samuel Tamares (1869-1931) addresses the timeless issues of ethics, morality, communal morale, and Judaism in relation to the world at large in these essays and sermons, written in Hebrew between 1904 and 1931. "For those who seek a Torah of compassion and pacifism, a Judaism not tied to 19th century political nationalism, and a vision of Jewish spirituality outside of political thinking this book will be essential." —Rabbi Dr. Alan Brill, author, *Thinking God: The Mysticism of Rabbi Zadok of Lublin*.

Return to the Place: The Magic, Meditation, and Mystery of Sefer Yetzirah by Rabbi Jill Hammer. A translation of and commentary to an ancient Jewish mystical text that transforms it into a contemporary guide for meditative practice. "A tour de force—at once scholarly, whimsical, deeply poetic, and eminently accessible." —Rabbi Tirzah Firestone, author of *The Receiving: Reclaiming Jewish Women's Wisdom*

Enlightenment by Trial and Error: Ten Years on the Slippery Slopes of Jewish Mysticism, Postmodern Buddhist Meditation, and Heretical Flexidox Spirituality by Rabbi Jay Michaelson. A unique record of the 21st-century spiritual search, from the perspective of someone who made plenty of mistakes along the way.

The Tao of Solomon: Finding Joy and Contentment in the Wisdom of Ecclesiastes by Rabbi Rami Shapiro. Rabbi Rami Shapiro unravels the golden philosophical threads of wisdom in the book of Ecclesiastes, reweaving the vibrant book of the Bible into a 21st century tapestry. Shapiro honors the roots of the ancient writing, explores the timeless truth that we are merely a drop in the endless river of time, and reveals a path to finding personal and spiritual fulfillment even as we embrace our impermanent place in the universe.

Embracing Auschwitz: Forging a Vibrant, Life-Affirming Judaism that Takes the Holocaust Seriously by Rabbi Joshua Hammerman. The Judaism of Sinai and the Judaism of Auschwitz are merging, resulting in new visions of Judaism that are only beginning to take shape. "Should be read by every Jew who cares about Judaism." —Rabbi Dr. Irving "Yitz" Greenberg.

Made in United States
North Haven, CT
24 September 2024

57821486R00173